IELTS
GENERAL TRAINING
ESSAYS & LETTERS
FROM THE PAST EXAMS

DR. KIRANPREET KAUR MAKKAR
(MBBS, DGO - Makkar Hospital, Phagwara)

ER. INDROOP SINGH MAKKAR
(MS in IE & OR Pennsylvania State University, USA)

Published by:**Makkar Publishing House**
4322 Sector 68 Mohali
M: 9646044322 | O: 9888998241
www.makkarielts.com | ravielts@gmail.com

Published by: Makkar Publishing House

Third Edition: 2019

First published in India in 2017 by **makkarIELTS**

Written by: Kiranpreet Kaur Makkar

Contributions: Sumeet Kaur, Indroop Singh, Ravpreet Singh, Anupam Kaur

Cover Illustration: Amrit Pal Singh

Cover Page Image Courtesy: John Cobb

Printed By: Chandigarh Publishing House, Sector 41, Chandigarh

ISBN: 978-93-5268-427-4

PREFACE

This book is the fourth in the series of my books for IELTS, which contains questions from the past exams. My earlier books on Academic Writing and Speaking have fetched remarkable sales. This book is meant to help the average student crack the IELTS essay. Over 12 years of my IELTS coaching experience has taught me a lot about what all would help the students do better in the writing module of the IELTS. Over the years, I have seen fairly good students getting 7+ in the other modules of the IELTS, fall to less than 6 bands in the writing module, but I have also seen those with less than 6 in the other modules, get a 6+ in writing. Over the years, I have coached thousands of students, checked their writings almost every day, and so I somehow know what precisely they have written in their exam. From their writing band scores, I have made important deductions as to what works, and what does not work in an IELTS writing section.

The IELTS essays and letters should have a plan. Time spent on the plan is time well invested. A plan is surely going to produce an essay or a letter which works. A crisp but brief and to-the-point introduction and conclusion, and two to three well planned paragraphs with sentences relevant to the topic is all that is needed for the IELTS Writing Section.

This book has over 300 essays and letters seen in the actual IELTS exams, most of which have been repeated many times. Valuable contributions have been made to the book by Sumeet Kaur (CELTA certified, and my top faculty), Ravpreet Singh (head of Mohali Centre), Mrs. Anupam Kaur (looking after the online students), and Indroop Singh (faculty and student counselor, Phagwara Centre). This book would not have been possible without their efforts.

Hope you enjoy going through the essays and letters in the book.

Kiranpreet Kaur Makkar

General Introduction

The IELTS General Training Writing Test lasts for 1 hour and includes 2 tasks.

Writing Duration   Test Parts

- Task 1 is a letter and you must write at least 150 words. You should spend about 20 minutes out of 60 minutes for Task 1.
- Task 2 is an essay and you must write at least 250 words. You should spend about 40 minutes for Task 2.

You are presented with a situation and asked to write a letter. The letter may be personal, semi-formal or formal in style.	are asked to write an essay in respons( )int of view, problem or an argument.)y can include a more personal respons( )pared to an Academic Essay.
You are required to write at least **150 words**	You are required to write at least **250 words**
You should spend about **20 minutes**	You should spend about **40 minutes**

Note: Task 1 writing is less important than Task 2 and to calculate the final writing marks, more weight is assigned to Task 2 than to Task 1. However, to get a good overall band, both tasks have to be well answered; so don't practice less for Task 1 or give yourscelf too little time to answer it properly.

General Training Writing Task 1 - Letter

The IELTS General Training Writing Task 1 asks you to write a letter of a minimum of 150 words in response to some situation or a problem. The task will probably ask you to complain about something, to request information, ask for help, to make arrangements and/or explain a situation. All these are fairly similar tasks.

Letter Structure

It is very important to organize the letter into paragraphs as it helps in building a coherent response. Following is the most commonly used structure while writing a letter, however the students can group the body paragraphs as per the requirement of the task.

1. **Salutation** - Example: Dear Sir or Dear John

2. **Opening statement** - This paragraph or sentence should include the purpose for writing.

3. **Body paragraph 1**- This paragraph should explain one point of the letter with details.

4. **Body paragraph 2**- This paragraph should explain one point of the letter with details.

5. **Body paragraph 3** - This paragraph should explain one point of the letter with details.

6. **Closing statement** — This statement should be written in a separate line, after covering the final point and before signing off Example: Hoping to see you soon.

7. **Signing off** - Example: Yours sincerely, Yours lovingly

8. **Name** - Could be any name

Letter Types and Salutations

Type of letter	Beginning	Ending
Formal, no name	Dear Sir or Madam	Yours faithfully
Formal, with surname	Dear Mr. Sharma	Yours sincerely
Semi -formal, e.g. neighbour or colleague	Dear Ramesh	Yours truly
Informal, e.g. friend	Dear Saira	Yours lovingly

Marking Criteria - Task 1

Each letter is marked on 4 different criteria, which share equal proportion of the overall band score.

1. Task Achievement (TA)

It means that you should cover all the points asked in the questions and answer the questions with appropriate tone. You should also clearly state the purpose of your letter and include a closing statement in the end. Lastly if your word count is less than 150 words, you will be penalized and lose marks in Task Achievement.

2. Cohesion and Coherence (CC)

It means that your letter should be well organized and there should be a logical flow of the information presented by using appropriate linking devices.

3. Lexical Resource (LR)

This criterion assesses how effectively and accurately you can use your vocabulary to develop your ideas. Big words and phrases might lead to your letter becoming forced and unnatural.

4. Grammatical Range and Accuracy (GRA)

This means, you can use simple, complex and compound sentences, along with proper punctuation   correctly

IELTS Band Descriptors for Task 1 -Band 7 Sample(Source: IELTS.org)

	Task Achievement	Cohesion and Coherence	LR – Lexical Resource	GRA– Grammatical Range and Accuracy
Band 7	- Covers the requirements of the task - Presents a clear purpose, with the tone consistent and appropriate - Clearly presents and highlights key features/bullet points but could be more fully extended	- Logically organizes information and ideas; there is clear progression throughout - Uses a range of cohesive devices appropriately although there may be some under-/over-use	- Use a sufficient range of vocabulary to allow some flexibility and precision Use less common lexical items with some awareness of style and collocation, although you may produce occasional errors in word choice, spelling and/or word formation	- Use a variety of complex structures - Produce frequent error-free sentences - Has good control of grammar and punctuation but may make a few errors

General Training Writing Task 2 - Essay

The IELTS essay is the second part of the writing section of the IELTS test. It requires you to write an essay with a minimum word count of 250, within a period of 40 minutes. There is no limit to the maximum word count. This part accounts for 2/3rd of the overall score of the writing section.

Essay Structure

The body of the essay should be divided into different paragraphs with each paragraph serving a clear purpose. The number of body paragraphs depend on the type of the question asked and ideas that you may have. Following is the most commonly used essay structure in the IELTS exam.

Introduction
- **Sentence 1:** Paraphrase the background information given in the topic
- **Sentence 2:** Thesis statement. For example, if the questions asks whether you agree or disagree with the given statement, you could mention that, "I agree with the given statement"

Body Paragraphs
First paragraph:
- Sentence 1: Topic sentence
- Sentence 2-5/6: Here you should mention your idea and then develop it further in the subsequent sentences. You can also include examples to support your idea. A paragraph can contain one or more ideas linked to the central theme of the paragraph. For every idea/reason you should follow the approach of Idea → Explain → *Example(Optional)*

Second paragraph:
- Sentence 1: Topic sentence
- Sentence 2-5/6: Here you should mention your idea and then develop it further in the subsequent sentences. You can also include examples to support your ideas. A paragraph can contain one or more ideas linked to the central theme of the paragraph. For every idea/reason you should follow the approach of Idea → Explain → *Example(Optional)*

Third or Fourth paragraph: (Optional – depending upon your ideas)

Conclusion: The restatement: Restate your opinion

Common Essay Types

1. Opinion essays
   - Opinion 1 – Agree/Disagree.
   - Opinion 2 – Is this a positive or negative development.
   - Opinion 3 – Are the advantages more than the disadvantages.
2. Discuss essays
3. Advantage and disadvantage essays
4. Problem and solution essays
5. Direct question essays (some might be two part questions)

Some important things to note

1. Contractions are not allowed (he's, she's, can't, won't).
2. Don't use informal language. However, you are writing for an educated non-specialist audience. Therefore, your language does not need to be as formal as that of university essays.
3. Always paraphrase or use synonyms when possible. Never copy the topic while writing the introduction.
4. Avoid using templates or memorized items for intro. Such templates can take a person from 4 to 5 or 5.5, but if your aim is 6 or above, these templates cannot help you. A simple but original introduction befitting the question asked will be better.
5. No clichés. For example, instead of writing 'every coin has two sides', it is better to write 'every argument has two sides'.
6. It is good to write complex sentences, but if the examiner has to read your sentence again to see what you mean, then it goes against you. So, write complex but clearly understood sentences. Avoid too long sentences.
7. In most cases you are expected to give your opinion. You may also have to include your life experience and relevant examples to support your opinion.
8. The topics of the IELTS writing questions are supposed to be of general interest, and they claim that no specialist knowledge is required. But it would be worthwhile to go through points of topics like telecommuting, gap year, genetically modified foods, globalization, rote learning, and many more. I believe that if you don't have ideas, even the best of language skills will not help you achieve your desired score. Ideas for some 100 such topics have been included in the speaking book, which is recommended along with this book for IELTS preparation.
9. Do not copy whole sentences or long phrases from the question. The examiner will recognize them, and they will not count towards the minimum number of words you must write.
10. The introduction should be approximately 35-50 words long. It is unnecessary for you to write a long introduction because it is the body that you need to focus on.

Opinion essay – Detailed Structure

General information

- An opinion essay is a formal academic essay, which requires you to state your opinion (usually "agree or disagree") on a given topic.
- You need to provide reasons and supporting details to convince the examiner of your answer.
- There are 2 common approaches to write an opinion essay: One sided and balanced.

One-sided approach

- A one-sided essay is an essay where your opinion is completely inclined to only one side of the argument, which means you either completely agree or completely disagree with the issue given in the topic.
- Always give 2 to 3 reasons to support your opinion, each of which must be analyzed and supported by specific details in each of the two or three paragraphs in the body.
- The third paragraph can contain the contradictory opinions with your refutation. In either case it will be a totally agree or disagree essay.

Let's see the complete structure of a one-sided opinion essay:

Introduction:

- Sentence 1: Paraphrase the background information given in the topic
- Sentence 2: State whether you completely agree or completely disagree with the issue.

Body:
First body paragraph:

- Sentence 1: The topic sentence (your 1st idea)
- Sentence 2-5/6: Give SPECIFIC examples or explanations to support the idea

Second body paragraph:

- Sentence 1: The topic sentence (your 2nd idea)
- Sentence 2-5/6: Give SPECIFIC examples or explanations to support the idea

Third body paragraph: (optional)

- Sentence 1: The topic sentence (your 3rd idea) OR The opponents view
- Sentence 2-5/6: Give SPECIFIC examples or explanations to support the idea OR Give arguments of opposite view and then refute with your view

Conclusion: Restate your opinion that you completely agree or completely disagree with the issue given in the question

Balanced Opinion Essay– Detailed Structure

General information
- A balanced essay is an essay where you are inclined to one side of the argument but you do not deny the other side, which means you partly agree or partly disagree with the issue given in the topic.
- **BUT -** Never sit on the fence,
- Even if you accept that there are 2 sides of the argument, you still need to choose which one you would agree with more.
- You need to analyze both sides of the issue and state which side you are in favor of at the same time.
- There are 2 places where you need to give you opinion: the intro, and the conclusion.

Let's see the complete structure of a balanced opinion essay:

Introduction:
- Sentence 1: Paraphrase the background information given in the topic
- Sentence 2: State that you partially agree or disagree with the issue. You can also say that you are more inclined on one side.

Body:
First body paragraph:
- Sentence 1: The topic sentence (your 1st idea)
- Sentence 2-5/6: Give SPECIFIC examples or explanations to support the idea

Second body paragraph:
- Sentence 1: The topic sentence (your 2nd idea)
- Sentence 2-5/6: Give SPECIFIC examples or explanations to support the idea

Third body paragraph: (Optional)
- Sentence 1: Your idea of the other view. But you can again say that you are more in favour of the first view even if this point also holds some water.

Conclusion: Restate your opinion that although both sides of the issue have solid arguments, which you agree upon, the arguments of one side are definitely more overpowering than the other.

Discussion Essay– Detailed Structure

General information
- Discussion essay is a formal essay where you are asked to discuss 2 sides of a given argument. The task may or may not ask for your opinion on the issue, only give your opinion if the task requires so. Try to find 2 ideas for each side of the argument.

Let's see the complete structure of a discussion essay:

Introduction
- **Sentence 1:** Paraphrase the background information given in the topic
- **Sentence 2:** Write a thesis statement saying that you will discuss both sides of the argument

Body
First paragraph: the first side of the argument
- Sentence 1: the topic sentence
- Sentence 2-5/6: Give 2 reasons and use SPECIFIC examples and explanations to support those reasons

Secondparagraph: The second side of the argument
- Sentence 1: the topic sentence
- Sentence 2-5/6: give 2 reasons and use SPECIFIC examples and explanations to support those reasons

Conclusion: The restatement: restate your opinion

IMPORTANT: _A discussion essay versus a balanced opinion essay_

A lot of people have a difficult time differentiating between these 2 particular types of essays since both of them require students to present 2 sides of the given argument with the same way of writing. However, the difference is that in a balanced opinion essay, you have to write about WHAT YOU THINK, whereas, in a discussion essay you have to write about WHAT OTHER PEOPLE THINK. This means there is a difference in the proper language you can use in each type.

In a balanced opinion essay
- You can use phrases to express your own opinion like "I think", "I believe", "I agree" … wherever you want.
- You can give examples of your own knowledge or experiences such as your family, your friends or a particular event you participated in to support your ideas.

In a discussion essay
- You can use the typical language for a discussion to express other people's opinion such as "people think", "people believe", "it is believed/considered"…

Advantage & Disadvantage Essays

General information

Basically, an advantage/disadvantage essay is a discussion essay that asks you to discuss the advantages and disadvantages of a given issue, for example the advantages and disadvantages of using public transport. DO NOT give any opinions if you are not asked to. Divide your body into 2 separate paragraphs, each of which develops either the advantages or disadvantages of the given issue.

Let's see the complete structure of advantages & disadvantages essay:

Introduction

- Sentence 1: Paraphrase the background information given in the topic
- Sentence 2: Answer the question

Body

First paragraph:

- Sentence 1: The topic sentence (advantages or disadvantages)
- Sentence 2-5/6: 2 advantages or disadvantages

Second paragraph:

- Sentence 1: The topic sentence (advantages or disadvantages)
- Sentence 2-5/6: 2 advantages or disadvantages

Third paragraph: optional (but on the same lines)

Conclusion: The restatement: Restate your answer

Note: If the task asks for your opinion or your favorable side then state your opinion

Problem/Solution or Cause Effect Essays

General information
Such essays ask you to discuss the causes and solutions/effects of a given issue, for example the causes and solutions/effects of overpopulation. DO NOT give any opinions if you are not asked to.

Your cause & effect/solution essays would be structured as follows:

Introduction
- Sentence 1: Paraphrase the background information given in the topic
- Sentence 2: Answer the question

Body
First paragraph:
- Sentence 1: The topic sentence (the causes of the given issue)
- Sentence 2-5/6: Explain in detail 2 causes

Second paragraph:
- Sentence 1: The topic sentence (the effects or solutions of the given issue)
- Sentence 2-5/6: Explain in detail 2 effects/solutions

Third paragraph:(Optional)
- You can add a third paragraph at the appropriate place. If the causes are more then you need to add it as paragraph number 2, and the solutions or effects will be at number 3. If the effects or solutions are more, you can add it at number 3.

Conclusion: The restatement: Restate your answer

Another way to handle a problem/solution essay:
- Make each body paragraph with a problem and its solution.

Difference between Academic and GT Essays

There are very few differences between Academic and GT Essays.

- The biggest difference is that the writing task topics for GT are gerneric and simple as compared to the Academic Exam. The topics for essays in GT are generally related to Family, education and job etc. whereas in Academic the topics can come from a wide variety of subjects such as science, economics etc.
- The essay can be less formal in style as you are normally asked to include personal examples in General Training essays.
- The marking criteria and essay types (Opinion, Problem-Solution, Discuss) are same for both GT and Academic Writing Task 2.

Marking Criteria - Task 2

Each essay is marked on 4 different criteria, which share equal proportion of the overall band score.

1. **Task Response(TR)**
   Answer the question given with relevant ideas and examples. Do not digress. For example, if your essay asks you to write the problems faced by cities because of rapid urbanization, and you write the causes of urbanization, you will be off track and lose out on task response.

2. **Cohesion and Coherence (CC)**
   Coherence means that your essay is easy to read and understand which goes with handwriting and language used in the essay. Cohesion means your essay stays on-topic and does not provide any irrelevant and redundant details.Cohesive devices or transition signals like 'however', 'despite this' and 'In conclusion' should be used more in academic writing. However, this does not mean that you should try to insert as many of these words in to your writing as possible. This is a common mistake in IELTS writing. Using too many of them, or using them inappropriately, can be detrimental. They are important, but must only be used at the appropriate time.

3. **Lexical Resource (LR)**
   This criterion assesses how effectively and accurately you can use your vocabulary to develop your ideas. Big words and phrases might lead to your essay becoming forced and unnatural.

4. **Grammatical Range and Accuracy (GRA)**
   This means, you can use simple, complex and compound sentences, along with proper punctuation   correctly.

IELTS Band Descriptors for Task 2 - Band 6,7,8,9 (Source: IELTS.org)

	Task Response	Cohesion and Coherence	LR – Lexical Resource	GRA– Grammatical Range and Accuracy
Band 6	- Address all parts of the task although some parts may be more fully covered than others - Present a relevant position although the conclusions may become unclear or repetitive - Present relevant main ideas but some may be inadequately developed/unclear	- Arrange information and ideas coherently and have is a clear overall progression - Use cohesive devices effectively, but cohesion within and/or between sentences may be faulty or mechanical - Use referencing clearly or appropriately, although at some places there may be flaws - Use paragraphing, but not always logically	- Use an adequate range of vocabulary for the task - Attempt to use less common vocabulary but with some inaccuracy - Be able to communicate, although you may have some errors in spelling and/or word formation (but they should not impede communication)	- Use a mix of simple and complex sentence forms - Be able to communicate, although you may make some errors in grammar and punctuation (but they rarely reduce communication)
Band 7	- Address all parts of the task - Present, extend and support main ideas, but there may be a tendency to over generalize and/or supporting ideas may lack focus	- Logically organize information and ideas; and have a clear progression throughout - Use a range of cohesive devices appropriately although there may be some under-use or over-use - Present a clear central topic within each paragraph	- Use a sufficient range of vocabulary to allow some flexibility and precision - Use less common lexical items with some awareness of style and collocation, although you may produce occasional errors in word choice, spelling and/or word formation	- Use a variety of complex structures - Produce frequent error-free sentences - Has good control of grammar and punctuation but may make a few errors
Band 8	- Sufficiently address all parts of the task - Present a well-developed response to the question with relevant, extended and supported ideas.	- Sequence information and ideas logically - Manage all aspects of cohesion well - Use paragraphing sufficiently and appropriately	- Use a wide range of vocabulary fluently and flexibly to convey precise meanings - Skillfully use uncommon lexical items but there may be occasional inaccuracies in word choice and collocation, and you have only rare errors in spelling and/or word formation	- Use a wide range of structures - Write a majority of error-free sentences - Make only very occasional errors or inappropriacies
Band 9	- Fully address all parts of the task - Present a well-developed response to the question with relevant, extended and supported ideas.	- Use cohesion in such a way that it attracts no attention - Skillfully manage paragraphing	- Use a wide range of vocabulary with very natural and sophisticated control of lexical features; rare minor errors occur only as 'slips'	- Use a wide range of structures with full flexibility and accuracy, with rare minor errors occurring only as 'slips'

Linking Words for IELTS Essay

Linking words, sometimes called as cohesive devices, discourse markers or transitional words are one of the most important parts of the IELTS Writing module as they bring overall structure and flow to your essay.

Most of the students pursuing IELTS exam, know these words as Firstly, Secondly, Furthermore, However, etcetera. But, once the students become aware about them, they tend to either overuse these words or use them inappropriately. So please make sure, that the linking words are used judiciously in your essay in order to get a high band score for Coherence and Cohesion.

Following is a list of the linking words that you can use in your essay, categorized according to the use.

- **Sequencing** - Firstly, Secondly, Next, Then, After, To begin with, First of all
- **Addition** - And, also, Furthermore, What is more, Moreover, Additionally, To further strengthen this view, another point/fact/factor is
- **Contrast** - In comparison, On the other hand, In Contrast, On the contrary, Admittedly, However, Although, Having said that, That said
- **Comparison** - Also, equally, similarly, likewise, compared with
- **Adding examples** - For example, For instance, To illustrate, To cite an example, To exemplify
- **Result** - So, therefore, As a result, thus, because, consequently, owing to this
- **Highlighting** - In particular, especially, mainly, particularly, above all
- **Restating** - In other words, Put more simply, rather, in simple terms
- **Conclusion** - To sum up, To conclude, To summarise, In conclusion

Useful phrases:
- Not only... but also
- This coupled with (to state an additional related point)
- Undoubtedly, Without a doubt, Indubitably (To state a fact)
- To state further points supporting the same view/point:
- Moreover, Furthermore, What's more, In addition, Additionally, To further strengthen my viewpoint, another point/fact/factor is
- To state opposite view/points:
- In contrast, By contrast, On the other hand, However, Having said that, That said
- To state an advantage regardless of a fact or evidence: Despite this, Nevertheless, Nonetheless, Notwithstanding.

Letters - Index

24.	Apology letter to the landlord for the damages you have done to the kitchen	Formal
25.	Apology letter to your manager because an important office bag was stolen from you	Formal
26.	Letter of thanks to a teacher who was very good when you did a short course in an English speaking country	Formal
27.	Letter to the travel agency to reschedule your flight tickets	Formal
28.	Letter to book a professional photographer	Formal
29.	Letter to offer your concert tickets to a friend as you can't go	Informal
30.	Apology letter to a friend because you can't pick him from airport as planned	Informal
31.	Complaint letter to tour agency who gave you wrong info about another city	Formal
32.	Thank you letter to colleagues who wished you well after you broke your leg	Semi-formal
33.	Letter to college about change of course which was different from its description in the brochure	Formal
34.	Letter to newspaper recommending the best neighbour	Formal
35.	Letter to a friend telling her about your new apartment and inviting her over	Informal
36.	Letter to a friend about a useful (for job) article in magazine	Informal
37.	Letter to the Environment Officer apprising him about the garbage problem in neighbourhood	Formal
38.	To a friend with whom you had lost contact for a long time	Informal
39.	To a friend who knows about a foreign country where you got a job	Informal
40.	Letter to accommodation officer in foreign university	Formal
41.	Letter to train's lost and found departmentabout an object you left behind	Formal
42.	To your manager of a new company overseas requesting for a job for your accompanying relative	Formal
43.	Letter to the producer of a TV show about a place on which a show could be made	Formal
44.	Complaint letter to a store for bad customer service	Formal
45.	Complaint letter to a transport officer about a problem	Formal
46.	Letter to real estate agent for changing your apartment	Formal
47.	Complaint letter to a hotel manager abouta bad experience	Formal
48.	Request letter to a restaurant manager to help organize a party for a friend	Formal
49.	Complaint letter to store manager about furniture item	Formal
50.	Complaint letter to supermarket manager about a faulty item you purchased	Formal
51.	Letter to editor of a magazine about wrong info about a place	Formal
52.	Apology letter toa friend because you damaged something you borrowed	Informal
53.	Letter to a bus company about something you lost in a bus	Formal
54.	Request letter to your neighbour to look after your house	Semi-formal
55.	Complaint letter to online store for two wrong items sent	Formal
56.	Resentment letter to authoritiesobjecting to the plan of making an airport in your area	Formal
57.	Thankyou letter to a friend in another city where you got a job, and he has offered	Informal

	to find accommodation	
58.	Letter to your manager complaining about a colleague	Formal
59.	Letter to your manager recommending a person who is good at translations	Formal
60.	Letter to a college whichis giving you admission in an alternative course	Formal
61.	Reply letter to a friend who has asked about a music academy for her children	Informal
62.	Letter to invite colleagues from a different department to attend a conference you are arranging	Semi-formal
63.	Letter to your manager who is offering some employees to work from home, requesting working from home	Formal
64.	Letter to your manager requesting working from home	Formal
65.	Letter telling your friends a good news and inviting them for party	Informal
66.	Letter to a football team mate as you have to leave the team for a while	Semi-formal
67.	Letter to a classmate about class reunion party	Semi-formal
68.	Letter to a foreign friend who is visiting your country	Informal
69.	Letter to acinema manager about a problem in cinema	Formal
70.	Letter to your friend who is moving to your hometown	Informal
71.	Resentment letter to authorities about plan to replace a library with a supermarket	Formal
72.	Apology letter for inability to attend friend's wedding in Britain	Informal
73.	Complaint letter to the flight manager about behaviour of crew member	Formal
74.	Request letter to teacher for a reference letter for an MNC job	Formal
75.	Letter to an NGO offering voluntary work to help children	Formal
76.	Letter of invitation to a friend in a different city for a family party	Informal
77.	Letter to a friend asking him to apply for a job in your company	Informal
78.	Apology letter to a friend for not keeping an appointment	Informal
79.	Request letter to a financial organisation to fund your course	Formal
80.	Letter to a friend asking her to participate in a public event in your town	Informal
81.	Letter to a travel company to re-reserve the same apartment which you hadon a previous holiday	Formal
82.	Letter to a friend about your relative who is visiting her country	Informal
83.	Letter to your manager telling him about an article in a magazine which printed wrong info about your company	Formal
84.	Letter to decline a full time job offer in a company where you are working part time	Formal
85.	Letter to a tour company appreciating a staff member who helped you	Formal
86.	Letter to a travel agent to change your accommodation in another country where you are going as student	Formal
87.	Letter to your manager asking permission to attend a conference which would help in your work	Formal
88.	Letter to apply for a job in anInternational Hotel	Formal

89.	Letter of complaint to your landlord as he is increasing the rent	Formal
90.	Reply letter to a friend who has asked suggestions about new business	Informal
91.	Letter to friend who is visiting your town	Informal
92.	Apology letter to friend because you damaged something while looking after her house	Informal
93.	Letter to a newspaper appreciating a restaurant	Formal
94.	Apology and thank you letter to a teacher because you couldn't return her book in time	Formal
95.	Application to the HR department against a job ad	Formal
96.	Letter to friends informing them about your new job and inviting them for a party	Informal
97.	Letter to a friend about unpleasant issues at work	Informal
98.	Letter to a language teacher to joinher classes	Formal
99.	Complaint letter to a store manager about a damaged TV	Formal
100.	Letter to an old friend whom you met in your last business trip and are going to meet again	Informal
101.	Complaint letter to a builder	Formal
102.	Complaint letter to sports centre about some problems	Formal
103.	Letter to your child's teacher asking for a day off	Formal
104.	Letter to your course organiser giving feedback about your course	Formal
105.	Letter to a friend telling him about your upcoming holiday in his country	Informal
106.	Letter to local authorities about traffic problems in your area	Formal
107.	Letter to the editor of a magazine which had written defaming things about a restaurant which you like	Formal
108.	Letter to your manager asking permission to give a presentation about a conference which you attended	Formal
109.	Letter to your professor about your dissatisfaction with a short part-time course you are doing	Formal
110.	Letter requesting your principal to issue you a duplicate certificate as you have lost the original	Formal
111.	Letter of thanks to an English speaking friend whom you visited recently	Informal
112.	Letter to college principal about a course you want to do	Formal
113.	Letter to a taxi company about something you forgot in their taxi	Formal
114.	Letter to foreign friend who is coming to attend a wedding in your home but you can't pick her up	Informal
115.	Letter to your employer expressing your inability to attend the computer skills training course	Formal
116.	Letter to a hotel manager about a family party in a private room	Formal
117.	Letter to a language teacher as your children need extra help in that language	Formal
118.	Letter to your manager seeking permission to attend a training course	Formal
119.	Letter to your professor about your inability to attend evening classes	Formal

120.	Letter to a friend requesting help with raising money for charity	Informal
121.	Letter to a café manager about the café you frequent	Formal
122.	Thank you letter to a person who returned something you lost	Semi-formal
123.	Letter to a camp organiser to apply for a job to help with children's summer holiday camp	Formal
124.	Letter to a friend for help in translating a document	Informal
125.	Letter to a colleague who is coming from another country to attend a meeting in your office	Semi-formal
126.	Letter to the manager of a new company declining his job offer	Formal
127.	To a colleague requesting for help with an equipment needed for a presentation	Semi-formal
128.	To the director of a summer school recommending your friend for the post of sports instructor	Formal
129.	To a hotel manager to organise the staff party, which is held every year	Formal
130.	To a hotel manager to book their facilities for a business meeting	Formal
131.	To the manager of a building company expressing resentment on the plan of construction of new housing in a vacant lot of land	Formal
132.	Letter to your ex teacher to borrow books to teach English	Formal
133.	To a friend requesting him to share your holiday photo because you have problems with your photos	Informal
134.	To a tour company because of the problems you faced with a taxi arranged by them	Formal
135.	To a friend to thank him for a meal at his home	Informal
136.	To a college in foreign country which has asked you to volunteer for an international day	Formal
137.	To a restaurant manager whose restaurant is next to your house to tell him about your plans to renovate your house	Formal
138.	To a museum manager to tell him about the problem you and your elderly friend faced	Formal
139.	To a shopkeeper in a different city from where you bought defective clothes	Formal
140.	To the city council because they want to demolish a historic building	Formal
141.	To a friend who had a baby and you want to see her and gift her something for her baby	Informal
142.	For a job to look after a house in Scotland where the owners are going away for some time	Formal
143.	To the manager of a company where you would like to do internship as part of a course.	Formal
144.	In response to a newspaper ad of helping to protect the environment	Formal
145.	To the neighbour because his animals cause noise	Semi-formal
146.	To your manager to critique an article which you have written for a magazine	Formal
147.	To a moving company who damaged some articles while moving	Formal

148.	To a friend who thanked you for helping in an interview.	Informal
149.	To your professor about recent internship and plans after graduation	Formal
150.	To an advertising company for wrong information contained in ad	Formal
151.	To a friend who has asked you to be a partner in a start-up business	Informal
152.	To a newspaper editor about a TV program you like	Formal
153.	To the airport manager regarding a flight you missed	Formal
154.	To your manager as you won't be able to do your job in full because of a minor surgical procedure	Formal
155.	To you colleagues thanking them in your working trip overseas	Semi-formal
156.	To your manager because some office equipment is not working properly	Formal
157.	To thank the manager of a company where you worked for a short period as part of study	Formal
158.	To a museum telling them you found something of historical importance	Formal
159.	To a cinema manager telling him that you lost your bag in the cinema	Formal
160.	To a friend who has offered to take care of your children while you are away	Informal
161.	To a friend who has offered to sell you something	Informal
162.	To the college administration complaining about the college facilities	Formal
163.	To the city council regarding the swimming pool proposed to be built in your hometown	Formal
164.	To a hotel manager thanking him for organizing a successfulparty	Formal
165.	To an NGO where you want to volunteer to look after the elderly	Formal
166.	To an international company where you wish to work without pay	Formal
167.	To a friend advising her what to study	Informal
168.	To a sports club suggesting improvements	Formal
169.	To the local council about the closure of a playground	Formal
170.	To a friend whose elderly parents are coming to visit you	Formal
171.	To a telephone company which sent your bill to the wrong address	Formal
172.	To a teacher who has invited you to her home but you cannot go	Formal
173.	To a travel agency for an unsatisfactory trip	Formal
174.	To the editor of a newspaper about your social meetings	Formal

Essays - Index

33.	Physical activities (sports) in schools	Education
34.	Should teenagers study all school subjects or only those in which they are interested in	Education
35.	Unpaid internships – pros and cons	Education
36.	Importance of the skill of handwriting	Education
37.	Importance of arts, drama, creative writing in schools	Education
38.	Students who don't do well become successful in life. Reasons for this. What is needed for successful life	Education
39.	Should teachers be friendly or strict//Should students be afraid or have friendly relationship with teachers	Education
40.	To be a good teacher is training required or is experience enough	Education
41.	Should public speaking be taught in schools	Education
42.	School starting age	Education
43.	Private tuitions - advantages/disadvantages	Education
44.	Nursery schools – advantages/disadvantages	Education
45.	Schools open till late – pros and cons	Education
46.	Science and technology vs. history and geography in primary schools	Education
47.	Academic subjects like history and physics vs. practical subjects like car machinery and cookery	Education
48.	Practical subjects like car maintenance and managing a bank account in addition to academic subjects	Education
49.	Traditional subjects like history vs. communication skills and business management	Education
50.	Music vs. science in primary schools	Education
51.	Should schools impart moral values	Education
52.	Who is better at learning a foreign language – Young or old	Education - Language
53.	What is the difficult part of learning a foreign language	Education - Language
54.	Should foreign language be mandatory in schools	Education - Language
55.	No need of human interpreters of language because computers can translate languages	Education - Language
56.	Some languages losing their importance and may become extinct	Education - Language
57.	Should schools invest in teachers or technology with their limited resources	Education
58.	Students and school administration	Education
59.	Road transport is taking over rail transport – positive or negative	Transport - Travel
60.	Cars vs. public transport -	Transport - Travel
61.	Should cars be banned in city centres	Transport - Travel
62.	Air travel has become cheaper – positive or negative	Transport - Travel
63.	Should roads be widened to solve traffic problems	Transport - Travel
64.	Increasing number of private cars is positive or negative	Transport Travel

65.	Decrease in international travel in future will be positive or negative	Transport/ Travel
66.	Youth tourism – travelling abroad is positive or negative for the youth	Transport/ Travel
67.	Travelling alone or with someone	Travel Tourism
68.	Free public transport	Transport Travel
69.	Should visitors follow host country's customs	Tourism
70.	Noise pollution	Environment
71.	Tourist destinations being damaged - Reasons and solutions	Environment - Tourism
72.	Negative environmental effects of tourism	Environment - Tourism
73.	Do tourists learn or not by touring	Tourism
74.	Why people are travelling. Is it good or bad for host country	Tourism
75.	Car vs. bicycle in city centres	Environment
76.	Should companies which cause pollution be taxed	Environment
77.	Why people don't care for the environment	Environment
78.	People prefer bicycles – effects of this	Environment
79.	Rubbish is increasing – Problem/ solution	Environment
80.	Garbage has increased globally – Solutions	Environment
81.	In spite of technological developments in transportation, many people believe that a bicycle is the best way to reach any destination. What are the advantages and disadvantages of using bicycles nowadays?	Environment
82.	Most countries allow 18 year olds to start driving a car. Some say it is good to allow driving at that age. Others think that the age to start driving should be at least 25 years. Discuss both views and opine.	Environment Age of driving
83.	Weekly pocket money is good for children – agree or disagree	Money matters
84.	Plastic money -	Money matters
85.	Money and happiness	Money matters
86.	Spending money on looks is good or not good	Money matters
87.	Spending on birthdays and other events	Money matters
88.	Death penalty or capital punishment	Crime
89.	People watching crime in movies – reasons and effects	Crime Media
90.	Prisons vs. education and job training	Crime Prisons
91.	Should the purpose of TV be to educate or to entertain	Media - TV
92.	Watching TV is enjoyable or is it a waste of time.	Media - TV
93.	TV vs. other form of media	Media - TV
94.	Radio vs. TV and internet	Media - Radio
95.	Which is the best medium for news	Media - News
96.	More media attention to celebs – Reasons and effects	Media and celebs
97.	Should media publicize people's private lives	Media and private lives

98.	TV contributes more than other inventions to the life of man	Media TV vs. other inventions
99.	National news vs. international news	Media - News
100.	Use of internet for shopping and information – Advantages and disadvantages	Media - Internet –pros and cons
101.	Films as educational tools for children	Media - Films
102.	Internet vs. traditional books	Media Internet and book
103.	Latest technology's effect on communication	Technology – Communication
104.	Is there less communication than past	Technology - Communication
105.	People use electronic equipment – Is it good or bad	Technology - Electronic equipment
106.	Computers have made the world better – Agree or disagree	Technology- Computers
107.	Adults playing computer games – reasons and whether it is good or bad	Technology – Computer games
108.	Manual jobs being done by machines is good or bad	Technology -Machine automation
109.	Mobile phones are more useful in personal or professional lives	Technology – Cell phones
110.	Social networking sites – Good or bad for making friends	Technology – Social network sites
111.	Many adults think that childhood and schooldays are the best years of a person's life. What's the reason for this? Do you agree or disagree?	Children - Childhood
112.	Should parents control the behaviour of children from a very young age	Children - Rules
113.	Children brought up in joint families	Children – Joint families
114.	Teenagers and their problems	Children – Problems
115.	Children and cell phones	Children – Cell phones
116.	Children and computer games – vs. outdoor games	Children – Computer games
117.	Children and computer games vs. reading	Children – Computer games
118.	Young people are less polite than past Reasons and solutions	Young people - less polite
119.	People marrying late	Family – Late marriages
120.	Paid maternity leave	Family
121.	Childcare courses for all parents-to-be	Family
122.	Children and violent cartoon characters on TV	Children and TV
123.	Children and too much TV	Children and TV
124.	TV can help in children's development or not	Children and TV

125.	Children wanting to watch same TV programmes and play same video games as friends	Children and parallel play
126.	Children leave parents homes and live on their own	Children living alone
127.	Family more important than friends	Children and family vs. friends
128.	Children learn more from team sports or solo sports	Children – team sports
129.	Why people live alone	Family
130.	Rural young people moving to cities, old people live in villages	Family
131.	Urbanization and its problems	Family Urbanization
132.	Children and toys	Children toys
133.	Generation gap	Children Family
134.	Children being brought up in cities or countryside	Children family
135.	Children and responsibility	Children
136.	Children and health	Children
137.	Childs success depends on parents bringing up	Children family
138.	Children and official adulthood	Children
139.	Should children obey parents or take own decisions	Children
140.	Old people looked after by children or old age homes	Old people
141.	Old people being looked after by professionals in their homes	Old people
142.	More old people than young – Why and advantages disadvantages	Old people
143.	Why people are living longer	Old people
144.	People and stress	People and stress
145.	Was life better in the past	People and life
146.	People like hot climate vs. cold climate	People climate
147.	Should government be held responsible for homelessness and unemployment	Government - homelessness
148.	Should hobbies be difficult to be enjoyable	People - hobbies
149.	Should old buildings be restored or new ones made	Buildings architecture
150.	Reasons why historic buildings are being destroyed and ways to protect them	Buildings/ architecture
151.	Modernization of cities	Buildings/architecture
152.	House vs. apartment	Buildings/architecture
153.	High rise apartments and people's loneliness	Buildings/architecture
154.	Should new houses be built in existing towns or should there be new towns	Cities / Urbanization
155.	Renting vs. buying	People housing
156.	Should zoos be abolished	Animals
157.	Purpose of zoos	Animals
158.	Should government preserve wildlife	Animals
159.	Ads - advantages and disadvantages	Ads

160.	Effects of ads	Ads
161.	Ads and children	Ads
162.	Modern clothes vs. traditional clothes	Globalization
163.	Food traditions are changing – reasons and solutions	Globalization
164.	Changing ones looks	Miscellaneous
165.	Fashion	Miscellaneous
166.	Modern lifestyle and health	Health
167.	People don't eat healthy and don't do enough exercise	Health
168.	People doing excessive exercise - Causes and solutions	Health
169.	Fast food	Health – Food
170.	International sporting events contribute to peace and stability in the world.	Sports
171.	Why people do dangerous sports	Sports
172.	Should dangerous sports be banned	Sports
173.	Hosting international sporting events	Sports
174.	Does technology reduce the role of Olympics	Sports
175.	Football hooliganism	Sports
176.	Professional sportsman behaviour on and off the field	Sports
177.	Competitive sport and children	Sports
178.	Why people are purchasing more second hand goods	Shopping
179.	Shopping as an entertainment or hobby	Shopping
180.	Shops open 24/7. Is it good or bad	Shopping
181.	Online shopping	Shopping
182.	Is it good that ordinary people copy famous people whom they see on TV and magazines	Famous people

Writing Task 1

Letter

1. Write a letter to local authorities by requesting additional sports facilities for your age group in your area.

- Mention about the current sport facilities available.
- What kind of additional sports facilities should be introduced?
- How the new sports facilities would be a help for the people in your age group?

Dear Sir,

I am Kuldeep Singh, a resident of Guru Hargobind Nagar, Phagwara. I am working in HDFC bank in the NRI branch. I am writing this letter to request you to provide some new sports facilities for the young people of this area.

Presently, there are not many sports facilities in this town. Children play sports like cricket and hockey in the ground of the Government High School. But, there is no facility for sports in the after office hours, where people of my age can play any sport.

Sir, there is an open ground next to the school, which has become a dumping spot for people to throw garbage and other waste materials. This area is under the municipal corporation of the city. This place would be ideal for an indoor stadium for games like badminton and lawn tennis. It is my humble request to use this place for the stadium.

This would benefit not only the young office goers, but also the children and youth of this area. Such a place is much needed as we are leading sedentary lives, and some physical activity is imperative for all of us.

Hoping for a careful consideration of this suggestion.

Yours faithfully,
Kuldeep Singh

2. You are getting married. Write a letter to an English-speaking friend to invite him/her to the wedding. In your letter

- Describe who you are going to marry.
- Tell what will happen on the wedding day (the schedule).
- Explain why it's important for him/her to be at the wedding.

Dear Sarah,

Hope this letter finds you in radiant health and the best of spirits. I am getting married on 5th March 2016 and I am writing this letter to formally invite you to the wedding. You always wanted to attend an Indian wedding and believe me you are going to enjoy all ceremonies that are attached with the actual wedding ceremony.

My fiancé, Tarun Sharma, is working with Dell International as a senior web developer. We met at my cousin's wedding 6 months ago for the first time and we had an instant liking for each other. He approached my parents through his parents and so it is an arranged-cum-love-marriage affair.

You must come one week in advance because on the 28th of February, we have the ring ceremony and on the 1st of March there is the 'Ladies Sangeet'. It is a very interesting celebration in which you will get to taste a lot of folk culture of Punjab. Then we have the 'Mehandi' ceremony on the 3rd of March and finally the great wedding day on the 5th. You know in a traditional Hindu wedding, the priest lights up a fire around which the bride and groom circle and take holy vows. After the 'Doli' ceremony, I shall leave my parent's home to go to my new home with my husband.

You are my best friend and I also heard you are doing a research on the Indian Tradition and Culture. Therefore, it is very important for you to attend the wedding so you get a first-hand experience of many things. After the wedding, you are welcome to stay with my parents for some time and my younger sister shall take you around to see some tourist spots.

Hoping to see you at the wedding.

Yours with love,
Kiran

---

3. Write a letter to the manager of a hotel where you stayed and left two important things.

- Give details of your stay.
- Why those two things are important?
- How he can return the things to you?

Dear Mr. Smith,

I am writing this letter to request you to check for my things, which I accidentally left in my hotel room. My name is Indroop Singh and I stayed in your hotel on the 23rd and 24th of January. I was in Room 203. When I arrived home, I discovered that I had left one of my trousers and a belt at the hotel. Could you please check with your housekeeping department and see if my things are there?

The trousers are black corduroy of Levi's brand in size 40. The belt is in leather and has a golden buckle. Inside one pocket of my trousers you will find several business cards, a fountain pen and a small address book. These things are not very valuable cost wise, but I need them all the same.

I would appreciate it if you could contact me as soon as possible, particularly since I need the address book urgently. If you could send the things by courier service, I would be most grateful. I would gladly pay for the service. I can transfer the money to your bank account or payTM account. My address is 341, Guru Hargobind Nagar, Phagwara. My phone number is 98xxxxxxxx, in case you need to call me for some information.

Thank you for your help.

Yours sincerely,
Indroop Makkar

---

4. A friend from abroad is visiting your country next month. She is planning to stay with you, but you can't accommodate her. Write a letter to her

- Tell her the reasons.
- Apologise.
- Make alternative arrangements.

Dearest Elaine,

I was overjoyed when I heard that you are planning a trip to India, and you have planned to stay with me, but when I came to know of your itinerary, I felt sad. My father's open-heart surgery has been planned in those days in Delhi, and so I will not be at home.. I am writing letter to apologise for my inability to accommodate you during that time.

My father had pain in his chest last week for which we got an angiography done. He has blockagesin two arteries of the heart and as he is a diabetic, he is not fit for angioplasty. So he needs a bypass surgery and will need hospitalization for three weeks.

If it is possible for you to postpone your trip, it would be great, but in case you have to come in these days only, then my cousin Suman, who is in Delhi would be happy to accommodate you and show you around. He works in an MNC in Delhi, but can take days off during your visit. Alternatively, I could plan a sight-seeing tour for you through Pack Travels, which is a domestic tour operating company. As your visit is for only ten days, they could plan a tour to Rajasthan, which would be very exciting for you.

Do let me know at the earliest, what you would prefer, so that I can make the arrangements accordingly.

Hoping to hear from you soon.

Yours lovingly,
Kiran

5. The company you work for has decided to close the cafeteria, as the staff is not using it much. You are not happy with the decision. Write a letter to the director

- Give reasons of low usage.
- How will it affect the staff?
- Suggest ways to improve it.

Dear Sir,

I am writing this letter to express my concern about the closing of the cafeteria within the company premises. My name is Kiran, and I work in the marketing department. I frequent the café two or three times a week, and I firmly believe that if the services of the café are improved, almost all the employees would start going there more often.

The cafeteria is a nice place to hang out with colleagues in the lunch and coffee break. I remember about a couple of years ago, it used to be always crowded. Now, only a handful of workers are working there, because of which it takes ages to serve an order. Out of the four microwaves, only one is working, so the staff has to wait a lot to reheat their tiffin. Now most of the employees prefer eating at their desks. That is why the cafeteria seems like a haunted place, with almost nobody there at times.

If the café is closed, there will be no place for the workers to sit and have their meals. If the café management employs a few more workers and gets the microwave ovens repaired, then the café will become a cheerful and crowded place once again.

Hoping for a kind consideration regarding this matter from your side.

Yours faithfully,
Kiran

6. You travelled abroad and faced some problems at the airport. Write a letter to the airport manager. In your letter provide

- Your flight details.
- What is the problem?
- Suggest some improvement you want to see.

Dear Sir,

I arrived in Houston, Texas, on 12th January for a business trip. I am writing this letter to complain about the problem I faced at the baggage recovery section of the airport.

My name is Sarabjeet Singh and I arrived in Texas on 12th January afternoon by flight number KL 881. I came from New Delhi. My flight was via Amsterdam, where I had a four-hour halt. After I checked in at New Delhi, I was told that I would get my baggage at Houston. When I arrived in Houston, my baggage did not arrive. I was told to report to the 'Lost and Found' section. When I went there, I was told to wait, as it was lunch hour. The concerned person came after two hours whereas the lunch hour is meant to be only one hour. The cab I had booked charged me extra for having to wait so long.

When people arrive after such a tiring journey, then such a long wait at the airport can be very irksome. The 'Lost and Found' department should work round the clock. There should be no lunch hour or at least someone should be there all the time.

I request you sir to do something about this matter, so that travelers do not face such problems in future.

Thanking you,

Yours truly,
Sarabjeet Singh

---

7. Your friend wants to send her/his children to your house for the weekend. Write a letter to him/her and say

- Agree to this arrangement.
- Say what time is suitable for you.
- Describe what you are planning to do.

Dear Sonia,

It was great to hear from you after such a long time. I would love to have Gia and Tanay over for the weekend. You know how much I love children. I am looking forward to having a splendid time with them.

These days I am on morning shift, so you can drop both of them any time after 2 pm. Let me know their favourite dishes, so that I can prepare them in advance, and then spend all the time with them.

I have planned many things for them. Friday evening will be movie time. There is a very nice animation movie 'Pete's Dragon', which they would love. On Saturday, I will take them to Hardy's World, which is a famous fun park, where there are many rides for children. I am sure they will enjoy that too. On Sunday morning I will take them to a mini zoo, which is in Chandigarh.

Hoping to see them soon.

Yours lovingly,
Kiran

8. You have recently faced a problem at the airport. An employee of the airport helped you with this matter. Write a letter to the airport manager and say

- What was the problem?
- How did that person help you?
- Suggest the manager to praise this employee in some way.

Dear Sir,

My name is Indroop Singh and my family and I have just returned from a two-week vacation in Goa. I am writing this letter to thank one of your employees, Mr Rohit Basu, who helped us with a problem we faced at the airport.

Last Monday, my family and I returned from our vacation in Goa. As we were going to the carousel to collect our baggage my son, Raju, fell from the escalator. Fortunately, he sustained only minor injuries, but we were all very upset. After some time my wife realised that her handbag was missing. Our passports and other important documents were in that purse. We searched everywhere but couldn't find it. Then we met Mr. Rohit Basu, who helped us search for our purse, which someone had deposited in the 'Lost and Found' department. We heaved a sigh of relief when we saw the purse.

Mr Rohit Basu also personally took care of my son who had suffered minor injuries because of the fall. What he has done for me cannot be compensated in any way, but it would be very kind of you if you could convey our thanks to him. We are highly indebted to him for his act of kindness. I have heard that you have an award for the best employee of the month. It would be very nice if you propose his name for the best employee of this month.

Yours faithfully,
Indroop Singh

9. You recently won a photography competition and your photo is going to be shown in an exhibition. Invite your friend for the exhibition. Please describe
- Competition and prize.
- About the photograph.
- Invite your friend.

Dear Elaine,

Hope this letter finds you in radiant health and the best of spirits. I am writing this letter to share with you the good news that I have won the first prize in a photography competition and this photograph is going to be displayed in an exhibition. I would love it if you could come for the exhibition.

You know very well how much passion I have for photography. My sister brought a Canon Power Shot camera for me three years ago and I have been clicking photographs of anything that fascinated me ever since. Last month, I went to my uncle's village and there I saw peacocks in their front lawn. My uncle told me that they were regular visitors. I could capture such close-ups of those peacocks and peahens, that even I couldn't believe my eyes when I saw those photographs.

Every year I participate in a photography competition conducted by an NGO of my hometown. They have a prize of Rs. 10,000 for the winner and then they display these photographs in an exhibition for sale and spend that money on charity. I am very excited that my photograph will be in the exhibition.

The exhibition is on 12th April in Club Cabana. You must come for sure. It would be great fun.

Hoping to see you soon.

Yours lovingly,
Kiran

10. Your friend bought tickets to the theatre for both of you. Write a letter to him to tell him that you cannot go to the theatre. In your letter
- Apologize.
- Explain the situation.
- Tell him what he can do with the extra ticket.

Dear Mankeerat,

I hope this letter finds you in radiant health and the best of spirits. It was really nice of you to buy theatre tickets for both of us, but unfortunately, I shall not be able to come as some unexpected guests have come from abroad and I have to be at home to attend to them. I sincerely apologise for the inconvenience it has caused you.

My uncle and aunt live in Canada. They arrived here three days ago with their daughter to fix her wedding with someone from my hometown. They have come here after five years. If the wedding is fixed, then all the arrangements have to be done and I am going to be very busy for the coming few days. Even now I have to be with them while they are finalizing things.

I was wondering, if you could invite our old friend Ramesh to go to the theatre with you. He is here on a holiday. He has come for the first time since he left for his higher studies in Australia two years ago. This would be your opportunity to catch up with him and your extra ticket will also not go waste.

Hope you have a nice time with Ramesh.

Yours lovingly,
Kiran

---

11. You had an appointment with the bank and now you realized that you can't make it for that. Write a letter to the manager

- Give details about your appointment and dates.
- Explain the reason why you cannot make it.
- Ask for other dates.

Dear Sir,

I have a meeting regarding a home loan fixed with you for the 24th of April 2018. Unfortunately, I shall not be able to make it on that day. I apologise for the inconvenience caused because of this.

My elderly aunt and uncle are arriving from Canada for one week, which happens to be the last week of April. I have to be with them during the entire week and therefore I have cancelled all my appointments for that week. Actually, they want to get their complete medical examinations done from here. Even after being in Canada for so long they trust our Indian doctors much more.

I would be very grateful if you could reschedule our appointment for any day in the first week of May. You can call me at 98xxxxxxxx to inform me the new date or alternatively you may e-mail me at kiranmakkar@hotmail.com.

Once again I apologise for the inconvenience and thank you for your kind consideration.

Yours faithfully,
Kiran

12. Write a letter to a restaurant manager to organise a party.
- Why you want to give the party?
- What special arrangements you will need?
- Any relevant questions.

Dear Sir/Madam,

My name is Sumeet and I frequent your restaurant, Zafraan. Your restaurant has a very good reputation and I personally have always experienced very good service, and even the quality of food is excellent. I am writing this letter to book your restaurant's banquet hall for a party on the 30th of November.

The party is on the occasion of my parents' Golden wedding anniversary celebration and there will be around 70 guests attending this party. So, the food and sitting arrangements need to be done accordingly. I have something in mind for the flowers and the table decoration. If you have an in-house florist, I can discuss and give them the details. However, if possible, I would like to get the decorations taken care of by a local florist I know.

In the food menu, Indian and Chinese dishes have to be included, which need to be both vegetarian and non-vegetarian. I would also request a corner reserved for the DJ and the dance floor.

I will be free to discuss the menu details and the cost of the entire arrangement over the weekend. Kindly let me know a suitable time to visit you at the restaurant on the weekend, so that we can discuss these details.

Looking forward to your response.

Yours faithfully,
Sumeet Kaur

13. You have a spare room in your flat/apartment and you want to rent it to a student. Write a letter to the accommodation office of the local college. In your letter
- Explain where your apartment is.
- Why you want to rent?
- What sort of person would you like to rent it to?

Dear Sir/Madam,

I am writing this letter to apprise you that I have an extra room in my house, which I would like to rent out to a student. I would be very grateful if you could find a suitable student tenant for me.

My name is Mukta Sharma, and I am working in New Ruby Hospital as a Resident Nurse. My house is just 5 minutes' walk from your college. I have seen that many students of your college live as tenants in apartments near my house. I also have a room, which I could rent out for some extra income. Moreover, my children are settled abroad and my husband and I would love to have some company.

This room has a separate entrance and an attached kitchen and bathroom. It would be nice if you could find a grad student, as they are more mature than the undergrad students. The rent I am expecting is Rs. 1200/- Per month. As my house is very near the college, the student will not have to spend extra on travelling to the college. I have a pet dog, so please make that known to the student beforehand.

Kindly let me know if there is any student needing a room for rent. My contact number is 9888195576.

Hoping to hear from you soon.

Yours faithfully,
Mukta Sharma

14. A college asked its graduates to give a speech to current students about their professional careers and future opportunities. You would like to participate. Write a letter and say
- What do you want to talk about?
- Why do you think students will be interested in it?
- Suggest a suitable date and time for your speech.

Dear Sir,

I am writing this letter to express my willingness to address your current students about their professional careers and future prospects, and at the same time I would like to thank you for thinking me capable of doing so.

I would like to talk about the various vistas open for them in the modern technological world. I did my graduation in science from your college, but after that I did my masters in Environmental Science from University of California. During that time I happened to work part time as a student counselor for the undergrads. There I learnt about the various new fields for the undergrad students. I would like to share all what I learnt there with your students.

Presently I am working as a research scholar in University of California. Fortunately, I am coming to India for a three-week vacation, next month. I would be free from the 10th to the 20th of December. Do let me know any day and time which would be suitable for you. I will be happy to interact with the new students and to revive some nostalgic memories of my college days.

Hoping to hear from you soon. My contact number is 98xxxxxxxx, in case you need to call me.

Yours faithfully,

Kiran Makkar

---

15. You were sent by your company to attend a meeting in another country, but you are not happy with the hotel your organizer booked for you. Write a letter to your organiser about
- The meeting you attended.
- Your complaint about the hotel.
- What you'd like the organiser to do about it?

Dear Sir,

I have just returned home after attending the business meeting which you had organised. I am writing this letter to express my dissatisfaction with the hotel arranged for my stay. I had to spend three nights at hotel Blue Skylark in Bangkok, Thailand.

The meeting went very well. I presented my products to all delegates who had come from different places and also asked their opinions on the same. They appreciated the quality of our products and were also very happy with the cost. Hopefully, we will be receiving a bulk order from them very soon.

I would like to apprise you with the problems I faced with the hotel. The location was very far from the place of the meeting, and I had a lot of problem in communicating with the staff of the hotel. There was no one who knew English. They only spoke Thai, and I had no knowledge of their language. As a result, I wasn't able to reach the venue of the meeting in time on the first day. I could also not order vegetarian food properly because they couldn't understand me.

I would like you to be careful about the hotel bookings in future. Kindly ensure that the hotel bookings in another country are made with proper research so that the employees, who have to travel abroad, are not inconvenienced.

Yours faithfully,

Kiran

16.Write a letter to a friend who is looking for a part time job to support his studies. In your letter
- Describe the job you found for him/her.
- Explain why this job is good for him/her.
- Say what he/she needs to do to get the job.

Dear Ravi,

Hope this letter finds you in radiant health and the best of spirits. When we met the last time you mentioned that you are looking for a part-time job, and this is the reason I am writing to you today.

Yesterday, I met up with our old friend Saranjeet, who owns a fast food joint in Hargobind Nagar, Jalandhar. He said that his business was really starting to grow and that he was looking for part time home delivery boys. When I mentioned that you were looking for a part time job, he seemed very eager to contact you and talk about employment possibilities. Apparently the job would involve delivering fast food orders to customers on bikes.

I thought this job would be perfect for you as you are free in the evenings and you know well how to ride a bike. Above all that, you know the streets of Jalandhar inside out as you have stayed there for three years when your father was posted there. This job is from 6 pm to 9 pm and you will get Rs.3000/- per month apart from the tips you would get from customers.

I hope this opportunity piques your interest. You should contact Saran if you are interested in the job. His contact number is 988819577698xxxxxxxx.

Yours lovingly,
Kiran

17.You found a small bag somewhere. The owner's address and name was there on the bag. Write a letter to the owner
- Inform where you found the bag.
- Write about the contents of the bag.
- How he or she can collect it?

Dear Mr. Singh,

I am writing this letter to inform you that I found your bag in the Golden TempleExpress train as I travelled from Jalandhar to New Delhi, yesterday.

New Delhi is the last stoppage of Golden Temple Express and as I was the last passenger to de-train, I saw this bag lying on aseat. Out of curiosity, I opened the bag and found your visiting card in it with some important papers and a bunch of keys. You probably got down at Ambala and forgot the bag in the train.

I can understand how worried you must be because the bag contains some papers, your driving licence and some keys. Now you can put your mind at peace because your bag is safe and secure with me. You can collect the bag from me on any weekend. My address is 341, Model Town, Jalandhar. Just give me a call before coming so that I am at home when you come. My phone number is 98xxxxxxxx.

Yours sincerely,
Narinder

---

18. Write a letter to your manger to nominate a person for best employee of the year award. Explain in your letter

- Who is this person?
- Why did you choose him/her?
- What are the characteristics of a good employee?

Dear Sir,

I am Kiranpreet Kaur from the marketing department of our company. I am writing this letter to draw to your attention an extraordinary colleague for the award of the best employee of the year 2017. Her name is Harpreet Kaur, and she is heading the manufacturing department of our company for the last two years.

I chose to nominate Harpreet's name because I have been associated with her for the last two years and I have found her to be very hardworking, conscientious and determined. Since I work in marketing, I get regular feedback from our customers about our products. No one has ever complained about the quality of any product for the last two years. Because of our quality control, our sales have grown more than five times in the last one1 year.

Harpreet fulfills all the characteristics of a good employee. She is punctual, cooperative with all her colleagues, respects others and has a great sense of humour. When she is around, everyone is in a happy mood and the work output goes up. I believe she deserves the best employee of the year award.

Hoping for a due consideration of my suggestion for considering Harpreet for the award.

Yours affectionately,
Kiranpreet

19.Your colleague has invited you to his farewell party. You will not be able to attend the party, write a letter to the friend.

- Explain the situation,
- Say why you will not be attending,
- Say something about the period you have worked together and his/her work.

Dear Nidheesh,

It was with mixed emotions that I got the news of your retirement because it also brings with it the fact that you are leaving us all. Thanks for inviting me to your farewell party, but regretfully I have to inform you that I would not be able to make it on that day because of an important family wedding on that very day.

It so happens that my first cousin's wedding is also on the same day. It is a family affair and I cannot be absent from there. I am an active participant in the arrangements of that day. Any other appointment could have been avoided or postponed but I just cannot miss this one.

Anyways, I wish you all the best in life. Whatever time I have spent with you in office will always have pleasant memories in my mind. It is from you that I have learnt how to meticulously plan my time. You have always been my friend, philosopher and guide. I shall always keep in touch through phone and e-mail. My e-mail ID is rajeshkakkar@rediffmail.com. Do let me know your new phone number so that I can keep in touch.

Yours truly,
Rajesh

20.You have rented an apartment recently, but you are facing some problems. Write a letter to the landlord:

- Describe the details of the problems.
- How are these affecting your family?
- Ask for possible solutions.

Dear Mr. James,

I am your new tenant from apartment number 341, Harrison Street. I moved in with my family one week ago. I am writing this letter to apprise you with some difficulties that we are facing in the apartment, and also to request you to find some solutions for these problems urgently.

The taps in the bathrooms are leaking because of which my two year old daughter has slipped twice. The shower is also not working properly. The lock of the main door is also not aligned properly. We have to push the door hard to lock it.

All these problems need immediate action. As you have rented out so many apartments, you must be having a tie-up with some plumber and carpenter. You may call them directly or give me their contact numbers so that I can call them at the earliest. As you know I have signed a lease of one year with you and the rent is also on the higher side because you have included the maintenance charges in that.

Hoping for a prompt action from your side.

Yours sincerely,
Kiran

---

21. You are shifting out of your accommodation. You think the place is suitable for your English-speaking colleague who is arriving next month. Write a letter to your colleague.

- Explain why you are shifting out.
- Describe your accommodation.
- Why is it suitable for your friend?

Dear Harry,

Hope this letter finds you in radiant health and the best of spirits. I heard from Nid that you have found a job in Long Island. Congratulations for getting such a good job. Unfortunately, I have to move to Madison this month. So, I shall not be able to meet you.

My company has given me a promotion and a transfer. So, I have to move by the end of the month. The apartment in which I have been staying as a tenant for the past 2 years is very good. The landlord is quite nice and he has provided many facilities, such as a gym and a swimming pool. It is a two BHK apartment and the rent is also very nominal. So, I would suggest you move in here after I leave. You can sign the lease after you move here. I can ask my landlord to hold the apartment for you.

This apartment would be very suitable for you. It is in the centre of the town so your workplace cannot be far away. Secondly, I have bought a lot of furniture, which I cannot carry with me. As it is I would have to throw it away but now it can be very useful to you.

In case you decide to rent this apartment, please let me know so that I can talk to my landlord about it.

Yours lovingly,
XYZ

22. Write to a friend who has asked you about a short course, which you have done.

- Write about the content of the course.
- The future benefit of the course.

Dear Sunita,

It was great to hear from you after a long time. You have asked me about the CELTA course which I did last year. Well, it is a great certificate course of one month, and you also must do it.

CELTA stands for 'Certificate in Teaching English to Speakers of Other Languages'. It is a one month course, which makes the person eligible to teach English anywhere in the world. CELTA trainees must be at least 20-years-old and have a first degree or equivalent.

The one-month CELTA experience was the best thing that ever happened to me in the sphere of my career development. The course as delivered by the CELTA trainers, brought out the best teacher in me. The entire course was filled with elements of learning, fun, enjoyment, activities and it not only gave me the opportunity to be a good teacher, but also to develop myself as a better person, as a better individual.

After doing this course, the future prospects are very bright. CELTA has changed my life for the better, and I have received job offers from educational Institutes in Turkey, Dubai and Vietnam. I am currently based in India as a full time ESL teacher involved with students from the age group of 3 years to 50 years. The pay package is also very lucrative. I would sincerely like to mention that, without CELTA, I wouldn't have been able to make it this far and attain success in my current position.

Hope I have satisfied your curiosity about this course. In case you are interested, you can get more information from the following link -
https://www.britishcouncil.in/teach/teacher-training/cambridge-celta.

Hoping to hear from you soon.

Yours with love,
Kiran

23. Write a letter to apply for a job as an English-speaking tour guide.
- Where you saw the advertisement?
- Justify the reason why you deem yourself fit for the job.

Dear Sir,

I am writing this letter to apply for the post of an English-speaking tour guide in your esteemed company, 'Pack Travels'. I saw your advertisement in the Tribune dated 5/12/2016.

I have done my Masters in History from Punjab University, Chandigarh, and my schooling has been in English medium throughout. I believe I would be the perfect candidate for the job. I love travelling and your job requires the guides to accompany foreign tourists to different tourist attractions all over India. My knowledge of history would also be very useful as a tour guide.

I am attaching my resume along with this letter. I assure you that if you hire me for the job, I would prove an asset to your company. Yours is a very reputed company in the travel and tourism business. It would be a great honour for me if I get an opportunity to serve as a tour guide in your company.

Hoping for a favourable response from you regarding my application.

Yours faithfully,
Kiranpreet Kaur

24. You caused some damages in the kitchen area of your flat. Write a letter to your landlord explaining the following
- How the damage occurred
- The extent of damages
- What would you like your landlord to do

Dear Sir,

I am Jagtar Singh, your tenant from apartment 1011, Western Creek. I am writing to apologise for some damages that I accidentally caused in the kitchen, and to request you to get them fixed as soon as possible.

I moved into your apartment about 15 days ago from India. I was not aware of the smoke alarm system. I started making paratha, an Indian flatbread, which needs some frying. Suddenly the smoke alarm started beeping and would not stop. In a panic I tried to remove it and its screw broke and it came off. Now, I cannot fix it back. I am aware that it would be risky to use the kitchen without the smoke alarm. Secondly, the kitchen drain is making noises, as I forgot to put the kitchen sink drain strainer on top, because of which maybe a spoon slipped inside.

The damages are not very major, but need immediate attention. It would be very kind of you if you could get these two problems, caused by me, fixed soon. I will be very careful in the future, so that such mishaps don't occur.

Thanking you,

Yours faithfully,
Jagtar Singh

25.A bag containing valuable company documents that you were carrying has been stolen. Write a letter to your manager mentioning:

- How the bag was stolen?
- What the bag contained?
- How important were the docs for your company?
- What you have done about it so far?

Dear Sir,

My name is Arun Mahala and I work in the accounts section of our company as senior accounts manager. I am writing this letter to inform you that my bag, which contained some important company documents, has been stolen. I would also like to apologise for my carelessness.

As I was going home on Friday in my car, I stopped at the petrol pump to get some petrol and to get the air checked in the tires of my car. I was out of my car for about 5 minutes over there. After that, I stopped at the chemist shop for about five minutes, as I had to buy some medicines for my mother. In my hurry I did not lock my car there. On reaching home I discovered that my briefcase was not there on the back seat. I remembered very well that I had put it there.

The bag contained all the account reports of this month, which I know are very confidential. The company's laptop was also in the bag, as I intended to sit and do some work on the weekend. I realise that the documents are very important for the company.

I have lodged an FIR in the police station. Both the chemist shop and the petrol pump have surveillance cameras fitted. I only hope the footage reveals some positive results. Once again I apologise for all this inconvenience.

Yours faithfully,
Arun Mahala

26. You have recently done a short-term course in an English speaking country and found one of your teachers to be very good. Write a letter to the teacher

- Thank him/her.
- Say why you liked his/her lessons.
- Say what your further planning of study is.

Dear Sir,

My name is Mohit and I am from India. I am writing this letter to thank you for your guidance, because of which I passed out with flying colours. It was wonderful being your student in the 'Business Management Course' this year at Melbourne.

I was always weak in Commerce but your exceptional communication skills and depth of knowledge made it very easy for me. You are really very good at coming down to the level of the student and guiding him properly. Because of your approachable nature, I never hesitated to come to you with my problems. The way you used the audio-visual aids also made the lessons very interesting.

I would like to pursue my masters in the same course. I have applied to the University of Melbourne and if I am fortunate enough to get admission, I shall again have the opportunity of learning from you as I have heard that you are taking the graduate classes too.

Thanking you once again for your valuable advice and guidance.

Yours faithfully,
Mohit

27. You have recently bought an airline ticket from a travel agency and unfortunately you are not able to fly on these dates. Write a letter to the travel agency manager to cancel the ticket. Explain in your letter

-
- What are the flight details?
- Why do you want to cancel it?
- What would you like him/her to do about it?

Dear Sir,

My name is Kiran Makkar, and I have booked a trip to Houston from New Delhi, India for September 15, 2017.

I am writing this letter to request you to reschedule my trip to October 15, 2017, as I cannot depart on the scheduled date because of some unforeseen family commitments.

My booking number is KM123456. I would appreciate if you cancel my reservation for this trip. I would appreciate if you adjust the amount I have previously paid for my upcoming flight. If you cannot accommodate me on the October 15 flight, kindly reimburse the paid amount to the credit card I have paid with. I am canceling this trip before 30 days of scheduled departure, so as per terms and conditions I am eligible for the full reimbursement of the paid amount.

I humbly apologise for the inconvenience this may cause to you. If you have any questions, please feel free to call me on 9898798987. You can also approach me at kiran@gmail.com.

Yours faithfully,
Kiran Makkar

---

28. Write a letter to a professional photographer saying you liked the photos of your family members taken by him and would like him to take pictures of another event in his family. In your letter mention

- What you liked in the photographs clicked by him?
- When is the next event in your family?
- Ask him about any special requirement.

Dear Sir,

My name is Rajinder Singh and I live in Rajinder Nagar New Delhi. I am writing this letter to congratulate you for the excellent photographs clicked by you on my cousin's wedding, last month. I would also like to book your services for my parents' silver jubilee function on the 15th of next month.

What I liked in your work was that every photograph brought out the best of everyone. You have the knack of capturing the perfect moments for a picture. Every photograph seems to be telling a story. You have such an eye for detail that you have captured the best emotions. The lighting and focus is also perfect. I have seen the album many times, and every time I have enjoyed seeing the photographs.

My parents' silver jubilee is on the 15th of next month. It would be great if you provide your services on that day. Do confirm at the earliest. The event will start at 6 pm and continue till 10 pm. There will be around 50 people in the party. In case you want to have a look at the venue beforehand, you can fix a day and time with me. My contact number is 988197556.

Hoping for a positive response from your side.

Yours faithfully,
Rajinder Singh

29. You have a concert ticket but you can't go. You want to give them to your friend. Write a letter to him or her telling

- What kind of concert it is?
- Why you can't go?
- How your friend can get the tickets from you?

Dear Sonia,

I hope this letter finds you in radiant health and the best of spirits. I just wanted to see if you would be interested in going to the Gurdas Mann's concert next week. He's playing here in Phagwara, and I've bought tickets for myself, and some friends. Unfortunately, I cannot attend the concert as my grandmother has suffered a stroke and is hospitalized. She will be in the hospital for minimum two weeks. It would be great if you could go on my ticket.

Every year Gurdas Mann performs for charity in a village near my hometown Phagwara. This year he is performing in Phagwaratown because last year the audience numbers exceeded the expectations of the organizers and so the event was a total disaster. He is going to sing all his famous songs and also some songs from his upcoming album. As a guest performer on his show he has also invited the famous folk singer Hans Raj Hans. I know that Gurdas Mann is your favourite singer too and I am sure you will definitely want to attend the concert.

Please, confirm your plan at the earliest so that I can arrange to send you the ticket in time. Alternatively, you can send someone to collect the ticket from me.

Hoping to hear from you soon.

Yours lovingly,
Kiran

30. Your friend is coming to your country from abroad, but you can't go to pick him up at the airport. Write a letter to him/her and say

- Why you can't pick him up?
- Suggest alternative ideas.
- Talk about what he can do in your country.

Dear Sarah,

I am anxiously awaiting your arrival on Friday morning. Unfortunately, because of unforeseen circumstances, I would not be able to come to pick you up at the airport as already planned. I would like to apologise for the inconvenience this might cause to you. However, I am suggesting some alternative plans for you to reach my home.

An unexpected business meeting has come up which I cannot avoid, so I am suggesting you some other means of reaching my house. One way would be to hire a cab from just outside the airport. That would be the most convenient option if you have a lot of luggage. However, if you are travelling light then I suggest you take the local bus from the airport. That would be very economical. I am very sorry for this turn of events.

I have planned a lot of things for you when you are here. There are a several historical places, which you must see. The Golden Temple at Amritsar and the Taj Mahal at Agra are on top of the list. Then, there are two museums and a lot of shopping centres where you can shop for souvenirs to take back home. Luckily, a wedding in the family is also there in these days, which will give you a taste of our rich cultural heritage.

Hoping to see you soon.

Yours lovingly,
XYZ

---

31. You have visited another city in your country. Prior to the visit you requested some information from a tourist centre, but the information was incorrect. Write a letter to the manager of the centre and say

- What information were you looking for?
- What was incorrect in it?
- What happened to you because of it?

Dear Sir,

I am writing this letter to complain about the problems I faced because of the wrong information that was provided at your Tourist Information Centre. My name is Jatinder Singh Gulati and I was on a seven-day trip to Mysore from 10th to 17th April 2016.

I reached Mysore on the 10th of April with my family and I wanted to know all the sightseeing available there. Your people told me about the Mysore Zoo, the Jaganmohan Palace, which has a museum, and the Mysore Maharaja's Palace. I asked them specifically if there were any special timings or days to visit these places, but I was told that these locations were open to tourists every single day and there were no special timings. I also asked them about some economical places to stay and they told me that SR Hotel was the cheapest and best.

I stayed with my family at SR Hotel and we chalked out our plan of visiting all these places. When we went to see the Jaganmohan Palace on Saturday, the 16th of April, we were told that the museum is closed on

Saturdays. The next day was our return, so we could not see the museum at all. I really wanted to see all the exhibits of the museum and also the world famous paintings of Raja Ravi Verma. We also came to know from other sources that there are economical lodges which include breakfast and at half the price of SR Hotel. It was not right on the part of your people to guide tourists in such a way just for some commission they get from SR Hotel. I spent double the amount and I also could not see the museum, which I really wanted to see.

Please look into the matter and firmly reprimand your staff against indulging in such malpractices so that other tourists are not misguided in the future.

Yours faithfully,
Jatinder Singh

---

32. You have broken your leg, and you have received cards and gifts from your colleagues. Write a letter to them. In your letter:
- Thank them for what they have done.
- Tell them about what you have been doing.
- And describe what the doctor said about your recovery.

Dear Samir and Arun,

Thank you so much for the get-well-soon card and the box of chocolates you sent for me. Ever since I met with the accident and broke my leg, it is the love and affection I am getting from friends like you, which is keeping my spirits up.

I have a fracture of the thighbone. It takes about three months to heal completely and my doctor has advised strict bed rest. So, I have a lot of free time. I do my regular study for two to three hours a day and after that I teach some children of the neighbourhood. I find it very interesting as I am being paid for it, and also these children keep me updated with what is going on around the town.

My physiotherapist comes at 8am and 8 pm every day for one hour of exercise session. He guides me very nicely and motivates me to push myself even if I have pain. With his help I am recovering very fast and I hope to start attending college by the end of next month.

Once again thanking you for your wishes and the card.

Yours truly,
Anil

33. You have started a course after reading its details in a brochure. Unfortunately it turned out to be totally different from the description in the brochure. Write a letter to the manager, including the following:

- Mention the details of the course.
- Explain how it was different.
- What course you would like to take instead?

Dear Sir,

I am writing this letter to complain about the wrong information provided in the brochure of your institute because of which I enrolled in the wrong course.

Your institute provides various courses related to cookery. I read all the details in your brochure and enrolled in the course C003, which deals with South Indian cuisine. I joined the course with great enthusiasm but the first day they started with North Indian dishes. I asked the instructors and they told me that C003 was a course in Indian cuisine and South Indian dishes were also a component of this course and they would be taught in the final week of the 12 week course.

I would like to enroll in a course covering purely South Indian cuisine. I very well know about the North Indian cuisine. I belong to North India and all these dishes I have learnt from my mother and grandmother. I love South Indian dosa and idli. I want to enroll in a course, which teaches purely South Indian dishes. If your centre provides this course, I would like to get a transfer to that course and in case such a course is not there, I would like a refund of the fees that I have paid for the wrong course. I would also suggest you to get the information corrected in the brochure.

Hoping to hear from you soon regarding this matter.

Yours faithfully,
Kiran

34.The local newspaper is holding a " Best Neighbour in the Area " competition. Write a letter to the newspaper to recommend your neighbour for this competition.

- Introduce yourself.
- Say whom you are recommending.
- Explain why this neighbor should be the winner of this competition.

Dear Sir,

I am Narinder Singh from 321 Bara Dari, Jalandhar. I would like to recommend Mr. Deol, my neighbour, as the most worthy competitor for the "Best Neighbour in the Area" contest. As I was flicking through the pages of your esteemed daily, I came across the notification of the competition that you are holding in our locality, and so I decided to recommend my neighbour's name for the same.

My neighbour, Mr. Deol is a retired army personnel. Ever since he has moved into this colony, he has brought dramatic changes in our area. It is because of him that our area is the most beautiful area in our city. He has planted more than 100 trees in the neighbourhood and nurtured them by watering them every morning and evening.

The park in our area was in a very bad condition. He went from house to house and collected money from all the residents and then hired workers to beautify the park. Now all the children play there and he sits there to keep an eye on them. All the people in our area love him because he is such a big help. He is always ready to help anyone in need with his time and money. Being from an army background, he is himself very disciplined and is a good role model for all of us. Mr. Deol rightfully deserves to win this competition. I recommend his name once again.

Hoping for a fair consideration of his name for the competition.

Yours faithfully,
Narinder Singh

35. You recently moved to a new apartment. Write to your friend and say

- Why did you move there?
- Describe the new apartment.
- Invite him/her to visit you.

Dear Sarah,

Hope this letter finds you in radiant health and the best of spirits. The good news is that I got a promotion and so I have moved from Phagwara to Chandigarh.

You know very well that I have been working with the HDFC Bank for the last five years. My promotion was long overdue. Last month I got my promotion and along with that I also got a transfer to the Head office at Chandigarh.

Chandigarh is a very nice and beautiful city. In fact it is the most well planned city of Punjab. I got my accommodation through the bank in sector 35. I moved in two weeks ago. It is a beautiful apartment. There are two bedrooms, a hall and a kitchen. The shopping centre is very near. My bank is also in this sector only, so I just walk there. I don't need to take out my car.

Why don't you come over for a few days. I am sure you will like it here. We would visit all these places together and also share some nostalgic memories of our college years.

Hoping to see you soon.

Yours lovingly,
Kiran

36. You read an article in a magazine recently, which might be useful for you and your friend's job. Write a letter to your friend and say

- Describe an article and its content to your friend.
- Explain why it is good for you.
- Why would it be helpful for your friend?

Dear Sarah,

Hope this letter finds you in radiant health and the best of spirits. I really miss the time we spent together in college. It was great that we both got placed in good companies, but unfortunately your company is in South India and mine in the North. Today, I am writing to you to share with you an article, which I read recently in my company's monthly magazine. The article is about time management and has been written by the CEO of my company 'Laxmi International'.

The article talks about managing time effectively between personal and professional life. This article is actually one chapter of the best seller 'Winning over Time'. This book has 10 more chapters and is full of interesting real-life examples.

This article is good for both of us, because I know that we are both very ambitious and in our quest of climbing up the ladder of success, we are somehow forgetting ourselves, and our families. The best part I liked was that if we give time to our family and keep them happy, it increases our efficiency in office also. Do go through the article and let me know if you liked it.

I am looking forward to hearing your personal views.

Yours lovingly,
Kiran

---

37. Your neighbourhood is having a problem with garbage. Write a letter to the environment officer in your area. In your letter:

- Describe what is causing the problem.
- Say why it is worrying you.
- And suggest a solution to fix the problem.

Dear Sir,

I am writing this letter to apprise you about the garbage which has accumulated in my street, and request you to do something about it as early as possible.

The sweepers appointed by the Municipal Committee have gone on strike as a result of which there are piles of dirt and garbage in lots of places. I have been living in Hargobind Nagar for the past 20 years, and such a situation has never arisen before.

The main problem we are facing is the stink coming from these heaps. On top of that mosquitoes and flies are prospering by leaps and bounds. If steps are not taken soon, there may spread epidemics of diseases.

Please look into the matter urgently. Whatever needs to be done to satisfy the workers, please do it so that they come back to work soon. If that is not possible, then please appoint some temporary workers to clean the street.

Hoping for a prompt action from you regarding this matter.

Immidiate.

Yours faithfully,
Kiran

An Act of assisting or Encouraging or done without delay.

38. You had lost contact with a friend, but you managed to get his/her contact lately and decide to write a letter. In the letter
- Explain how you got hold of his/her contact.
- Explain why you want to contact him/her.
- Ask questions about himself/herself.

Dearest Aveena,

You must be very surprised to receive this letter from me. We have been out of touch for the last five years. I've really missed you badly. Luckily I ran into our old friend Amika, in Delhi last week. She gave me your address and contact number. So, I decided to write to you.

What have you been doing these past five years? Amika told me that you've had a tough time finding a good job. You know, I got a job in a big IT company, Sigma Solutions. I have been promoted twice in the last five years, and now I am in the HR department, in charge of interviewing new applicants. As I got this post, I thought of all my friends, whom I could help get a job in my company. You know, this is a nice American company, and they give handsome pay packages and good perks. So, if you are interested, send me your resume, and I can push it forward. It would be great to be together again and revive all our nostalgic memories of the past.

make or become more cheerful or interesting.

Do convey my regards to your mom and dad and love to your little sister. Waiting eagerly to hear back from you.

Revive → Restor to life
Nostalgic →

Yours lovingly,
Kiran

39. You found a job opportunity in a foreign country. Write a letter to your friend who knows about the country. In your letter mention the following:
- What is the nature of your future job?
- Why did you apply for that job?
- Ask for details and his/her advice about the country.

shinning or glowing brightly

Dear Elaine,

Hope this letter finds you in radiant health and the best of spirits. I applied for a job in Barclay's Bank in Leeds and have received their job offer. I heard that you have also worked in the same bank in Leeds a couple of years ago.

My job is in their insurance section. It mainly involves meeting people and convincing them of our insurance policies. It also has a lot of fieldwork. I have done an MBA in finance and my resume was very impressive. That is why, perhaps, I got the job. The pay package is also very good.

I applied for this job because I have good communication skills and I love meeting people. The fieldwork involved in this job would help me in developing my network. Ultimately, I would love to open my own company and this experience would help me a lot.

Do tell me something about the country and the people there. What sort of weather I shall have to face and what kindof accommodation should I look for. It would really be helpful to know about the culture and traditions of the people there. It would help me get adjusted there sooner and mingle with the locals. It would also be good for my job.

Waiting eagerly to hear from you. Do convey my regards to your parents.

Yours lovingly,
Kiran

---

40. Write a letter to an accommodation officer in a foreign university in which you have taken admission. In your letter

- Ask him to arrange an accommodation for you.
- Brief him about what kind of accommodation you would need.
- Describe what you would need when you arrive there along with arriving details.

Dear Sir,

My name is Tawmit Singh, and I have enrolled as an undergraduate student in the Business Management Course. I am writing this letter to request you to arrange an accommodation for me in the University Halls of Residence.

My classes start from the 13th of August, but I will be reaching on the 1st of August. I have been in touch with some senior students through email, and they have very kindly offered to pick me up from the airport and accommodate me for 3-4 days. I have heard that the University Halls of Residence fill up very soon. That is why, I am writing well in advance so that I am sure of getting a room.

I would like a single room, but in case that is not possible, I can share a room. It would be nice if I have another student from India to share my room. It would be very helpful, if you can give me a room in the 'A' Wing as it would be very close to my class building. Please let me know if I can be allotted a room in the University Halls of residence.

Hoping for a prompt response from you regarding this matter.

Thanking you.

Yours faithfully,
Tawmit Singh

---

41. You have recently left something in a train, write a letter to the manager of the Lost and Found department and specify:
- When you lost it?
- Describe the object you have left.
- Tell the manager what you want them to do with it.

Dear Sir,

I recently travelled from Delhi to Mumbai on Shatabdi Express. I am writing to report about something that I lost on the train, and to request you to kindly look for it in the lost and found department of Chhatrapati Shivaji Terminus, Mumbai.

When I returned home I discovered that I had left my black, leather laptop cover in the train. It is a rectangular bag of Dell Company. I was working on my laptop in the train. I had my small suitcase also with me. When the train reached Mumbai, I picked up my suitcase and laptop , but forgot its bag in the train. The inside pocket of the bag has my visiting card with my name and address on it. There are some other important papers in it.

I would really appreciate if you take some efforts to find the bag. If the case is found, please inform me. My contact number is 98xxxxxxxx.

Hoping to hear from you soon.

Yours faithfully,
Kiran Makkar

42. You are moving to a new country to join a new company. One of your family members is moving with you too and is willing to work with your company too. Write a letter to your manager.

- Introduce yourself.
- Tell him/her about your family member.
- Tell how he/she suits your company.

Dear Sir,

My name is Mahendra Singh, and I have been placed in the IT department of your company, Bayer Healthcare, as senior web developer. I have heard that you are recruiting more new employees in the IT department. I am writing this letter to request you to consider my younger brother Jogendra Singh for this post.

I intend to move from India to work in this company next month. My mother and my younger brother are also moving with me, as there are only three people in my family. My brother has recently completed his MCA (Masters in Computer Applications). During his course, he did 6 months internship in the IT department of Ranbaxy Pharmaceuticals. I think he will be perfectly suited for the posts you are hiring for.

I am attaching his CV (Curriculum Vitae), along with this letter. I hope his credentials measure upto your expectations.

Hoping for a favourable response from you.

Yours affectionately,
Mahendra Singh

---

43. A TV program wants to create a show about a place and they want ideas from people about where to go. Write a letter to the producer of the show and say:

- What your suggestion is?
- How you know about the place?
- And why you think it would attract viewers?

Dear Sir,

My name is Kiran Makkar, and I belong to Phagwara, a small town between Jalandhar and Ludhiana. As I was watching your TV show 'Peoples and Places' last Sunday, I came to know that you are asking people for ideas on places, which deserve to be on this show of yours. I am writing this letter to suggest an attractive place on which to create a TV show.

There is a small village, Plahi, about 4 km from my hometown. It is the most hi-tech village of India. This village developed so much because of the efforts of the NRIs of this village. The local people of the village set up an NGO – National Rural Development Society. This NGO has transformed the lives of 3800 people. This NGO is providing free Internet to all residents. There is a big soundproof community hall, which can accommodate more than 1000 people. There is a stadium and a polytechnic also in the village. It has a well-maintained public park and an energy park. It is the only village in Punjab, which runs almost entirely on renewable energy sources. From streetlights, water heaters, pumps to cookers, everything is solar. People have smokeless stoves and biogas plants in their homes. No wonder, it is called the energy village.

If you dedicate one episode of your TV show to this village, it would be an eye-opener to many people who think that villages are backward and can never match up with the cities.

Hoping to see a show on this village on your TV channel soon.

Yours faithfully,
Kiran Makkar

44. You recently visited a store and didn't like the customer service there. Write a complaint letter to the store manager and say
- What was the issue there?
- Why wasn't the staff helpful?
- Suggest what can be done about it.

Dear Sir,

I am writing this letter to complain about your staff members who were very unfair and rude with me when I visited your store last Sunday. My name is Kiran Makkar, and I belong to Phagwara. When I came to know that a new store, 'One Stop Shop', has opened in my hometown, I was very excited and went there with my parents last Sunday.

We were awed to see that a store of this magnitude had opened in our small town. We picked up our shopping cart and started moving through the aisles, picking up all we needed. We saw a room heater, which we liked a lot and put it in our cart. There was an attractive discount offer on it and it was the last piece. Then we came to the billing counter and started waiting for our turn. There was a long queue and we told the person behind us to look after our cart while we went to drink water. When we came back, we saw that our heater was not in our trolley and someone else had already got it billed in his name. We complained to the salesman who knew that we had picked up the last piece, but he sided with the other person and said that he had seen and liked the heater first. I could not understand his logic, but as the heater had already been billed, I could do nothing. Your other staff members also did not cooperate with me. We were so upset that we didn't buy anything and came out of the store.

You have CCTV cameras fitted all over in your store. Please go through the footage and you will come to know that we have been wronged. Please admonish your staff for such behaviour, or you will never be able to build your customer network.

Hoping to hear from you soon regarding this issue.

Yours faithfully,
Kiran Makkar

---

45. Write a letter to the transport officer about a problem with transport system in your area. Please say

-   Describe the situation you are facing.
-   Why do you consider it a problem?
-   What changes would you like to recommend?

Dear Sir,

My am Narinder Singh from Hargobind Nagar, Phagwara. I am writing this letter to apprise you with a problem with the transport system, which is causing a lot inconvenience to the people of Phagwara, and to request you to do something to mitigate the problem as early as possible.

You know very well that a flyover near the bus stand is under construction, because of which there is a lot of chaos in the traffic in front of the bus stand. To add to the confusion, the private buses stop on the roadside, instead of going inside the bus stand, and keep waiting for their buses to fill with passengers. This causes problems for people on their personal two wheelers and cars. The traffic lights on the crossroads are also not working at many places, causing a lot of accidents.

It is my humble request to stop the buses from stopping on the road and not going inside. And also please get the traffic lights in working order again. Hoping for a prompt action from you regarding this matter.

Yours faithfully,
Narinder Singh

46. You are living in a rented apartment, but your family situation has changed. You need a new accommodation. Write a letter to the real estate agent asking for a new arrangement. You should say

- What is your family situation?
- What are the requirements for the new accommodation?
- When do you want to move?

Dear Sir,

I am Mohit Sharma, your new tenant from apartment number 341, Netkalappa Circle. I moved in with my family a year ago. I am writing this letter to request you to change my apartment to a bigger one as I my parents are also moving in with me.

I moved to Bangalore from Punjab, as I got a job in Sigma Tech Solutions. My wife and two children also shifted with me. Now, I have somehow persuaded my parents also to move here, as it is not possible for me to go to Punjab very often to look after them.

They are arriving next week. Sir, it is my humble request to change my two bedroom apartment to a three bedroom one. It would be very kind of you if you find me such an apartment as soon as possible.

Hoping for a positive response from you regarding this matter.

Yours faithfully,
Mohit Sharma

47. Write a letter to the hotel manager about a bad experience you had while staying there. Include the following in your letter:

- Where and when did you stay?
- What had happened?
- Suggest a solution for the situation.

Dear Sir,

My name is Indroop Singh, and I am from Punjab. I am writing this letter to complain about a bad experience, which I had when I stayed in your hotel, SK Inns Mysore, from 14th to 19th December 2016.

I had booked your hotel online from 14th to 19th December. I was to reach by 6 pm. My flight was till Bangalore and from there I took a taxi to Mysore. It takes 4 hours normally, but unfortunately, I got stuck in a traffic jam and reached Bangalore at about 9 pm. When I arrived, the person at the reception, Biju Thomas, told me that my room had already been let out to someone else. I couldn't believe it, because I had paid well in advance. To add to my dismay, Mr. Thomas was mad at me for not informing him that I would be late. When I told Mr. Thomas that I would lodge a complaint against him, he gave me another room, but that was in the corner, and there was no internet connection over there. The next morning, I went to the restaurant for the complimentary breakfast, but that too was pathetic, in terms of quality.

I am not at all satisfied with my stay at your hotel. It was a disaster. I believe you should refund me some of my payment, which I made for my stay, because I did not get what was included in my stay, and what I got did not meet the basic standards.

Hoping for a prompt response from you regarding this matter.

Yours faithfully,
Indroop Singh

---

48. Write a letter to the hotel manager to make arrangements for hosting a party for one of your friends. In your letter

- Tell the manager about the reason for the party.
- Explain what requirements you have.
- Ask about the availability of facilities and the menu.

Dear Sir,

My name is Kiran Makkar, and I belong to Phagwara. I am writing this letter to book a party hall in your hotel, Cabana Palace, for the 15th of April. I would also like to request you to make all the necessary arrangements for the party.

My friend, Surjit is turning 25 on the 15th of next month, and I want to make the day special for her by inviting all our common friends. I would like to book the hall from 4 pm to 8 pm. Please arrange a party for a gathering of 20 people. My total budget is between Rs.10,000 and Rs.12,000. Please arrange the snacks and soft drinks within that amount.We would also like to play housie and musical chairs, so if you could arrange the music system and the chairs, it would be great.

Do let me know if your party hall is free on that day, and also let me know a suitable time when I can come and finalise the menu for that day with you.

Yours faithfully,
Kiran Makkar

49. You have recently purchased a piece of furniture, but you noticed a problem when it was delivered to you. Write a letter to the store manager and say

- What is the problem?
- How did it happen in your opinion?
- What do you suggest the manager should do to resolve the problem?

Dear Sir,

My name is Mukhinder Singh. I visited your shop on the 2nd of April, and placed an order for a dining table and a centre table. I am writing this letter to complain about the defective furniture that was delivered by your company.

The eight piece wood-and-glass dining set (Order number 77779) that I ordered on April 2 was delivered yesterday. As I was away on business that day, my neighbour, who has a key to my apartment) accepted the packaged set and signed for it without question. However, when I opened the teak wood dining table myself with great care, I found that two of the glass inserts were badly scratched and one was broken.

I cannot accept the table in this state and want to receive a replacement as soon as possible. In my opinion the damage seemed to be caused by inadequate packaging. In case you have any questions feel free to call me at 98xxxxxxxx.

Hoping for a prompt reply from your side!

Yours faithfully,
Mukhinder Singh

50. You recently bought an item in the supermarket but later found out that something was wrong with it. You came back to the supermarket, but the staff wasn't helpful. Write a letter to the supermarket manager and say

- What item did you purchase?
- What was the problem with it?
- What do you want the manager to do about it?

Dear Sir,

I am writing this letter to complain about the poor after-sales service I received from your employees at the shop. My name is Kiran Makkar, and I am one of your regular customers.

I purchased a personal computer from your shop last month. I discovered that the computer's graphics card was not properly assembled. I could not use the computer to play any video game. Therefore, I went to your shop and asked one of your staff to fix this issue. Unfortunately, he was very impolite and disregarded my request. I approached the store manager and he told me that I have to buy a brand new graphics card. He refused to provide me with a free graphics card and claimed that the computer had no problem prior to my purchase.

My computer comes with 2 years of full service warranty. You should follow the terms and conditions of your service warranty and fix my computer. Therefore, I would like to recommend that you contact your staff and ask them to respect their customers and solve their technical problems.

Hoping for a prompt and positive response from you regarding this matter.

Yours faithfully,
Kiran Makkar

---

51. You have read a magazine article that mentioned a place you are familiar with. There was a mistake in the article. Write a letter to the editor of the magazine and say

- What the error was?
- Explain that you are familiar with the place.
- Why is it important to correct the error?

Dear Sir,

My name is Raghav Bharadwaj from Jalandhar, Punjab. I am writing this letter to apprise you with some wrong information printed in your magazine, Punjabi Virsa. There was an article in your esteemed monthly, which contained some incorrect information about Phagwara.

I do not belong to Phagwara, but my relatives live there and I visit them very often. In fact I know it as well as my hometown. I know about each and every historical place and worth-seeing place of this city.

In the December 2016 issue of Punjabi Virsa, there was an article on the historical and religious places of Phagwara. It was written that that there is a temple of Lord Ganesha, which is about 50 years old. This temple is of Lord Shiva, and is not just 50 years old; it is more than 150 years old. I have been to that temple many times and I know the history and the religious significance of this temple.

The information in your article may have been just a misprint but still I feel you must correct it and re-post the article with the correct information. It is very important to publish the correct information because it is a religious and historical place and people are entitled to get the correct information.

Hoping to read the article again in the next issue with the correct information.

Yours faithfully,
Raghav

---

52. You borrowed something from your friend a while ago, but it has been damaged somehow. Write a letter to him/her and say

- Remind him/her what you borrowed.
- Explain what happened to it.
- Suggest what you are going to do about it.

Dear Elaine,

I hope this letter finds you in radiant health and the best of spirits. You remember, you lent me your beautiful silk stole for my sister's wedding party. Unfortunately, it got damaged and I would like to apologise for that.

It was so kind of you to lend me that stole. The stole complemented my dress so well that I got a lot of compliments that day. Alas, I ruined your stole by mistake. It so happened that we were all dancing on the dance floor and suddenly the tassels on the stole got stuck in my shoe heel and I heard a loud ripping noise. My heart skipped a beat when I saw the stole completely torn from the middle. I tried to get it darned, but the tear is still showing.

Please forgive me for this. I would be happy to buy you a new stole. Please let me know where you bought it from, so that I can buy a similar one from there. I hope the new one will be as good as the old one.

I am looking forward to hearing for you soon.

With love,
Kiran

53. Write a letter to a bus company about something you lost on a bus. In your letter

- Give details of your bus trip.
- Tell them what you lost.
- Explain what you'd like them to do.

Dear Sir,

I am Kiran Makkar from Jalandhar. I travelled in your 2.30 pm bus from Phagwara to Chandigarh on 3rd February 2017. I am writing this letter to request you to check with the conductor of that bus for a tote bag containing two silk suits, which I forgot to pick up while disembarking at Chandigarh.

I had a laptop bag, a purse and this tote when I boarded the bus at Jalandhar. I put this tote bag under the seat in front of me. The tote bag had two silk suits, which my sister-in-law had gifted me. I remember, I was very tired and I went off to sleep. The next thing I knew was that the passenger sitting next to me was shaking me telling me that the final stop at Chandigarh had come. I got up and picked up my laptop bag and purse, but totally forgot about the tote. There is a strong possibility that as it was the last stop, the conductor or the driver of the bus may have spotted it later on.

Sir, I would be highly grateful if you help locate my tote bag for me. In case you are able to find it, kindly call me at 98xxxxxxxx. I can come to the bus stand at Jalandhar and collect it.

Hoping for a prompt response from you regarding this matter.

Yours faithfully,
Kiran Makkar

54. You are going away from home for one week and you need to ask your neighbour to look after you house.

- Why you want to go away?
- What you want your neighbour to look after?
- If there are any problems then give instructions.

Dear Elaine,

I hope you are well. I am writing this letter to request you to look after my house for one week as I have to go on a business tour to Mumbai.

You've already informed me that you'll be at home next week, and that is why I am asking this favour of you. If you could just check my house from time to time to make sure everything is fine, it would be great.

The plants in the living room need to be watered once a week only and placed near the window when it is sunny. In terms of taking care of the house that is all I require you to do. I also gave your telephone number to the TV repair company who will be returning my set on the 8th of April. Kindly open the house for them so they can install it for me.

Thank you for all your help and I'll remember to bring back the souvenir you requested from Mumbai.

Yours truly,
Kiran

---

55. You ordered two items through the Internet and you received two different items. Write a letter to the manager:

- Explain about what you ordered.
- Ask why the two other items were different.
- Ask about how would he solve this problem.

Dear Sir,

Today morning I received my order of the external hard disk and the camera that I had ordered over the internet from your website www.lears.com . I was shocked to see that both the things were very different from what I had ordered.

I ordered an external hard disk of WD Company and I specifically ordered a 500 GB one. What I received was a hard disk of 250 GB and that too of Sony. The second item I ordered was a Canon Power Shot camera of 12 mega pixels but you sent me a Sony Cyber Shot of 7.2 mega pixels.

I have been a regular customer from your website but such a problem has occurred for the first time. I paid online for the two things I ordered and I printed out the receipts. I fail to understand how this mistake could have been done.

I would like you to either send me the refund or the actual items I purchased. Also please advise how you want me to send these things, which I got, back to you.

Hoping for a prompt reply from you regarding this matter.

Yours faithfully
Kiran Makkar

56. Government plans to construct an airport in your locality. Write a letter to the authority.

- Explain where you came to know about the news.
- Describe the negative effects of airport construction.
- Ask to consider alternate site for airport construction.

Dear Sir,

I am writing this letter to express my concern about the plan of construction of an airport in Model Town. I got this information from a local newspaper of our area.

My name is Indroop Singh and I am a resident of Model Town, Ludhiana. This area is very well developed and there is a school, a college and a very big multi-speciality hospital. The hospital in our area is a big asset for the people. It has been here for the past 50 years now and has benefited not only the people of our locality but also the people of the neighbouring areas. An airport in this area would bring a lot of noise pollution and congestion in the area. The big park, which you intend to include in the airport site would also be a big loss for the people.

Our area is already very congested. An airport here would bring even more congestion. As it is, there is an international airport at Amritsar, which is only 200 km away. So, I urge you to please reconsider your plan and drop the idea of an airport. If at all you have to construct an airport at Ludhiana, please make it in the suburbs, so that city people are not affected negatively.

Hoping for a prompt consideration of this urgent request.

Yours faithfully,
XYZ

57. You are going to work in another city for a year. A friend who lives there offered to help you find a place to live. Write a letter to your friend and say

- Express your gratitude to him/her.
- Describe the area that you want to live in.
- Explain what type of accommodation you are looking for.

Dear Simar,

Hope this letter finds you in radiant health and the best of spirits. It was so kind of you to offer to find a place for me to live in. I am writing this letter to thank you and to let you know what type of accommodation I am looking for. It would be great if it would be near you.

I will be moving with my family to Leeds next month. I would like a two-bedroom apartment, preferably on the ground floor. I am prepared to spend anything between $800 and $1000 per month as rent. The bedrooms should be pretty spacious and the kitchen should have a window that opens to the outside. The kitchen should also have the basic things like the refrigerator, dishwasher and a microwave fitted in it.

The apartment should be close to the shopping centre and should have a playground in the neighbourhood as I have two children 3 and 7 years old. Good educational facilities for children should also be there for children. Last but not least, public transport should be available in that area because I am not sure when I would be able to buy my own car.

I would be arriving next month. Please let me know as soon as you find a suitable apartment for me. I am really looking forward to spending a year in your country. We would be able to meet often and revive nostalgic memories of our college days.

Yours lovingly,
Kiran

---

58. You are an employee in an office, working on one big project together with your colleagues. Write a letter to your manager to inform him/her that one of the employees makes mistakes that affect your work. In your letter say

- What mistakes have you encountered so far?
- Explain that other employees complained about the same mistakes.
- Suggest a solution to solve this problem.

Dear Sir,

I am Mohit Bhalla, working in the IT department of our company Sigma Healthcare. Presently, I am part of the team working on the project of development of an app for direct marketing of the products of our company. I am writing this letter to apprise you that one member, Sumit Sharma, is slowing down the project by constantly making mistakes. I would request you to please do something about it.

Sir, our project is an integrated project and six of us are working on it simultaneously. Sumit Sharma does not have the knowhow of the software we are using in making this app. As a result he makes mistakes, requiring us to to undo and redo our work many times, which is very confusing and frustrating. All the other team members are facing the same problem.

Sir, I would like to suggest that you can assign some other project to Sumit Sharma, and remove him from this project. It is my humble request.

Hoping for a prompt response from you regarding this matter.

Yours faithfully,
Mohit Sharma.

---

59. You came to know that your company is looking for an interpreter for meetings, and you know a person who is good at interpretation. Write to your manager -
- Describe this person.
- Explain why he/she is suitable for this role.
- Give his/her contact details to your manager.

Dear Sir,

I am Mohit Bhalla, working in the IT department of our company Sigma Healthcare. I came to know that you are looking for an interpreterfor our company meetings. I am writing this letter to recommend my acquaintance, Rajeev Verma for this job.

I met Rajeev Verma when I took a tour with Pack Travels, a tour company based in Chandigarh. I was surprised to know that he can speak 17 languages comfortably. He became a good friend, and we are in touch through a social networking site. He just mentioned that his work for the tour company involves lot of travel, which he is finding very cumbersome at times. He is on the lookout for a stable job, and you are looking for an interpreter as our company is expanding globally.

Sir, I believe Rajeev Verma would be perfect for our company. I am attaching his CV along with this letter, with his contact details.

Hoping for a favourable response from you regarding this matter.

Yours faithfully,
Mohit Bhalla

60. You had applied to City College recently. Now the college has written back saying the course you applied for is full and they have even suggested an alternative course. Write back to them stating

- Why you chose the first course?
- Your views on the suggested second course.
- Your plan of action.

Dear Sir,

I received your letter dated 13th March in which you have denied me admission in the 'Graduate Diploma in Computer Animation' for the fall 2010 session. You have written that I was late in applying and the seats were already full. You have also suggested an alternative course in 'Web Designing'. I am writing this letter to say that I don't want to do the other suggested course. I would appreciate if you give me a seat in the next intake.

I chose the Computer Animation course because it is an upcoming field nowadays and yours is the first college in Punjab to start this course. My friends have gone to Delhi to do this course. There are many job openings after doing this course. As it is a relatively new course so the competition is also not so severe yet.

I have done my masters in computer science from Khalsa College Jalandhar. Web Designing was a component of that course. Therefore, I don't think I need to do the course in web designing.

I would be very grateful if you consider my application for 'Graduate Diploma in Computer Animation' for the spring 2011 session. It would be worth waiting for that course. Please reply soon so that I can plan accordingly.

Thanking you.

Yours faithfully,
Kiran

61. Your friend wants to send her/his child to learn music. He/she asked you for some information about the music academy that you went to. Write him/her a letter and say

- Describe this music academy.
- Suggest a teacher or a class to go to.
- Explain why you recommend it.
- Provide some extra information that may be needed.

Dear Shabana,

It was great to hear from you after a long time. You wanted some information on a place where you could send your daughter to learn music. Well, I learnt music from Rajeshwari Kala Sangam, Jalandhar. They teach classical and vocal and many other genres of music, and all the teachers are very nice.

This academy is in New Jawahar Nagar, Jalandhar. They have very good teachers. They teach music in small groups of four students in each group. The timings are also very convenient for school going children. Although all the teachers are very good, one of the teachers, Santosh Vyas, was my favourite.

I am recommending this academy because I did a lot of research and went to many other academies before joining. I found this to be the best. They have very up-to-date musical instruments and other infrastructure needed to teach music. Many other people also recommended it to me. Parents are allowed to sit outside in the reception area while their children attend the class.

I hope this information will help you make your decision. If you want to know anything more, do not hesitate to ask.

Yours lovingly,
Kiran

62. You are arranging a conference for your company next month. Write a letter to your colleagues from a different department and invite them to attend it. In your letter say

- What the conference is about?
- Why you want them to attend the event?
- Provide some information on the arrangement of the conference.

Dear Gaurav and Mohit,

Hope everything is going well with you. I am writing this letter to formally invite you to attend a conference, which I am organising in the manufacturing department of our company.

You know very well that this conference is held every year in our company. The conference is mainly to make our products well known to our dealers and distributors. This year our CEO made me the project director. I have a team of 20 people working under me. We have spent two months in preparing for this Conference. This year more than 200 delegates have registered from all over India and abroad. It is going to be a mega event.

I would like you both to attend the conference and give me some feedback on our work. You know we joined the company together, and we have had good rapport with each other. I really value your comments and suggestions.

Hoping to see you in the conference.

Yours truly,
Kiran Makkar

---

63. Recently your employer offered some employees the opportunity to work from home. Write a letter to your manger requesting the same arrangement. You should say

- Why do you want to work from home?
- Why would it be beneficial for the company and yourself?
- Suggest a suitable arrangement for you to work from home.

Dear Sir,

I am Vikas Gaba, senior web developer in our company. I have been working for the last five years. I came to know that you are offering the opportunity of telecommuting to some employees. I am writing this letter to request you to allow me also at least two days of telecommuting per week.

As I work in the IT sector, much of my work is online, which can be done from home. Actually, my house is about 15 miles from our office, but there is a new flyover being constructed, because of which I have to take the longer route. It takes me two hours to reach office. This construction is going to take another 6 months. I am not able to cope up with 4 hours of commuting everyday. It is eating into my family time, because of which there is a lot of stress at home.

If I am allowed to work from home, I assure you that no work will suffer and it will be good for the company also. I can work from home on Tuesdays and Fridays. I will be connected to my other colleagues and can even do video conferencing with them.

Hoping for a kind consideration of my humble request.

Yours faithfully,
Vikas Gaba

64. Write a letter telling your friend about your good news.
- What is it
- Why does it affect your life
- Invite him/her over for celebration.

Dear Hannah,

Hope this letter finds you in radiant health and the best of spirits. I am writing this letter to give you the good news that I have got admission in Harvard University in Business Administration course and that too with a scholarship. I would like to celebrate this good news and it would be great if you can come over.

You know it was my dream to study in Harvard University, Boston USA, but it was beyond my reach. As you know very well the fee structure of Harvard is very high. I worked very hard and got a very high score in GMAT and IELTS. I read about this scholarship and as my academic credentials were good, I decided to apply for it. My joy knew no bounds when I received the mail that I had been selected for the scholarship.

This opportunity would affect my life in a big way. After doing this course I hope to get a highly paid job, and then I would be able to help to improve the financial status of my family. I have seen my parents slog hard to make both ends meet and I would definitely want to give them some rest now.

I will be leaving next month, but before going I would like to have a get-together with my friends on the 16th., that is, next Saturday. The party would be incomplete without your presence. So, please do come.

Waiting eagerly for you.

Yours lovingly,
Kiran

65. You are a football player, but you have to leave the team for a while, write a letter to your team-mate and say:
- Why you have to leave,
- How much you love the football team,
- When you are coming back.

Dear Anil,

Hope this letter finds you in radiant health and the best of spirits. I am writing this letter to inform you that I shall not be able to play for our team for some time as my grandfather has suffered a stroke and I am going home to look after him.

You know how much I love football and our team. Playing football is a passion for me and the best time of my life is when I am on the football ground. However, one has to set priorities in life and my family comes before anything else. My grandfather is the most important person in my life. He has always been my friend, philosopher and guide. He is the one who motivated me to play football. Whatever I am today is because of him. Now he has suffered a stroke and his left side is paralysed. He needs good care and a lot of physiotherapy, which I can provide better than anyone else.

I shall be back as soon as my grandfather is fit and able to walk on his own. It may take a few weeks to a few months, but I am sure I shall be able to get him on his feet very soon. Hoping to see you all very soon.

Yours truly,
Mohit

---

66. Write a letter to one of your classmates and invite him to a class reunion. Write
- When and where is the party
- Give some details about what is going to happen at the party
- Tell him/her what you have been doing recently

Dear Vibha,

Hope this letter finds you in radiant health and the best of spirits. It has been a long time since we met and so just to catch up with everyone I am organising a reunion of the class of 1999. Do take out time to attend this reunion, because it would be incomplete without your presence.

It has been 12 years since we all passed out of high school. Then everyone chose different careers and got busy in higher education. Some are doctors, some chose engineering and some got into business. Out of all our class-mates, I am the only one in our hometown. Therefore, I decided to organise this get-together. The party is on 12th of March at Club Cabbana, Phagwara. I hope you can make it to the reunion.

I am sure there will be fun and frolic all around. At the same time we shall be reviving the nostalgic memories of our school days. I have also arranged a gourmet dinner and a DJ so that we can all dance to the beat of music. I have invited all of our class fellows. It was really tough to get the addresses of some of them.

After doing my MBA, I joined my father in our family business. My father runs his own business of building materials. I am the only son, so he wanted me to join him. I have been able to take our business to new heights by applying what I learnt in MBA.

Looking forward to seeing you on the 12th of March.

Yours lovingly,
Kiran

---

67. Write a letter to your friend from an English speaking country, who wants to visit your country. In your letter

- Invite him and his parents.
- Tell him what places they should visit in your country.
- Give him some useful advice.

Dear Karen,

Hope this letter finds you in radiant health and the best of spirits. I was really very happy when I heard from Nisha that you are planning to come to India with your parents. I would suggest you to come in November or December because it is very pleasant here in these months. It would be my pleasure to host you during your stay in my country.

There is a lot to see in India. It depends on how long you are going to be here and what specifically you have in mind for your holiday. The Taj Mahal in Agra and the Golden Temple at Amritsar should be on top of your list. You know India has a rich cultural heritage and I am sure you will enjoy every moment of being here.

I can also plan a leave for two weeks and show you all these tourist places. We shall also revive some nostalgic memories of our college years when we studied together at Leeds University. Please send me your detailed itinerary so that I can plan out your time fruitfully.

Hoping to see you soon.

Yours lovingly,
Kiran

68. Write a letter to a cinema manager you have previously been to regarding a problem you had. In your letter mention
- Which the movie was and when you saw it?
- What the problem was ?
- What the manager should do to rectify the problem?

Dear Sir,

I am writing this letter to complain about a problem I faced last week when I saw the movie Avatar in your cinema hall.

My name is Gagan Singh. Last week I came with my friends to see Avatar in Sarb Multiplex. We were about five minutes late and the movie had already started when we reached. One of your ushers pointed out our seats to us, which were in the third row, and we had to walk down a few steps. As it was dark inside the theatre, I could not see that the first step was broken, and tripped and fell sideways, spraining my ankle in the process. It spoiled the whole movie for me. I had so much pain that I had to leave immediately and consult a doctor.

Please look into the matter urgently and get the step repaired as soon as possible so that other people do not suffer in this way. Till that time, please advise your staff to guide the people up to their seats when it is dark inside.

Hoping for a prompt action from you regarding this matter.

Yours faithfully,
Gagan

69. Your friend is planning to move to your hometown, and is asking you for some information about it. Write a letter and tell him/her about:
- Housing (the places to live) in your hometown.
- Schooling (choice for schools) for his/her children.
- Socializing (making new friends) with the locals.

Dear Sabina,

It was great to hear that you are planning to move to my hometown, Phagwara. Although my hometown is small, yet it offers all the facilities any big city can provide.

All types of housing are available. Two big colonies are Model Town and Hargobind Nagar. You can get a suitable apartment on rent in any one of them. I am in Hargobind nagar. So, if you need I can start looking for a suitable accommodation for you.

Education facilities are also of topmost quality. There are schools affiliated to ICSE Board, CBSE Board and also Punjab School Education Board. You can select one according to your need.

People of my hometown are also very friendly and nice. There is a City Club, which you can join. Most of the elite citizen of the town are members and there are regular get-togethers in the club, which can help you to acquaint yourself with the locals.

If you have any other query in your mind, do not hesitate to ask. Waiting eagerly to see you in Phagwara.

Yours lovingly,
Kiran

---

70. Write a letter to the local council regarding the plan of replacement of a library with a supermarket. You need to write the following:

- Where did you get this information?
- The disadvantages of having a supermarket instead of the library.
- Importance of the library.

Dear Sir,

I am writing this letter to express my resentment about the plan of replacement of a library in Model Town with a supermarket. I got this information from a local newspaper of our area.

My name is Indroop Singh and I am a resident of Model Town, Phagwara. The library in our area is a big asset for the people. This library has been here for the past 50 years now and has benefited not only the people of our locality but also the people of the neighbouring areas. The elderly people of our community sit there for hours enjoying the latest newspapers and magazines and the children often go there to find matter for their school assignments.

Our area is already very congested. A supermarket here would bring even more congestion. As it is, there are already many supermarkets in our town and people do not need another one. So, I urge you to please reconsider your plan and drop the idea of a supermarket. People need the library more than anything else.

Hoping for a prompt consideration of this humble request.

Yours faithfully,
XYZ

71. You are unable to attend to your friend's wedding in Britain. In this letter
- Tell her what you think about her wedding plan.
- Apologize for not attending.
- Suggest date for future meeting.

Dear Samaira,

It was such a pleasant surprise when I received your wedding card today afternoon. Unfortunately, I shall not be able to attend the wedding as my parents' silver jubilee falls on the same day and I have planned a surprise party for them here on that day.

I have read from your card that you have planned an eco-wedding. All decorations will be in green and even your dress will be green. This is a new concept and a very nice one. You always wanted to do things in different ways. This is also a novel idea. We all know how important it is to save our environment and you have tried to give this message on your wedding day.

I am really sorry that I shall not be able to come, but, I have a suggestion. Why don't you two come to India for your honeymoon? The backwaters of Kerala are a wonderful choice for honeymooners. Then you can also spend a few days with me. Please consider this proposal.

I wish you a very long and happy married life. Hoping to see you soon!

Yours lovingly,
Kiran

72. Write complaint letter to the airline manager regarding the behaviour of one of staff members on your flight. In your letter
- Give full details of your flight.
- Say what the problem with the staff member was.
- What would you like the manager to do regarding this matter

Dear Sir,

I am writing to complain about the behavior of one of your staff in my last flight with your airline.

My name is Kiran Makkar and I am one of your regular customers. Unfortunately, the last time I used your airline I felt totally ignored. Last Monday on August 12, I flew from Delhi to London and my flight number was B203. Everything was good, until I had eaten my dinner. After dinner, I felt some hyperacidity, so I called one of flight attendants, Jyotsna, and asked her for some soft drink. She did not reply and went away. I thought she would come back with something, but she didn't turn up.

You can imagine how unhappy I was, when I saw this behavior. I was in great discomfort throughout the flight. She could have easily managed something for me. I am very disappointed with your airline. You must reprimand your staff for such behaviour. An apology letter from Ms Jyotsna would be very welcome.

I am looking forward to hearing from you.

Yours faithfully,
Kiran Makkar

---

73. You have applied for a position in an international organization and you need to provide a reference letter. Write a letter to your former teacher asking him/her to write it for you.

- Give your full details.
- Describe the job that you are going to do there.
- Say why it is important to you.

Dear Mr Phillips,

My name is Kiran Makkar, I was a student in your Bachelors of Commerce class in 2012. I was among the toppers of your class. I am writing this letter to request you for a reference letter for the job, which I've applied for.

I recently applied for a full time position in 'Universal Enterprises', an international company. The position is for a Financial Researcher in their 'Research and Development' section. I think it is quite an interesting job and will help me develop my research skills further.

This job is really important for me because it is a great opportunity in a really good company. They have offices overseas as well and there is the possibility of working on projects with staff from other countries around the world. This is something, which has always interested me.

Your reference would carry a lot of weight and will surely help me in getting the job. Thanks for your help in this matter.

Yours sincerely,
Kiran Makkar

74.A local community group is looking for part-time volunteers to help take care of children. Write a letter to the organizer of the group. In your letter

- Tell the organizer why you are interested.
- Say why you are suitable for the work.
- And provide details of when you are available.

Dear Sir,

I am Kiran Makkar from Phagwara, Punjab. I came to know through your advertisement in the local tabloid, Jagdambay Times, that you are looking for volunteers for taking care of children. I am writing this letter to request you to consider me for this job.

I am working as a staff nurse in a cancer hospital. I work in the ward for the terminally ill. It is a very depressing job, as I have to see people in great pain every day. I also see people dying before my very eyes every other day. Working with children would give me great happiness and peace of mind. I can look after children very well. I would love to spend some time with children every day.

My working hours are from 9 pm to 2 pm. After that I am free for the rest of the day. I can spare 2-3 hours in the evenings. It would be a blessing for me if you give me this opportunity to look after children. I am attaching me resume with my contact details.

Hoping to hear a prompt and positive response from you.

Yours faithfully,
Kiran Makkar

75.You are having a family party at your house. Write a letter to a friend who is living in a different city. In your letter:

- Tell him or her about your party.
- Say why you want to invite him or her to your party.
- Provide information about how to get to the party.

Dear Suman,

Hope all is well at your end. It has been a long time since we met. I am writing this letter to invite you to attend the silver jubilee party of my parents. They have been married 25 glorious years and so my brother and I have decided to make the day special for them by organising this surprise party for them.

You know very well that my mom and dad have a special liking for you. They would love your presence there. I have another selfish motive for inviting you. You can make the party rock by your singing talent. It would make it an event to remember. You have to come. I am not taking no for an answer. I am telling you well in advance, so whatever your prior commitments are, you can adjust them on any other day and time.

The party is on the 15th of next month. We have booked a hall in Ashish Continental hotel. It is a new hotel between Phagwara and Jalandhar. If you come by car, it would take you two hours from your city, but if you come by bus or train, then I can arrange to pick you up from the bus stand or railway station.

Waiting eagerly for you at the party.

Yours lovingly,
Kiran

76.The company you work for has got some work, which they need help with. Write a letter to your friend and say:

- Why he/she should do this work?
- The job description.
- And how he/she can apply for the job.

Dear Sahil,

Hope this letter finds you in the best of health and spirits. I am writing this letter to inform you that my company is expanding globally and is hiring interpreters for their meetings, and it would be great if you apply for and get the job.

I remember last time we met that you want to leave the tour company in which you are working, as it involves a lot of travelling. This job would be a golden opportunity for you to get a stable job. I am sure you will be hired, because they need people who know many languages, and you have done certificate courses in five languages.

It is easy to apply for the job. My company is going to advertise in the Economic Times, this coming Sunday. Apply immediately, because it is a lucrative job, and I feel that many applications would pour in. I will push your application forward and provide a letter of recommendation for you. Our company welcomes recommendations of the current employees.

Hoping to see you soon in my company.

Yours lovingly,
Mohan

77. You had an appointment to meet your bank manager regarding your home loan, but you were not able to make it and you couldn't inform him. Write a letter

- Apologize for not coming.
- Explain the reasons why you couldn't be there.
- Tell him/her how you tried contacting him/her.
- Request another meeting.

Dear Sir,

I had a meeting regarding a home loan fixed with you for 24th April 2011. Unfortunately, I could not make it on that day. I apologise for the inconvenience caused because of this.

My elderly aunt and uncle are arrived unexpectedly from Gurdaspur on that day. My uncle was suffering from a heart problem for which I had to rush him to the hospital. I had to be with them during the entire week he was at the hospital. He was quite serious but fortunately he has recovered completely now because of timely medical help. It was a very tense period and in all that hustle and bustle I could not inform you in time. I am sorry for that.

I would be very grateful if you could reschedule our appointment for any day in the second week of May. You can call me at 98xxxxxxxx to inform me the new date or alternatively you may e-mail me at kiranmakkar@hotmail.com.

Once again I apologise for the inconvenience and thank you for your kind consideration.

Yours faithfully,
XYZ

78. Write a letter seeking financial assistance to an organization whichgives money to meritorious students who would like to take a part-time course. Mention

- Qualifications and work experience.
- Details about the course.
- How this course will help you?

Dear Sir,

I recently read about a scholarship programme that you are offering students who wish to do a part time course in Australia. I would like to be considered for the scholarship. I am enclosing my resume for your consideration.

My name is Indroop Singh and I belong to India. I have done my Bachelor's of Computer Engineering from IIT Chennai and now I want to do a part time diploma course in International Business. I have always been a topper in my class and I have heard that you encourage meritorious students. The fee for the course is very high and if I don't receive funding I shall not be able to continue my studies.

The course would be very beneficial for me as today we belong to a global village. Whatever we do in life, we must know the basics of 'International Business'. Only then can we survive the tough competition we have to face in today's time. The scholarship I receive from you will help me to study further and also take some burden off my parents' shoulders. I will also be able to concentrate on my studies more as I will not have to worry about the expenses incurred.

You may contact my professors at IIT Chennai in case you need to ask anything about me. My contact number is 98xxxxxxxx, if you have anything to clarify from me.

Yours faithfully,
Indroop

79. There is a public event coming up in your town. Write a letter to your friend who you think would be interested to take part in it. In your letter

- Describe the event.
- Say why you think he / she would be interested.
- Suggest an arrangement to meet there with him / her.

Dear Elaine,

I hope this letter finds you in radiant health and the best of spirits. I am writing this letter to invite you to celebrate our traditional festival Deepawali with us this year. Apart from having a great time, it will also help you in the project you are doing on 'Globalisation and Tradition'.

Deepawali is our national festival. It falls in the month of October or November. It literally means rows of lights. It is celebrated to commemorate the return of Lord Rama to Ayodhya after fourteen years of exile. This is one festival which all Indians celebrate. A month before Deepawali, we whitewash our homes and buy new clothes to wear on that day. On the day of Deepawali we worship Goddess Laxmi, the symbol of wealth and also burn crackers. There is lots of fun and frolic.

We would be honoured to have you as our guest for your entire stay here. You are welcome to bring your parents along if they can spare the time. Ever since I finished my course at Leeds University and came back home, I have talked so much about you to my parents that they are all very eager to see you. You will see that we Indians have not forgotten our traditional celebrations even if we have become a part of the global village, which is influenced by western culture. I assure you we will make it a memorable holiday for you.

Hoping to see you soon.

Yours lovingly,
Kiran

---

80. Write a letter to request a reservation of the apartment that you rented during your last vacation. Please say

- What did you like about the apartment
- What weren't you happy with
- Provide your date of arrival and length of stay.

Dear Sir/Madam,

I am writing to request you to book apartment number 203 on the Calungate Beach, from the 24th of November to the 8th of December. My family and I intend to visit Goa during this period and I wanted to share the same experience I had the last time I was there with them. We all liked the apartment and would like to secure the same this time too.

This apartment is in the perfect location facing the seaside. The rooms of the apartment are very spacious and the view of the sunset from the balcony is spectacular. We intend to have a relaxing holiday, which I am sure would be possible in this apartment.

I would like to bring to your notice an inconvenience we faced last time. The AC of the master bedroom was a bit temperamental and would stop working for hours at a stretch. Please make sure that everything is in perfect order.

Looking forward to making the trip and hearing back from you.

Yours faithfully,
Suneet Broca

81. Write a letter to your friend to inform him/her that one of your relatives is traveling to his/her country and say

- Describe your relative.
- Why is he traveling there?
- Why do you think they should meet?

Dear Christine,

I hope this letter finds you in great health and cheer. I am writing to inform you that my aunt Meena is visiting Germany next month. She is to visit some friends on the occasion of their daughter's wedding. I am sending some Indian saris for you with her. It would be great if you could meet her to collect your things.

Aunt Meena would be staying at the Merry Land Hotel at Berlin, which I believe is only two blocks away where your university. She is in her mid-forties, and is not tall, but very beautiful. She is as passionate about fashion and culture as you are. She is also very knowledgeable about Indian history and as you are working on a project on Indian culture, this would give you the opportunity to learn a lot from her. She would be delighted if you attend the wedding ceremony with her. You could also show her around a bit.

Hope you can manage the time to attend the wedding with her and also get ideas for your thesis.

Yours lovingly,
Suneet

82. You recently read an article in a business magazine about the company you work for. Some information in the article was incorrect. Write a letter to your manager and tell him/her about the magazine article.

- Give details about the article.
- What was wrong in your opinion?
- Suggest a solution to correct this error.

Dear Sir,

I am an employee in your company "The Triple Travel" in the Overseas Division. Recently I read an article about the leading travel companies in the April issue of "Travel Today" magazine written by Jagat Vishwas. As you are aware Mr Vishwas is the leading travel expert in India, I would like to bring it to your notice that this article conveyed certain incorrect facts about our company's achievements.

The article conveyed that our profits were 15% in the year 2015-16, whereas we have registered a profit of more than 20% in the given financial year. This information lowers our company's standing to the fifth position amongst other travel companies.

Moreover we have started some overseas projects also, which have not been reported in the article. Overseas projects are very important for a global outlook. We must convey the right facts to the editor and have them corrected at the earliest.

I feel that these facts have been intentionally misrepresented/omitted to lower the standing of our company. I would advise that we should immediately convey these issues to the editor of the magazine so that they can issue an amendment in their next issue. As an employee of the company I felt It is my duty to inform you so that these facts can be rectified at the earliest.

Yours faithfully,
Anupam

---

83. You are studying and doing a part-time job. A full time position recently opened in the company and your manager is asking you to quit your studies and start working full-time. Write a letter to him/her and say

- What is your decision?
- Why did you make this decision?
- Suggest a solution that will suit both you and the company.

Dear Sir,

I am writing this letter regarding your offer to take up the full time position of an assistant auditor in CSL. I have decided to humbly decline the offer, so that I can finish my diploma, which has only six months to go.

The reason for my decision is simply that I have dedicated 18 months to my Diploma course, and it doesn't seem right to discontinue it at this stage. Further on in my career, this course might help me in getting a promotion. So, it seems more practical to me to complete this first. My part-time job in your organisation is helping me in translating my theoretical knowledge to a practical one, and I am learning a lot. In my opinion, if I finish this course, I would be a far better asset to the company, than what I am now.

I would suggest that I continue as a part timer, and then six months down the line, I could transition to a full time role. Emily, who has just joined as an intern, and has been working on our project for the last one month, would provide you with the manpower you need for the current projects.

I hope you would understand my situation and keep this job open for me for the very near future.

Yours faithfully,
Suneet Broca

---

84. You have recently visited a tourist attraction and were very pleased by the help given to you by the staff. Write a letter to the staff manager and say
- Give details of your visit.
- Describe how the staff helped you.
- What do you want the manager to do?

Dear Sir,

I am working in Shimla and along with my family I visited Red Fort in the month of January this year. I am writing this letter to thank one of your staff members who helped us during that trip.

We reached Red Fort by a bus. Red Fort is a very intricately designed and an imposing monument. We were confused about how to go about the visit. At the entrance we noticed that there was an office, which I figured could offer us some assistance about the monument. I went to the office and politely inquired from the person manning the office if he could offer me some advice as to how to go about visiting the Red Fort. The official whose name was Mr. Vijay Singh was very positive and dynamic. He first gave us a brief glimpse into the history of Red Fort and then explained the various sections of the Fort. Hetook great pains to explain us in detail as to how we should go about the visit. He even went out of the way and got us a good guide at very cheap rates. The official spent a good 30 minutes with us even though he was very busy. It was due to his positive attitude and painstaking efforts that the visit to the Red Fort was very educative and interesting.

I wish to place on the record the helpful and positive attitude of Mr. Vijay Singh, as it was due to him that our visit to Red Fort was fruitful. I am sure if all tourist officials function in this manner it would lead to great deal of satisfaction amongst the tourists.

Yours sincerely,
Mandip Singh

85. You are going to take course in another country and you have finalized your accommodation through a travel agent. Now you want to change your accommodation. Write a letter to him and mention

- What was your previous accommodation, which you requested?
- Why you want to change your accommodation?
- What new accommodation you want this time?

Dear Sir/Madam,

I am Kiran Makkar, from India. I have joined a Diploma in International Cookery course in Hamilton University, and have booked an apartment through your company for one year. I am writing this letter to request you to kindly change that apartment, which is near the North Campus, to another one, which is near the South Campus.

I understand that I had finalized the apartment you suggested to me, but then I did not know that the course I am applying for is in the South Campus. I was also not aware that the two campuses are 2 miles apart. It would be very difficult for me to go for my classes every day on foot, from the present accommodation, which is near the North Campus.

Please book a 1 BHK apartment for me, preferably near North Campus and the student market. I am sorry for the inconvenience caused, but as I am informing you within the notice period of three weeks, I hope you will be able to change it without any hassle.

Hoping to hear from you soon!

Yours faithfully,
Kiran Makkar

86. You recently saw an advertisement about business conference that can be helpful for your work. Write a letter to your manager asking permission to attend the conference. In your letter say

- What is the conference about?
- How did you get to know about the conference?
- Explain to him/her why it is important that you attend this conference.
- Inform him/her about the schedule and venue of the conference.

Dear Ma'am,

I am writing this letter to request permission for attending a conference being organized by the British Council on the topic of 'Managing and Teaching Large Classes'.

I saw an advertisement about this conference in today's newspaper, The Tribune. It will focus on the different strategies for the management of students and improving teaching in large classrooms. As you know, in our college there are a minimum of 40 students per class and it becomes a challenge to keep everyone engaged. This also sometimes leads to a compromise on the quality of our teaching, as we are unable to cater to the needs and the learning pace of all the students.

I believe this conference will be extremely helpful for our institute, as it will enable us to develop and use strategies and methodologies to ensure that our classrooms are managed better. We need to maintain and improve the quality of education to meet and live up to the expectations of the parents of the learners.

The conference is scheduled to be held on the 15th of June, from 9:00AM – 5:00PM, at Club Cabana in Phagwara. After attending this conference, I can then organize a training session for the other teachers at the college.

I hope you will grant me the permission to attend this conference.

Thank you.

Yours faithfully,
Sumeet Kaur

87.A new international hotel has posted various job vacancies. Write a letter to the manager. In your letter:

- Say what position you want to apply for.
- Say why it interests you.
- And provide your qualification and experience.

Dear Sir/Madam,

I am writing with regard to the vacancy for a Restaurant Manager in The Windsor Hotel, which I saw advertised in 'The Times' dated 15th April. I hereby extend my interest in this position and am attaching herein a copy of my CV and certifications.

I am currently working as a Restaurant Manager at the Pancake Parlour in Malvern. I have over 10 years of hospitality experience in the roles of Team Leader, Chef and Supervisor. Recently, I have been promoted to a managerial position. I have heard a lot about your esteemed Azaaria Restaurant. I am looking forward to work there as a restaurant manager.

I am seeking to move to a bigger organisation with an internationally acclaimed business. I believe I meet and exceed the key skills and attributes needed for the post. You require someone with a Diploma in Hospitality and 5 years of experience. I hold a bachelor's degree and 10 years' experience. You want someone who can speak French. To this I would like to mention that I am qualified in French, Spanish and German.

Being a part of your organisation would bring mutual benefit to you and me. It would allow me to share all that I have learnt at Pancake Parlour, and at the same time allow me to hone my skills and widen my career prospects at a global scale within the hospitality industry.

Looking forward to your reply.

Yours faithfully,
Suneet Broca

---

88. You have lived in an apartment for a year and your landlord wants to increase the rent. You are not happy with it. Write a letter to the landlord and –

- Introduce yourself
- Explain why he should not increase the rent
- What you would do if he increases the rent

Dear Sir,

I am Ravinder Walia, your tenant from apartment number 131, Bissonet Enclave. I am writing this letter to express my dissatisfaction about your decision to increase the rent.

I signed the lease for this apartment last August. It was clearly mentioned in the lease deed that if the current tenant wants to continue staying there, then there will be no increase in rent for 3 years. This policy is being followed by most of the landlords of this area.

If you are adamant to increase the rent, then I would not be signing the lease for the next year. The newly built apartment block, just across the road, is offering their apartments at much lesser rent for the first 20 people who sign the lease. I had not thought of it before, because I did not want to go into the hassle of shifting, but I may have to do so now, because it would be a saving for me. Please reconsider your decision and let me know at the earliest.

Hoping to hear from you soon.

Yours faithfully,
Ravinder Walia

89.A friend of yours has started a new trading business in a foreign country. He or she needs some suggestions from you. Write a letter to your friend. In your letter:
- Suggest some products from your country.
- Provide details about where it is available.
- And explain why your suggestion is good for him or her.

Dear James,

What a surprise to receive your letter yesterday! I am thrilled to read that you're planning to start an import-export business in Southhall. I feel honoured that you have asked for my advice regarding a product to import from India.

I would suggest that you import traditional Punjabi Suits from here. I have seen that Southall is full of Punjabis. In fact people call it the mini Punjab. People crave for traditional Punjabi suits over there and I am sure you will get a good business. You can add matching accessories like bangles and other jewellery with it.

I can help you in this endeavour. You just make one initial visit and after that I shall take care of things. You can buy stuff from Delhi, Amritsar and Patiala. For the jewellery you can visit Jaipur. You can get very good jewellery in all colours to go with the dresses.

I have recommended this product to you because my cousin is already in this business and I know that he exports these dresses to many parts of the world. So, I know they are popular in the west and you will also do well. Moreover, my cousin can guide you where to get the latest variety at reasonable rates.

Hope you like my suggestion. Looking forward to hearing from you soon.

Yours lovingly,
Preet Mohan

90.Write a letter to your English-speaking friend who is visiting you soon and asking you what presents your family would like. Write
- Who your family consists of?
- What kind of presents each member would like?
- How you feel about your friend coming to visit?

Dear Hannah,

It was a very pleasant surprise to hear from you after such a long time. My joy knew no bounds when I read that you are coming to visit me.

My parents and my younger sister too are very excited about your visit. It is very generous of you to ask what they would like as a present from you. Believe me Hannah, your presence here would be the biggest gift for them. As far as material things are concerned, nowadays everything is available in India. So, please don't bother yourself for this.

It would be great if you send me your detailed itinerary so that I can plan the best for your holiday. You know, India has a rich historical background and I would like you to visit as many places as possible. There is the Taj Mahal at Agra which is a must-see. Then the Golden Temple at Amritsar, the temples of South India, the beaches of Goa and the back-waters of Kerala are all awaiting your visit.

Fortunately, there is a summer break going on in my college, so I shall be completely at your disposal. I am really excited about your visit. We shall have a great holiday together and also revive some of the nostalgic memories of the great time we had four years ago when we were both studying at Leeds University.

Waiting eagerly for you.

Yours lovingly,
Kiran

91. You recently stayed at your friend's place to look after the house while he/she was away. You accidentally damaged something in his/her house. Write a letter to your friend and say

- What was the accident?
- When did it happen?
- Suggest how the damage can be fixed.

Dear Manwinder,

Hope this letter finds you in the best of health and spirits. It was my pleasure to look after your house in your absence. Unfortunately, the glass pane of your living room's window broke down accidentally when I was playing with my children in the garden. I am writing this letter to apologise for that damage.

Yesterday, while I was playing football with my children in your front garden, they passed the ball to me. I could not stop the ball, and the ball went beyond the boundary of the garden smashing the window. I know that the window has to be repaired soon. I have closed the opening temporarily with a thick cardboard from your attic. It would be very kind of you if you could tell me the store from where you bought the glass, so that I can get it fixed before you and your family arrive.

Looking forward to your reply.

Yours lovingly,
Anu Gandam

---

92. You have recently had a good meal in a local restaurant with your family. Write a letter to your local newspaper about your experience

- Describe the restaurant.
- What meal did you have there?
- Why do you think this restaurant is worth visiting?

Dear Sir,

I recently visited the local Hot Millions Restaurant for a family dinner and am writing to share my experience there.

The restaurant is located right in the heart of the city and has ample parking space with valet service. The interiors are designed to provide a great dining experience with large glass windows providing a view of the city. The dining hall is spacious and the seating is worth a watch. To add to the experience is their staff that provides service within no time and with a smile. They serve traditional and local dishes along with a select range of Continental cuisine.

We had ordered Chicken in Clear Lemon Soup for appetizer and Grilled Mutton Chops, Vegetable Stew and Italian Brown Pasta Salad in the main course. For dessert, we ordered their specialty, Kiwi Fruit in Nutty Cream. The food was scrumptious and a treat to the eyes. The display and plating was beautiful. My kids loved the dessert in particular.

I highly recommend this restaurant as a must-visit for your readers. To attract new customers, they offer a 10 percent discount.

I'm sure your readers will have a great experience there.

Yours truly,
Simran

93. You recently completed a course and you borrowed a book from your teacher, which you couldn't return in time. You would like to return the book now. Write a letter to your teacher and say

- What book was it?
- How helpful was the book?
- Explain why you couldn't return it in time.

Dear Mrs. Joshi,

I am writing this letter to thank you forthe book – 'The Photographer's Eye' by Micheal Freeman, which you had lent me to study during the final semester of my Journalism course. I also want to apologise for having failed to return it immediately after the exams were over.

The book is a masterpiece on practical aspects of digital photography and it helped me a lot in the exam of Digital Photography. It throws light on every aspect of framing, exposure, compositions and light. The routine text books of our course could've never matched to what this book taught me. It was only because of this book that I bagged the University position in the subject of Digital Photography.

The reason why I have been unable to return the book even after 4 months of my course completion is that I had received an invitation for internship in a fashion magazine. They wanted me to join immediately after my exams and I did the same. In this rush, I totally forgot that I had to return your book.

I am back from the internship programme and will come to you soon to return that marvelous book.

Yours sincerely,
Simran

---

94. You would like to apply for a full-time position at an international company. Write to the human resources department and say

- What job are you interested in?
- Explain what you are currently doing.
- Why do you think you are best candidate for the job?

Dear Sir,

I am writing with reference to your advertisement in the local 'Employment News' magazine for vacancies various categories of workers in New Zealand. I consider that my credentials match the category of Certified Nursing Assistants and I want to apply for the same. I am enclosing my CV for this job.

Presently I am deputed as a nurse at the Regional Hospital. I have been working here for the last two years. During these years I have equipped myself with knowledge of all the nursing functions, which include taking and recording temperature, blood pressure, pulse and respiratory rates along with cleaning, sterilizing and preparing treatment trays. Strong communication skills and reacting actively to emergency situations has made me a well- organised nursing assistant.

Although I am enjoying my present job, I am looking for new opportunities in the developed world. I am sure that working in New Zealand would broaden my horizons even further, and on coming back, I would be able to serve my people even better.

If you have any questions please feel free to contact me at 98xxxxxxxx. I look forward to hearing from you soon.

Yours faithfully,
Kiran Makkar

---

95. You have recently started a new job. Write a letter to your friends to tell them about it and invite them for an evening meal.

- Describe how you feel about the job.
- Give directions to a meeting place.
- Give suggestions on where to stay, if they come from a different city.

Dear Robin and Ajay,

I hope this letter finds you in good health and cheer. I am writing to give you the good news that I have started working in Delta International. I just started last week. I would like to celebrate with you. Why don't we have dinner together at Club Cabana the coming Saturday.

I saw the ad for this job vacancy two months ago and applied for it. My joy knew no bounds when I received this offer letter. I have the post of Senior Web Developer. I am very happy about this job. This is something I was looking forward to doing.

Do let me know when you can come. Club Cabana is just 10 miles from Phagwara on the National Highway 44. I can make arrangements for your pick up from the railway station and then you can stay the weekend at my place. It would be great to revive some nostalgic memories of the college times.

Looking forward to see you.

Yours lovingly,
Narinder Makkar

96. You are having some unpleasant issues at work. Write a letter to your friend who does the same job as you in a different company and say:

- Describe your job.
- Describe the issues that you have.
- Ask your friend for some advice.

Dear Joseph,

I am writing to inform you that I have been promoted to the post of Senior Journalist recently and I also want to discuss with you certain issues that I'm facing with this bigger role. Since you hold a similar position in Journalism, it makes you the best person for me to talk to about this.

As a Senior Journalist, I have to handle a team of three other Journalists. I also am responsible to coordinate the Journalists of four other cities that fall under the head office I work for. Apart from my own news coverage, I have to be the link between the head office and all the Journalists under me.

With added responsibilities have come some unpleasant issues too. The head office needs to be updated about the news every two hours and the final news items go in the evening. I have to make the two-hourly news update chart of all the journalists under me and keep sending it to the head office. During this time, I have to cover the news events that are under my direct responsibility. In this rush, I miss on my own news items.

Since you've been working as a Senior Journalist for a fairly long time now, please advise me on how to simultaneously handle the work load of news update charts and my own news items. I also want your suggestions on ways to finish my work a little early in the evening.

Looking forward to your advice.

Yours lovingly,
Simran

97.Your mentor recommended you to learn a new language and gave you contact details of a teacher. Following his advice, you need to write a letter to the teacher and say

- What is your motivation to learn a new language?
- How can the teacher help you?
- When will you be ready to start?

Dear Sir,

I am Anu, pursuing my Bachelor's degree in Technology at Chandigarh University. My mentor Dr. Kiran has given your reference, as I have been shortlisted for a student exchange programme in your country, Germany. It is an advanced Diploma course for duration of eleven months. I am writing this letter to request you to accept me as a student of your online course at the earliest.

It has been my dream to study in Germany, as it is a country known to be technically advanced. But to study in Germany, it is very important to know how to speak and understand the language. I have already started to learn German with the help of material available on the Internet. I am also planning to enroll at the Max Muller Language Centre for weekend classes. However, I still need personalized guidance.

My mentor has informed me that you provide online classes that are moulded as per the student's requirement. My requirement is not only to be able to speak and interact in the country but also to work part time. I will be permitted to work only if I know the language well. Kindly mail the requirements and fee details to join your online course.

I want to leave no stone unturned in my efforts to ensure that I do not lose this golden opportunity. I want to start at the earliest and lose no time. I will wait eagerly for your reply.

Yours sincerely,
Anu

98.You have recently bought a TV and it arrived damaged. Write a letter to the store manager and say:
- When and what TV did you buy?
- Describe the damage.
- How can the issue be solved in your opinion?

Dear Sir,

I am writing this letter to complain about a damaged TV set, which I bought from your store. I visited your Sony Centre, Model Town, Jalandhar on the 13th of May, 2017 and placed the order of item no. 23506-Black, Sony LED 32". I paid the sum in full. I received the item today on the15th of May, 2017.

I opened the box with great enthusiasm, but to my dismay, I noticed that the thermocol packing was completely damaged, and when I took out the TV, the front corners were all scratched badly. Obviously, it was not packed properly and due to mishandling or careless handling the user booklet wasalso in two-pieces.

I am highly disappointed with this service. I would like to get the TVreplaced on priority basis. Kindly make sure the item functions properly and is wrapped thoroughly to avoid any damage. Do let me know when will you be delivering the new item.

Eagerly awaiting your reply.

Yours faithfully,
Aditya

99.You have met an old friend in another city on your last business trip. Now you are going on another business trip in the same city and want to meet him/her again. Write a letter to your friend and say
- Express your excitement about the last meeting.
- Give details about your new business trip.
- Suggest an arrangement to meet again.

Dear Raghav,

I hope this letter finds you in the pink of health. I am writing this letter to give you the good news that I am again coming to Chandigarh for abusiness trip. Our last meeting was reallyunforgettable. It was amazing catching up after so long. My mother loved the scarf you sent for her and I have put the schedule pad to use. It really helps me plan the daily routine and meetings.

I will be arriving in your town next Friday i.e. the 26th of May by the morning flight. On the very same day, I have two back-to-back meetings followed by lunch. Later in the evening I have to report the minutes of the meetings to the head office through a video call. Therefore, I will see you on Saturday noon. I will be flying back on Sunday at 10 p.m.

Why don't we explore the Hill Resort we were talking about last time? I have surfed through the Internet and it is a great place, and serves a variety of cuisines. Also, we can visit the Sukhna Lake in the evening. I am really excited to meet you again. Do let me know if you are available on Saturday, else we can meet on Sunday.

Looking forward to see you.

Yours lovingly,
Aditya

---

100. A builder has recently completed some renovation at your house, but you are not satisfied with his work. Write a letter to him. In your letter,

- Tell him what work has not been completed properly.
- Tell him what you want him to do.
- Suggest some times when you will be available at home.

Dear Mr. Oberoi,

I was happy and surprised to know that you have completed the renovation of my home earlier than your stated commitment. Unfortunately, there are a few problems, which I have noticed. I am writing this letter to express my dissatisfaction about your unsatisfactory performance.

Firstly, the wall-paint of the living room has not been done properly. Anyone can make out the differences in the color concentration on various spots of all walls. Secondly, the new tap of the kitchen is leaking. It seems it is a defective piece. Furthermore, the door closer of the backyard door has not been tightly screwed. It may fall any moment the door opens and is dangerous.

I will be available at home before 11 in the morning and after 3 in the noon for this week. I strongly feel that you should rectify all these problems as early as possible so that I can release the remaining payment. I hope a week's time is enough for you to complete the work.

I look forward to hearing from you.

Yours sincerely,
Aditya Kalra

101. You have recently joined a sports centre and encountered some issues during your visits. Write a letter to the centre manager about it and say

- What do you like about the centre?
- Mention the problems that you have had there.
- Give your view on how to solve those problems.

Dear Sir,

My name is Parminder Singh. I have recently joined your sports centre. I am writing this letter to complain about the problems I am encountering in the changing rooms.

The bolts on the doors and windows are all broken as a result of which anyone can budge into the room while we are changing. To add to it, the curtains are so dirty that they smell. The urinals attached to the changing rooms also stink. The dustbins are also very dirty.

On behalf of all the members, I request you to look into the matter urgently. We all feel very disgusted at the services we are receiving. We have all paid a very heavy membership fees and we feel that we deserve the best.

I would suggest you to call in a plumber and a carpenter to rectify the sanitary and wooden fittings. The curtains need to be changed. Last but not least, I would urge you to make regular inspections of the changing rooms so that the staff in charge of the mopping and cleaning, do their work properly.

Hoping for a prompt action from you regarding this matter.

Yours faithfully,
Parminder Singh

102. You have seen a man a few days ago in your local park, causing damage. Write a letter to the park management and say
- What did you see
- Who are you
- What do you think should be done about it

Dear Mr Sethi,

I am living in House No 1633 Sector 47A Chandigarh, and all people of this area enjoy the park of this sector, which is maintained because of your able management. I am writing this letter to apprise you that some irresponsible person is damaging the beauty of the park.

On 12 May, while I was taking my morning walk in the Park, I noticed that a person who lives in House No 1534 of the same Sector was causing lot of damage to the flowerbeds. He was walking through the newly planted saplings of the flowers. Realizing that his irresponsible actions would damage the flowerbeds and not allow their proper growth, I requested the person not to walk through the flowerbeds. However, he paid no heed to me and told me that I had no right to question him on his actions and he continued to walk through the flowerbeds. It appeared that he wanted to spoil the flower beds on purpose.

May I request you to look into the matter and take necessary action so that there is no further damage to our beautiful park. Notices should be put at regular intervals that any person who causes damage to the park would be fined heavily. In case such wanton acts are not arrested, our park will cease to be the pride of our Sector.

Yours sincerely,
Mandeep Singh

103. You have finished a course. Write a letter to the course organizer to give your feedback. In your letter include: You have finished a course.
- The details of the course.
- What you enjoyed during the course?
- Any suggestions you would have.

Dear Sir,

My name is Raghav Ghaie. I have recently finished a certificate course in 'Computer Hardware and Maintenance' from your institute. I am writing this letter to apprise you with my experiences during the course.

The course I attended was of six months duration. I must appreciate the faculty who taught us each and every thing in a very nice manner. What I enjoyed most was the hands-on practical training that they gave. I feel so confident after doing the course that I am thinking of opening my own computer repair centre in the near future.

However, I must suggest that some latest models of computers be provided there. The computers which are presently there are outdated now. Technology is developing by leaps and bounds and therefore the computers have to be updated regularly. If this suggestion is given due consideration then definitely the course would be the best.

I pen down by thanking you once again for the wonderful experience I had while doing this course at your institute.

Yours faithfully,
Raghav Ghai

---

104. You are planning to go on a holiday in an English-speaking country where one of your friends resides. Please write him a letter and let him know about the upcoming trip. In your letter:
- Ask for recommendations for places to visit during your trip.
- Ask about accommodations.
- Advise on a program that you and your friend can do together once you will meet him.

Dear Samaira,

Hope this letter finds you in radiant health and the best of spirits. It has been a long time since we met. I am writing this letter to inform you that I am coming for a holiday in your area with my husband and I wanted to take some information from you.

First of all, I would like to know how the weather would be like in the month of April. Actually, my husband is getting two week's leave, and we would like to come at that time. Secondly, I would like to know what all is there to see and do in your area. If we plan in advance then we shall be able to make the most of our time. Finally, I would be very grateful if you suggest some economical but good place to stay in.

Please write at the earliest so that I can rest easy about the arrangements. I would also like to spend some time with you. It would be great to share some nostalgic memories of our college years after such a long time. Do let me know if you would like to have anything from India, I shall be too happy to get them for you.

Waiting eagerly for your reply.

Yours lovingly,
Kiran

---

105. You have recently noticed an increase in traffic in your residential area. Write a letter to the responsible person at the local council to inform him/her about the problem and say

-   Introduce yourself and describe the problem.
-   What are the reasons for the traffic in your view?
-   Suggest a solution to the problem.

Dear Ma'am,

My name is Kiran Makkar and I am a resident of Guru Hargobind Nagar, Phagwara. I am writing this letter to apprise you of the worsening traffic situation in this area.

The traffic through this area has always been heavy. Besides the regular traffic, buses also use this road to get to the bus stand. Over the last one month, the traffic on this road has become heavier and the situation has worsened. Accidents have become commonplace and there is too much congestion on the roads. It takes almost 5-8 minutes to cross this road on foot at anytime during the day.

This is mainly because this area has developed a lot recently and there are many new banks and shops that have opened up. People park their cars and two-wheelers anywhere on the road, while they go into the banks and the shops for their work. This leads to the flow of traffic being disrupted and traffic bottlenecks are created.

I have some suggestions that may help alleviate this problem. There should be a few parking assistants assigned to make sure that people park their vehicles properly. This can be done by the council or by the shops, offices and banks on this road. Also, there should be random checks by the traffic police and those who have parked their vehicles incorrectly and irresponsibly should be fined. Lastly, I believe that spreading awareness among the people about being more responsible when driving and parking will help alleviate this problem to a great extent. This can be done by organizing traffic drives, through seminars, advertisements in the local newspapers and TV channels and posters put up on the roads.

This issue needs your immediate attention, so that it doesn't escalate further. I hope you will take the required action at the earliest.

Thank you.

Yours faithfully,
Kiran Makkar

106. **You have recently read an article in a newspaper about your favourite restaurant. The writer did not like the restaurant, but you disagree with his/her opinion. Write a letter to the editor and say**

- Where the restaurant is and its name?
- Describe your last visit to the restaurant.
- Why you disagree with the writer's opinion?
- What should the editor do about this?

Dear Mr. Vinayak,

My name is Manpreet Kaur and I am a resident of Chandigarh. I am a patron of your newspaper, The Tribune. I am writing this letter to express my discontent with an article that was published in the Chandigarh Tribune supplement, on May 1, 2017.

In this article. Ms. Kaveri, a well-known chef, has critiqued the restaurant, Under the Willows, which is located in Sector 26, Chandigarh. She has mentioned that the food there is excellent, but the ambience of the restaurant is very dull and it is not decorated tastefully. I have been a regular at this restaurant since it opened last year in August. I visit it at least once a month; in fact I was there for a family lunch just last week. In my opinion, the restaurant is decorated very aesthetically and its ambience is very pleasant. I think it has a very nice theme of willows and the interiors have been designed keeping that in mind.

I understand that everyone has a right to their opinion and we all may have different choices. However, the tone used by the writer is more of a judgment than an opinion, which is not fair and not a responsible way of assessment. I suggest that when such an article is published, it should have a disclaimer that it is only the writer's personal opinion and doesn't reflect the views of all the customers in general. A disclaimer to this effect should be printed at the beginning of such articles.

I hope you understand my perspective and would consider my suggestion.

Thank you.

Yours sincerely,
Manpreet Kaur

107. You have recently attended a conference and found it very informative. Write a letter to your manager and ask hispermission to give a presentation on the same topic to your colleagues. Include the following details in your letter:

- What was the presentation about?
- Where was the conference held?
- How can it be useful to your colleagues and the company?

Dear Ma'am,

I am Suman Singh, team manager Tech Support. I am writing this letter to request your permission to conduct a presentation on the subject of 'Effective Reporting' to the other managers in the department.

As you know, I recently attended a conference on effective reporting and analysis of data, using MS Excel and other such tools. It was held in New Delhi, at the InterContinental Hotel. Many managers from organizations from across India attended this conference. It was an insightful and enlightening experience. I learned about many useful practices that we should follow when making and analyzing reports.

In our organization also, making team reports is one of the main responsibilities of the managers. These reports not only need to be sent out to the senior managers, but they also help to analyze and track the progress of the team. I have prepared a presentation on some useful tips and tricks we can use for the reports and I believe that it will be very helpful for all the managers to track, analyze and improve upon the performance of their teams.

This session will be for an hour and a half and we can conduct it in the coming week. I am sure this presentation will be beneficial for the Team Managers.

I hope you will consider this request and allow me to conduct this session for the team.

Thank you.

Yours faithfully,
Suman Singh

108. You have a permanent job, and few weeks ago you have started a part-time short course. You are not satisfied with it and want to change this part time course. Write a letter to your professor explaining

- Why you are not satisfied with your present part-time course?
- Stating which course you would prefer and why?

Dear Sir,

My name is Sharad Pahwa and I am working in a bank. I am writing this letter to express my dissatisfaction with the part time course in 'Computer Basics' that I am doing under you.

I was not aware of the contents of the Course when I started. While working in my bank, consulting friends from the IT Dept. by hit and trial and by consulting with friends, I have already learnt whatever is being taught in this course. What I actually want to learn is Basics of HW trouble-shooting: how to identify is a problem is due to the Hard Disk or RAM or Modem.

I have heard that you also have a part time course in Hardware Management. I would be very grateful if you enroll me in that course instead of the present one. I apologise for the inconvenience caused due to this.

Hoping for a kind consideration of this urgent request!

Yours sincerely,
Sharad Pahwa

109. Your company had sent you to an English speaking country to do a course. You have finished it and got a certificate, which unfortunately you have lost. Write a letter to the college principal to issue a duplicate certificate. Write

- An explanation of how you lost that certificate.
- Tell him why the certificate is important to you .
- What you want them to do?

Dear Sir,

My name is Mohit Bhasin and I work for Dell International, India. I am writing this letter to request a duplicate certificate for the 'Business Administration' course which I did in your college in 2010.

I did the 'Certificate Course in Business Administration' in your college from January to July 2010. I got the certificate also but as I travelled back to India, British Airways misplaced my baggage. I got my baggage after 5 days and when I opened it many things were missing including the certificate.

This certificate is very important for me as my promotion is based on this course and that certificate is a proof that I have done the course.

I am sending a self-addressed and stamped envelope along with this letter. I would be very thankful if you issue me a duplicate certificate and post it as early as possible.

Thanking you in anticipation.

Yours faithfully,
Mohit

---

110. Write a letter to your English-speaking friend whom you visited recently. In your letter

- Tell him/her how wonderful the experience you had in his country was.
- Invite him to visit your country.
- Tell him what you can do for him during his visit.

Dear Sally,

Hope this letter finds you in radiant health and the best of spirits. I am writing this letter to formally thank you for such a wonderful experience that I had in your country. It was all because of your meticulous planning that I enjoyed so much in these two weeks. All the places we visited and all the activities we did during this period will always have an everlasting imprint on my memory.

Now it is your turn to visit my country. I assure you there is a lot to see and do in India. Please take at least a month off from work and believe me you will enjoy every second of it. Fortunately, my brother is getting married in May. Why don't you come then? You will also get to attend a typical Indian wedding.

We can cover historical places of Punjab, Delhi, Agra and Rajasthan during these days. I have a network of relatives in all these places and they would all be willing to extend their hospitality and accommodate us during the time.

Once again I thank you for all you have done for me. Hoping to hear from you soon!

Yours lovingly,
Kiran

111. You have planned to study in Australia. You have sent a letter to a college, but you have not received a reply from the college. Write a letter to the college principal. In your letter

- You should give details of the course that you wished to do.
- Say why do you choose to study at the college.
- Say why you need the reply soon.

Dear Sir/Madam,

I am writing this letter to enquire about the 'Diploma in International Cookery' that your college is offering. I wrote earlier also, but unfortunately did not get any reply.

I wish to do the 'Diploma in International Cookery' in your college. This is a very interesting course and after doing the course I would have a very bright future in this field. Chefs are earning telephone figure salaries nowadays. I would like to know when the next intake of the course is, so that I can apply in time and I would also like to know the fee structure. Please also let me know if there are any pre-requisites for doing this course.

I have chosen your college to study because elsewhere, this course is of two years duration but in your college it is of 15 months duration. Moreover, I have heard that you have got very good faculty and infrastructure. Campus placement rate of your college is also the best. So, for all the above reasons, your college is my first choice for doing this course.

It would be very kind of you if you could reply soon so that I can make alternative arrangement for my future studies if I cannot get admission in your college.

Hoping for a prompt reply from your side.

Yours faithfully,
XYZ

112. You have forgotten an important thing or document in a taxi on your recent trip. Write a letter to the taxi company manager and say

- Give details of your journey.
- Describe the importance of what you left in that taxi.
- What do you expect the taxi company manager to do?

Dear Sir,

My name is Mohini Makkar. I travelled by one of your taxis from Hotel Demon to the airport on Tuesday, the 15th of April at 3 pm. The driver was a young boy, with curly hair, and his name was Jisu. By mistake, I left my small paper bag containing a book and my certificate on the back seat.

My flight was at 4.30 pm. The taxi was in time, but there was a traffic jam on the way and instead of taking the usual 20 minutes, it took us one hour to reach the airport. In my hurry, I forgot that bag in the taxi. As I boarded the plane, I realised that the small carry bag was missing.

The bag does not have any costly things, but what it has in invaluable for me. The book, a novel 'Many Lives, Many Masters', was gifted by one of my friends and the certificate is a proof of the conference I attended. Both things are important for me.

Please courier the items to 341, Guru Hargobind Nagar, Phagwara. Do let me know the courier costs and your account number, so that I can transfer the required amount..

Hoping for a positive reply from your side.

Yours faithfully,
Mohini Makkar

113. You have invited your English-speaking friend to a family wedding and reserved a room at the hotel for him/her as you agreed before. You won't be able to meet him/her at the airport. Write a letter to your friend, describing:

- The reason why you can't meet him/her.
- How he/she can get to the hotel from the airport.
- The hotel where you made the reservation.

Dear Sarah,

I am anxiously awaiting your arrival on Friday morning. Unfortunately, because of unforeseen circumstances, I would not be able to come to pick you up at the airport as already planned.

An unexpected business meeting has come up which I cannot avoid, so I am suggesting you other means of reaching the hotel that I have booked for you. One way would be to hire a cab from just outside the airport. That would be the most convenient option if you have a lot of luggage. However, if you are travelling light then I suggest you take the local bus from the airport. That would be very economical. I am very sorry for this turn of events.

The hotel's name is Mount View and it is about 30 km from the airport. It is very near to my home, though. Normally I would have made you stay at my home but because of the wedding many relatives are already there and so for your convenience, I have booked the hotel. The wedding in the family will give you a taste of our rich cultural heritage.

I have planned a lot of other things for you when you are here. There are a lot of historical places, which you must see. I will be happy to accompany you and ensure that you have a hassle free visit.

Hoping to see you soon.

Yours lovingly,
Kiran

114. You have been selected for a training course on computer skills that you cannot attend. Write a letter to your employer and say:
- Explain how this training course would help you.
- Why won't you be able attend it?
- Suggest a way to have that training again.

Dear Sir,

I am Mohit Ghaie from the Accounts department. I am writing this letter to thank you for selecting me for the training course onComputer Skills. Unfortunately, I cannot attend this course right now because of some family commitments. I apologise for the same.

This training course would have been a boon for me. Computer skills can add much more efficiency to my work. However, attending this course now would not be possible for me. It would mean an extra 2 hours after office for two months. My grandfather has suffered a stroke and is bed-ridden. He needs me more than ever now. He is showing good recovery, but it may take another 6 months before he can be on his own.

I could attend this course after July. I have heard that the company is going to provide such training courses twice a year. Please consider my name for the training post July. I apologise for not being able to avail this offer now.

Hoping to hear from you regarding this matter.

Yours faithfully,
Mohit Ghaie

---

115. You are going to have a family party in a private room of a hotel. Write a letter to the hotel manager and say

- Why do you need to use this private room?
- What do you need them to provide for the party?
- Inquire about the price of the food you are ordering.

Dear Sir,

I would like to celebrate my nephew's 10th birthday at your hotel on 6th April. I am writing this letter to book a private room for a gathering of 25-30 for this purpose.

The party is to be on 6th April at 7.30pm. There will about 25 guests. I have invited all my near relatives and a couple of very close friends. I have plannedthis party as a surprise for my nephew. I intend to have some games like housie and musical chairs, which I think will be enjoyed by all. There should be soft music in the background and a lot of snacks. The preparations should be very delicious and not at all spicy. The snacks should reach each and every table and even the cake cutting ceremony should be very nicely arranged.

Do call me at 9811898118, so that we can plan the menu. Please let me know what three savory and three sweet snacks would roughly amount to, for this size of a gathering. Do also let me know what advance I have to pay for the booking.

Hoping to hear from you soon.

Yours faithfully,
Kiran Makkar

116. Your children are learning a foreign language at school, but they need some extra help. One of your friends suggested to contact a language tutor. Write to him/her and say

- Why are you writing to him/her?
- What do your children need help with?
- Ask the tutor about his/her experience and suggestions.

Dear Madam,

I am Kiran Makkar from Phagwara. I got your reference from my friend Mrs Bambah, who knows you personally. I am writing to seek your help in providing French classes to my children on weekends.

My children are in 5th and 7th class in Sophia School. They both have French classes at school. Somehow, they are not being able to catch up with this language at school and so their grades are suffering. Would it be possible for you to provide them weekend classes? Mrs Bambah was telling me that you have your own innovative ways of teaching French, because of which your students develop a love for learning the language.

Please let me know at the earliest when you will be able to give these classes to my children. Any suggestions from your personal experiences regarding learning French would be highly welcome.

Hoping to hear from you soon.

Yours faithfully,
Kiran

117. Write a letter to your manager asking for a training course, which you would like to attend. In your letter explain

- What the course is?
- Why it is required for your job?
- How you will manage your work while doing the course?

Dear Sir,

I am working as a Senior Web Developer in the company and write to request you to allow me to attend a two month Certificate Course in Computer Hardware. It is imperative for me to attend this course to improve our company's efficiency.

Our company basically deals with software development. We develop software for our clients and then as part of our after-sale service, we help them use the software effectively. In doing so, sometimes we face hardware problems such as those with the RAM or hard disk. That is why I would like to do this course. After doing the course I would feel more confident and I will be able to serve our clients even better.

By doing this course, my overall work efficiency would improve which would in turn help in the company's overall performance. I can manage my work from home during that period. I assure you that I would not let any work suffer as a result of this course.

Hoping for a favourable response from you in this matter.

Yours faithfully,
Kiran

---

118. You have recently joined an evening class in a college, but you are not able to attend the classes. Write a letter to your professor

- Introduce yourself and describe about your course.
- Why you are not able to attend the classes?
- Say what you want them to do.

Dear Professor James,

I am writing to inform you that I will have to discontinue the part time course "Introduction to Gerontology", which I am doing in the evening batch in Khalsa College. However, I would like to thank you for making the subject very interesting, and I would surely like to re-enroll in the next intake.

The reason for dropping off from the course is that my mother is not keeping very good health lately. She has recurrent attacks of asthma and cannot be left alone in such a situation. She is a known case of asthma but this time the attacks are more severe because of super added viral infection.

The course in Gerontology involves caring for the elderly. Today, we belong to an ageing society and we are part of a graying population. I would be better placed in today's job market after doing this course. Your innovative way of teaching and depth of knowledge have aroused my interest in the subject.

I would definitely like to continue this course in the next intake, which is in August. It would be very kind of you if you give me admission in the next intake starting in August.

Thanking you once again for your valuable support and guidance from time to time.

Yours sincerely,
Kiran

119. Write a letter to you friend to ask for help with collecting money for a charity organization.

- Why do you want to collect money for this charity?
- How will you collect the money?
- And how your friend can help with collecting money?

Dear Ravi,

Hope this letter finds you in good health and the best of spirits. I am writing this letter to request your help in raising money for a local NGO in my hometown, Phagwara.

As you may be well aware, the number of stray dogs has increased everywhere, and my hometown is no exception. Even if it is illegal to kill these dogs now, people do it secretly and this leads to many disputes in the society. The SPCA and the PFA have not yet reached small places like my hometown.

A lady, Ms. Nidhi, has taken up the initiative and has got her organisation approved as an NGO, which works under SPCA. I have joined her and so have many other people. Funds are needed urgently to get all the dogs neutered, so that no further pups are born. We are also asking people to adopt these dogs and are getting all of them vaccinated for free.

I know you are also an animal lover, and will put in some efforts to raise some funds for this cause. I am going door to door and doing my bit. You have good communication skills and as you are working in a local tabloid, you can advertise about this in your paper. Any help you can provide will be sincerely appreciated.

Hoping to hear from you soon.

Yours lovingly,
Ajay

120. Write a letter to a cafeteria you use

- Express your satisfaction.
- Tell about boring food.
- Give suggestions.

Dear Sir/Madam,

I am a regular customer of your café as it is reasonably priced, convenient and has a friendly atmosphere. I am writing this letter to apprise you with some shortcomings, which if looked into would increase the traffic to your café.

Firstly, the menu is very limited, and it tends to get very boring at times. It would be highly appreciated if you add some more items in the regular menu and have daily specials, which we would look forward to while visiting the café.

Secondly, although the staff tries to keep the tables clean, there are not enough workers at peak times. So either you should put up notices in bold that the students should clean their tables before leaving, or you will have to employ more people, which may increase the cost of running the café.

Hoping you take my feedback and suggestions positively and make some changes to make your café better.

Yours faithfully,
Kiran Makkar

---

121. You lost something and someone found it and sent it to you. Writing a letter to that person

- Thanking the person.
- Explain how you must have lost it?
- Explain what was there in it and why it was important to you?

Dear Mr. Rohan,

Thank you so much for returning my briefcase containing my important documents to me. I received the package by courier only today morning.

Actually, last week I travelled from Bombay to Delhi on the Shatabdi Express. My briefcase was in my suitcase but I had to see an important phone number and so I took it out. But somehow, absentmindedly, I forgot to put the briefcase back. When my stop came I just rushed out with my suitcase and forgot my briefcase in the train. Fortunately it came into your hands and you tracked my address from my diary inside the briefcase.

There were many important documents inside the briefcase. My driving licence, my business papers, my contacts diary and many more important documents were in there. I don't know what I would have done without them. Thank you once again for this kind gesture.

Do let me know if there is anything I can ever do for you. My contact number is 98xxxxxxxx.

Yours sincerely,
Kiran Makkar

122. Write a letter to a camp organiser about a job advertisement asking for people to help in a summer holiday camp for children. You should write

- Why do you think you are good for this job?
- When can you attend?
- What questions would you like to ask about the camp?

Dear Sir,

I am writing to apply for a job opening in a children's summer holiday camp. I came to know about this job from an ad in a local newspaper.

I think I would be good for this job because I am a music teacher in a public school at Chandigarh, and music is something, which would be good for the children to learn especially during the summer vacation. Music is a very important subject, but unfortunately, it is only an optional subject in our schools and very few students opt for it.

I can offer my services from 15th May to 15th July, as there will be summer vacations in our school. Please let meknowthe remuneration you are offering for this job, and also what would be the working hours.

I am attaching my CV with my contact details with this letter. Please feel free to contact me if you need to ask anything.

Yours faithfully,
Kiran Makkar

123. Write a letter to your friend and ask him to translate an important document in the foreign language. Please write:

- Why the document is important?
- Why you want him to do the translation?
- How he can get that document?

Dear Ravi,

Hope this letter finds you in good health and cheer. I am writing this letter to seek your help for translating an important office document, which is in German.

The company for which I am working is collaborating with a German firm. They have sent some documents to be read and signed before finally signing the partnership. My manager has asked me to go through the document thoroughly and see if there is any point needing further discussion.. I have used online translators, but am a bit sceptical about machine translations. You have done your master's in German and are adept at this language. So, I will be very grateful if you take out some time to help me in this translation.

I am sharing the document through Google Drive. Please do it as early as possible, because I need it imperatively by Monday. Thank you for your help in advance.

Hoping to hear from you soon.

With warm regards,
Rahul

---

124. Write a letter to a colleague who is coming from another country to attend a meeting at your office. Write about

-   The pick-up arrangements you have made.
-   The accommodation arrangements.
-   The arrangement for the meeting.

Dear Nick,

I am Rohan Sobti, your colleague from our India Office. I am writing this letter to inform you that I have been assigned the privilege to pick you up andarrange for your stay during your forthcoming visit .Dofeel free to contact me at 9123491234 in case you need to ask something.

I have been informed that you flight is landing at 6 pm next Wednesday. A person with an orange placard with our company's logo and your name on it will be waiting for you at the airport.He will take you to the Hotel Hilton, which I have booked for you. I have booked a single room facing the beach for you. I hope you are satisfied with the arrangements.

The meeting is on Thursday, at 9 am at the company's meeting room. There will be other colleagues from our other overseas offices also. Our company has entered into an important collaboration with another international company. That is why this meeting is very important.

 Hope to see you at the meeting.

Yours truly,
Rohan.

125.   You recently met a manager of a new company that has started in your city. After the meeting, the manager wrote you a letter offering a job at this company. Write him back and say

- How do you feel about the job?
- Why can't you accept it?
- Provide a reference of your friend who might be interested.

Dear Mr. Timmins,

It was a real pleasure to meet you last week in the Rotary Club meeting. Your mail regarding the job offer also came as a pleasant surprise. Thank you so much for considering me suitable for working as Senior Manager in your Company – 'Kundi International'. However, after careful deliberation I have decided to decline this position.

As I mentioned in our discussions last week, I am currently working for Delta International and immensely enjoying my sales position there. Now my company has offered me a promotion, which I feel I cannot let go.

However, I would like to recommend my friend Amit Gaba as a strong potential candidate. He has an extensive sales background and is currently looking for a change. He can be reached onhis mobile number 98xxxxxxxx.

Thank you once again for your confidence in offering me an opportunity to work for your organisation. I am sorry if I have caused you any inconvenience.

Yours sincerely,
Mohit Ghaie

126.   You have a business presentation in which you want to use equipment for which you need one of your colleagues to help you in its operation. Write a letter to your colleague and ask him to help you.

- When and where is your presentation?
- Which equipment you have to use?
- How he can help you ?

Dear Harmeet,

I am writing this letter to request you to help me with my presentation related to what our company 'Delta International' is doing to spreading its foot print across the globe.

I have to make this presentation on 15th June at the Conference Hall of Club Cabana. I need to use the projectors, which our company has purchased recently. This is a very important presentation which I am making before delegates from different parts of the world. You know that interested parties are coming from France, Germany, Italy, Japan and Korea. This presentation has to be really good so as to lure those people to become our business associates. It has to bring out all our achievements so far, and also our future plans.

You are very adept at handling projectors and computers, and making Power-Point presentations, and you have proved your mettle many a time in company meetings. I would really be grateful if you lend a helping hand to me this time. I need your help in connecting the projectors to my laptop. I also need your help in selecting the background theme and also to add some audio clips to some slides so that they become very catchy. I know you are an expert at all this and I would appreciate if you spare some of your precious time to help me in making this presentation a success.

Looking forward to a positive response from you.

Yours truly,
Kiran

---

127. Write a letter to the director of a summer school recommending your friend for the post of a sports instructor for teenagers.

- How do you know him?
- Talk about his past experience.
- Why do you think he is suitable for the job?

Dear Sir,

I am writing to draw your attention to a most extraordinary young man, Indroop Singh, for the post of sports instructor. He has applied for the job in your summer school. I have known Indroop Singh for the past 10 years as we both have been working in a local public school since 2007. I hold the post of a history teacher, whereas Indroop is a physical education teacher. During this time he has consistently excelled in everything he had to do. He has always had a good rapport with the students and other members of the staff.

Indroop has extensive knowledge of teaching various sports to school children. I have found him completely reliable and enthusiastic in performing whatever he is asked to do. He has led our school in various sports competitions and under his able guidance our students have won trophies for the school in cricket, hockey and badminton.

You need a good sports instructor for your summer school. You are also offering a lucrative salary. Indroop would be very suitable for the job because that is what he has been doing and is very good at. I will personally be very sorry when he moves on, but I am confident that wherever he goes he will be a great asset. I recommend him whole-heartedly.

Yours faithfully,
Richard

---

128. Your company holds a staff party every year in the same hotel. This time you are tasked to organize the party and you have to write a letter to the hotel's manager. Include the following in your letter:

- Write about your past experience with the hotel.
- What are your impressions with the hotel's service?
- What you want to ask the manager?

Dear Sir,

I am Robin Taneja working in the HR department of Bell International. I am writing this letter to book your banquet hall 'Fusion' for the annual staff party of our company, which we have been holding in your hotel for the last 10 years. Although we are very happy with your services, I would like to bring to your notice some problems, which we faced last time, so that these can be avoided.

In the past our meetings at your hotel have been a very pleasant experience. However, as our company has grown, the employee strength has also grown. Last time we felt that the number of waiters could have been increased. Some employees were complaining that the snacks did not reach their tables in time.

Sir, I would like to ask you if you have a slightly bigger hall, and if more employees of your hotel could be put to duty on that day, it would be perfect. The date we have planned for the party is July 15. If you have any queries, please feel free to contact me at 9123481234. Please let me know how much deposit I have to make in advance for the booking.

Hoping to hear from you regarding this matter.

Yours faithfully,
Robin Taneja

129. **Write a letter to a hotel manager to inform that you are coming with a group of people to have a business meeting at his hotel.**
- Introduce yourself and the group.
- Tell about the business meeting.
- Inform if accommodation is necessary.

Dear Sir,

My name is Sumit Singh from Model Town, Phagwara. I am writing this letter to book a conference hall in your hotel, Club Cabbana, for a business meeting for which I have invited my business associates from many other states of India.

I am running a manufacturing unit of automobile spare parts. I am planning to open retail outlets in other parts of India for which I have invited interested parties. I would like a hall, which can accommodate about 100 people. I have some power-point presentations to show about my manufacturing and quality-control unit. I have heard that you have a room for such type of meetings. The ambience of your hotel is great and I would like to make this meeting to be an unforgettable event for them.

I would also like to book 10 rooms as some delegates from the South would like to stay the night and do some sight-seeing the next day before returning home. Please inform me in writing if the hall and rooms are available for the 25th. and 26th. of next month, and I will respond with a deposit. If you need any other information, please do not hesitate to call me at 98xxxxxxxx.

Hoping for a prompt reply from you

Yours faithfully,
Sumit Singh

130. A building company is planning to build new houses on some land near where you live and has asked the people to give their comments. Write a letter to the manager of the building company and

- Say how you heard about the plan of the building company.
- Give your opinion of the plan.
- Say what you hope the building company will do.

Dear Sir,

I am Gurmeet Singh Lyal from Model Town Phagwara. I am writing this letter to express my concern about your plan to build new houses in the vacant land near my residence. I came to know about this plan from the local tabloid.

Yesterday, as I was flicking through the pages of the local 'Jagdambay Times', I came across your ad related to this housing colony you are proposing for this site. Honestly speaking, I was shocked. This open space is needed for the children of the surrounding areas to play outdoor games. Every evening you can see young people play cricket and football here. This is the only open space in this locality. As it is, this whole area has become a concrete jungle. More buildings here would add to the congestion of the area.

If at all you have to make houses here, I hope your building company leaves a green belt all around and leave some space for a small park. On behalf of all the residents of my locality I humbly urge you to consider this request and do the needful. I am sure this step would also be welcomed by the people who would buy your new houses. It would be a win-win situation for all.

Hoping for a favourable response from you regarding this appeal.

Yours faithfully,
Gurmeet Singh Lyal

131. Your friend asked you to teach his son English. You need to borrow some English books from your teacher. Write a letter to your teacher requesting these materials. In your letter you should share:
- Details about the child.
- What type of books you need?
- When and where you are going to teach this child?

Dear Mr Sharma,

I am Kiran, your ex-student from the 2007 batch. I am writing this letter to request you to lend me some books for teaching English as a second language. I remember well that your teaching material used to be excellent and your way of teaching was also superb.

Actually, my friend has a son who is 13. She wants to change his school from a Punjabi medium to an English medium one. The school wants to test the child for his English skills. So, my friend has requested me to prepare him for that entrance test. I am sure you will be able to guide me as to what books I should follow to teach him and also lend me the relevant books for about a month.

I would be teaching the child at my place after my office hours, in the late evenings. On weekends, I would be able to give him more time. My friend requested me specially because my language skills in English are pretty good, but I attribute my skills to you.

Please let me know if you can lend me some material so that I can come and collect them from you. If you need any other information, please feel free to call me at 98xxxxxxxx.

Hoping to hear from you soon.

Yours sincerely,
Kiran

132.   You and your friend recently went on a holiday together. You have a problem with your photos taken during the holiday. Write a letter to ask your friend for a particular photo and say

- What is a problem with your photographs?
- Which photo would you like from him/her?
- Why do you need this photo?

Dear Manveer,

I hope this letter finds you in radiant health and the best of spirits. I really enjoyed the holiday we spent together and hope you enjoyed it as much as I did. I am writing to ask whether you could send me a copy of the photo you took for me on the Tiger Hills we visited on the second day of the trip.

The memory card of my camera was full as I had made a lot of videos and as a result some photographs were saved. I remember, you clicked some photographs of me. There was one particular photo in which I am standing on the top of the hill. I would like to upload that photograph on my Google account and share it with all my near and dear ones.

The reason I'm after that particular photo is that that photograph has also captured the spectacular view of the whole area. I did copy all the fantastic pictures from your camera, but by mistake I deleted this one on my laptop. It would be great if you could email a copy to me if you have it.

Waiting eagerly for your mail

With love,
Jimmy

133.   Write a letter to a manager of the taxi company to complain about the problem with the taxi service used by you.

- When and where you used the taxi?
- Describe a problem you have faced.
- What do you expect the manager to do?

Dear Sir,

I am writing this letter to complain about the problem I faced last week because of the taxi I hired from your company 'Express Travels'.

Last Monday, I travelled from Kochi to Trivandrum with my family. Till Kochi we went by air as we had a conference to attend there. We booked a taxi for one whole week. We had paid all expenses in advance and our itinerary was planned upto the minute.

We faced a lot of language problems. The driver didn't know Hindi or English and we did not know any Malayalam. As a result, we could not communicate properly and a lot of time was wasted. We wanted to go boating in Kovalam beach and he took us to some private beach where we had to pay four times more for the boating in the backwaters. On top of that he kept asking us for money for this and that from time to time. When we booked the taxi, we were told that there were no hidden costs and we had paid everything in advance.

I would suggest you to appoint drivers who can communicate well in English so that tourists don't face any problem. Secondly, I expect a refund of the two thousand odd rupees I shelled out to the driver.

Hope for a prompt response from you regarding this matter.

Yours faithfully,
Kiran Makkar

---

134. One of your friends invited you for a meal with his/her family in their home. Write a letter to your friend:

- Thank them and tell what you have enjoyed the most.
- How do you feel about his/her family?
- Suggest him/her to visit you.

Dear Sonia,

Hope this letter finds you in radiant health and the best of spirits. Thank you so much for inviting my family to dinner at your home last Sunday. We were overwhelmed by your hospitality and had a wonderful time at your place.

I must say your mother has excellent culinary skills. She had prepared so many dishes which were all lip smacking. I loved the Chinese style okra and mixed vegetables in hot garlic sauce the most. The apple pie as the dessert was just superb. Your father and younger brother also attended to us very nicely. Your whole family is very loving and caring.

I also take this opportunity to invite you and your family over to my home for lunch next Sunday. My mother also has a gifted hand in cooking and I am sure you will enjoy her dishes too. Do let me know if next Sunday suits you or we can fix it up for some other day.

Waiting eagerly for your reply.

Yours lovingly,
Kiran

---

135. You are studying in a different country. The college has invited you to volunteer to conduct an International day. Write a letter to college coordinator stating

- Do you like the idea of conducting an international day?
- Do you know to prepare any special dish of your country?
- Any activity that you plan to do on the particular day.

Dear Mr. Smith,

I am writing this letter to commend you for the wonderful idea of conducting an International day. I would also take this opportunity to thank you for giving me the opportunity of doing voluntary work for the special day.

Our college has students from across the globe. There are students from Thailand, China, France, India and Japan. This International Day would be a stupendous opportunity for cultural exchanges and getting to know the other students. I would readily take care of the stall for India. I willprepare traditional Punjabi food, which I am sure everyone will love.

I would also like to organise a dance competition on that day in which students would dance the traditional dances of their countries and have lot of fun and frolic. It would be nice to know when you intend to celebrate this day so that I can plan the arrangements accordingly.

Once again thanking you for considering me for the arrangements for this day and please feel free to contact me at my number 98xxxxxxxx for any arrangements.

Yours sincerely,
Kiran

136. Write a letter to the restaurant manager whose restaurant is next to your house. Inform him about the repair work of house that you're going to undertake
- Tell him what could be the possible problems.
- Also suggest possible solutions to him/her.

Dear Sir,

I am Narinder Singh and my house is right next to your restaurant. I am going to get some repair work done in my home, which is likely to cause some inconvenience to you and your customers. I am writing this letter to apologise in advance for the inconvenience it may cause you. However, I assure you that I will complete the work within a fortnight and your cooperation in this matter would be highly appreciated.

The front wall of my house has developed huge cracks and the stairs, which run from the side to the first floor also need to be renovated. So there will be some building material dumped in front of the house, which will block some part of the entrance of your restaurant. I hope you understand the situation and bear with me for a few days.

Your restaurant has another gate on the other side, which you normally do not use. If you open that gate for your customers for a few days, it will solve the problem.

I apologise for the problem which you may have to face and hoping for your kind consideration regarding this matter.

Yours faithfully,
Narinder

137. You went to a museum with your elderly friend last week. However he/she found it difficult to walk around the museum. Write a letter to manager and say
- Whom did you visit the museum with?
- What problems/inconveniences did he/she face?
- Suggest a solution that will enhance the museum visit experience for an elderly person.

Dear Sir,

I am writing this letter to complain about the problems faced by my elderly friend when we visited the Science City Museum last week. I would also like you to look into this matter at the earliest, so that other people do not face such problems again.

Last Tuesday, my friend Darshan, who is in his 70s, had come from Delhi and I decided to show him the Science City Museum. We reached there well in time to buy the tickets. There was a long queue but there were no benches for people to sit and so Darshan had to stand for half hour while I was in the queue. It was very tiring for him.

When we went inside, the laser show and the Earthquake simulator were very good but there was no one to guide us there and people were literally pushing each other to get a seat. Then we had to go to the second floor for the 3D movie but unfortunately the lift was out of order and so we had to take the stairs. It was very difficult for my friend.

I would request you to have special arrangements for senior citizens. There should be a separate queue for the senior citizens. There should be wheel chairs and proper sitting arrangement and the elevators should be in proper working condition all the time. If all these things are looked into then certainly it would be a worthwhile experience for everyone especially the elderly.

Hoping you would look into the matter and improve the things over there so that the people don't face problem over there.

Yours faithfully,
Kiran

---

138. You have bought clothes from a shop in a different city, and one garment turned out to be defective. Write a letter to the manager of the store and explain

- What did you buy there?
- What defect did you find?
- How would you like to solve this issue?

Dear Sir,

I am writing this letter to complain about the defective tracksuit that I bought from your shop two days ago. Last week I visited Chandigarh with some friends. We did a lot of shopping from your store, Kultham Garments. I also bought two tracksuits, one in red and one in blue colour.

On reaching home that night, I opened my shopping bags to show my purchases to my parents. I was shocked to see that the red tracksuit top was in 'L' size, whereas the pajamas wereof XL size, which is my size. The salesman must not have checked properly before packing my tracksuit otherwise this mistake would not have happened.

I have the bill with me. I have to come to Chandigarh next week for a business meeting. Please keep a red tracksuit in my size on hold for me so that I can get a replacement for my defective one, or if you don't have another piece in red colour in my size then I would like a full refund.

Hoping for a prompt reply from you regarding this matter.

Yours faithfully,
Kiran Makkar

139. There is a historical building in your town and the city council wants to pull it down, because there is no money for repairs. You are not happy with this decision. Write a letter to the city council and say
- Why is the building important?
- Suggest a solution to finance the repairs.

Dear Sir/Madam,

I am Kiran Makkar living in Phagwara, Punjab, India. I am writing this letter to express my resentment on the decision of knocking down the Municipal Committee building. You know that this building was once the home of the Maharaja of Kapurthala and now is serving as an office of the Municipal Committee, Phagwara.

This building is very important because it gives a unique identity to Phagwara. It is on the National Highway 1 and is a landmark for many other places. It is a beautiful building, which reminds us of the grandeur in which our early rulers lived.

It is understandable that a lot of money is needed for its repairs, but if this is brought to the notice of the local people then there would be many who would come forward to contribute for this cause. Fortunately, Phagwara is a rich belt of Punjab because there are many NRIs who would be all too happy to help. Some charity shows could also be organised and funds could be collected.

I hope you will re-think your decision. Looking forward to a favourable response from your side.

Yours faithfully,
Kiran Makkar

140. Your friend has had a baby recently and you bought a present for baby.

- Describe what you bought.
- Why you chose that present?
- Suggest some arrangements to visit your friend to bring the present.

Dear Kalyani,

Last week I heard the news of your beautiful baby girl. Congratulations to you and Anshul and baby Gia. I am so happy for the three of you.

I have bought a crib for your baby. I went to the 'Toys R Us' store to look for some gift for Gita and my eyes fell on this crib. It is made by Graco company and can be converted into a toddler bed later on. I know it will be very useful for a long time to come. I bought itimmediately and now am waiting for an opportunity to visit you and hand it over.

I was wondering if next weekend would be convenient for me to visit you. I can come on Saturday or Sunday. Please let me know what time will be more convenient. Please contact me at 98xxxxxxxx to finalize the time.

Hoping to see you soon.

Yours lovingly,
Kiran

141. Write a letter to apply for a position to look after a house in Scotland where the owners are going away.

- Provide personal details
- What qualities you have for this position
- And ask for information.

Dear Sir,

I am writing this letter to apply for the post of housekeeper for your house in Scotland as advertised by you in the Daily Tribune.

My name is Andrew Smith and I have recently completed my 'Diploma in Hotel Management' from Yorkshire University. After completing the course, I found that there is stiff competition in this field. So, I decided to go for the Masters course in Hotel Management. The intake for that course is after 6 months. The job you have advertised is a perfect fit, time-wise, and can be of mutual advantage to both of us.

A copy of my resume is attached. I will be happy to provide references from my college professors and other members of the community. I am confident of my abilities and assure you of a high standard of service.

Please let me know the exact nature of my duties and if there are any pets or domestic animals at home.

Looking forward to hearing from you soon.

Yours faithfully,
Andrew Smith

---

142. You are taking a business course at a college. As a part of the course every student has to choose a company to study and visit. Write a letter to the manager of the company

-    Tell what course you are doing.
-    Why you are interested in your company?
-    Suggest arrangements for the visit.

Dear Sir,

My name is Kiran. I am a final year student of 'Master of Business Administration' at State University of New York at Buffalo. I am writing this letter to request you to allow me to visit and study your company 'Bell Enterprises' as a part of my course.

I am interested in your company because I have heard a lot about your company. Many of my seniors have done their training in your company and they have told me how the owners of your company started from scratch a few years ago and how they have grown their small firm into a mighty empire with 10,000 workers in just five years. Your auto parts are excellent quality wise but just having good quality products is not enough for any company to succeed. It has been possible only because of your sound business acumen and your employer-employee relationship.

I would like to start my study project in your company during the summer break, which is of three months. I would like to spend a few days in each department and study the work pattern there as part of my assignment. I assure you I would be an asset to your company during my stay. Please let me know if I can start my project in May this year and if you provide paid accommodation for trainees like me.

Hoping for a positive response from your side.

Yours faithfully,
Kiran

143. Your local newspaper published an advertisement asking people to help with protecting the environment. Write a letter to offer your help to the project manager and say

- Why are you interested?
- What can you help with?
- When can you start?

Dear Sir,

Your advertisement dated 28th July about improving the environment was a real eye-opener. Environmental degradation is a serious issue and I would commend your paper to raise awareness about it. At the same time I would like to contribute my share in your endeavor.

I am really interested in it because global warming is a burning issue and we humans are the cause of it. I realise that if all of us put a little contribution in saving the environment then we can make a huge change for the better.

I can help by going house to house and telling the people to recycle things; by telling them to say 'no' to plastics; by planting trees and by making the people aware about the benefits of public transport.

I can start right away and I am available every day from 5 pm to 7 pm. I have good communication skills and I will be very grateful if you give me a chance to join hands with you in saving our planet Earth. My name is Kiran Makkar and my contact number is 98xxxxxxxx.

Hoping to hear from you soon.

Yours sincerely,
Kiran Makkar

144. Your neighbour has animals and they cause noise. Write a letter

-   Describe the situation.
-   Suggestion to solve the problem.
-   Tell him what will you do if he will not solve the problem.

Dear Sir,

I am Madan, your next-door neighbour. I am writing this letter to complain about the problems my family is facing because of your pets.

I recently moved into your neighbourhood with my family. There are five members in my family. My parents, my wife and my son aged 17. My son has to appear for his medical entrance examination this year. It is his usual habit to study during the night. Your two Pomeranians and the German shepherd keep barking all night long. He can neither study nor sleep because of them. During the day time also, these pets are creating a lot of nuisance. Only yesterday, one of them ran into our garden and my mother had to run inside to save herself.

It will be very kind of you if you take some steps to handle this problem. One solution would be to keep them separate in the night. The three of them together create a lot of noise. Secondly, you should keep them leashed in the daytime. Finally, I will urge you to keep their immunisation up-to-date so that in case they bite someone, that person should not have to go for the anti-rabies vaccine.

Hoping for a prompt consideration of this urgent request.

Yours truly,
Madan.

145. You have written an article for a magazine about the job that you do. Write a letter to your manager and ask for his/her comments regarding the article, which will be published in a famous magazine next month. In this letter, you should say

-   Explain why you have written this article.
-   Give a short description of what you have written.
-   Specify what particular things you want him/her to comment on.

Dear Mr Makkar,

I am writing this letter to request you to critique my article, which I have written for the 'Jobs Today' magazine. This monthly magazine it describes various job opportunities for the young people of today. This month their focus is on various jobs related to industry. I have written this article to throw light upon the ways in which a fresh graduate can join jobs related to the manufacturing industry.

In this article I have written about the qualifications needed for the various levels of work done in the industries. For example, what different opportunities are there for diploma holders, degree holders in technology and business management, and also for those who want to step into the working world right after senior secondary education. I have also written about our company's policies on hiring and training the fresh employees and about the prospects of promotion.

I will be very grateful if you spare some of your precious time to go through my article and see if I have missed out something important or if there is any other mistake in my article. 'Jobs Today' is a very popular magazine and this article will also act as an advertisement for our company. Therefore, it should be flawless and at the same time interesting to read.

Hoping to hear from you soon regarding this matter.

Yours sincerely,
Rajesh

---

146. You have recently used the services of a moving company. At the new place you found out that some of your items were badly damaged. Write a letter to the company manager including the following:

- Give details of your move.
- List items that were damaged.
- Say what you expect the manager to do.

Dear Mr. Singh,

I hired you company 'Packers and Movers' for shifting my belongings from Amritsar to Chandigarh two weeks ago. I am writing this letter to complain, as my experience with you has been rather bad because my expensive dining table and dressing table are totally ruined.

I hired you after reading an advertisement in the local paper in which you have bragged about your excellent service. My dining table had a toughened glass topping which now has an ugly crack on the corner. The dressing table also has scratches all over it. I believe it is because of inefficient packing done by your men.

The solution that I can suggest is that you get a new glass top for my dining table and the dressing table re-polished. Alternatively you can reimburse me for the amount that I have to spend on both these things. I cannot use these items in their present condition. I hope you realise the value of a satisfied customer.

Hoping to hear from you soon! My contact number is 98xxxxxxxx.

Yours sincerely,
Indroop Singh

---

147. Write a letter to your friend thanking him/her for guiding you for an interview. In your letter

- Explain what happened at the interview.
- Say how his guidance helped in the interview.

Dear Suman,

I hope this letter finds you in radiant health and the best of spirits. I write to thank you from the core of my heart for your guidance and tips for the interview of staff nurse at Ivy Hospital, Phagwara. Your suggestions and advice helped me crack the interview and I got the job.

I reached half an hour before the interview time and registered myself at the reception. After about an hour they called me in for the interview. Most of the questions they asked were what you had asked me to prepare. It was easy for me to answer all the questions as I had already prepared them.

You told me to go through the background of the hospital and what all services they provide. Had you not guided me, I would have just prepared myself along technical things. This hospital is the first super-specialty hospital in North India and they wanted to know how aware I was of the stature of the hospital and whether I was dedicated enough to give my best. I was able to satisfy them and they immediately appointed me.

Next Sunday, I have my off day. Why don't you come over and we will celebrate. Once again thanking you for your guidance.

Yours lovingly,
Kiran

148. Write a letter to your professor about your recent internship and future plans after graduation. In your letter
- Thank him.
- Tell about your duties at internship.
- Share your plans for after graduation.

Dear Sir,

My name is Mohit and I am from India. It was wonderful being your student in the 'Business Management Course', this year at Melbourne. Thank you so much for your guidance because of which I passed out with flying colours.

I have recently done my Internship at Sears International at Melbourne. My duties there were very diverse. All interns were given an orientation on the first day and after that we were sent in small batches to various departments for few days each. It was a very nice experience. It was as if we were converting our theoretical knowledge into practical. My theoretical concepts were very clear because of your guidance and so I learnt a lot there.

After seeing the work there I feel that I should pursue my Masters in the same course. The salary you receive after a Masters course is much higher than that after an Undergraduate course. I have applied to the University of Melbourne and if I am fortunate enough to get admission, I shall again have the opportunity of learning from you as I have heard that you are taking the graduate classes too.

Thanking you once again for your valuable advice and guidance.

Yours faithfully,
Mohit

149. You saw an advertisement recently and bought the advertised product. Upon receiving the product you discovered that the information in the advertisement was incorrect. Write a letter to the person responsible for the advertisement and say:

-   What is the product?
-   What information in the advertisement is incorrect?
-   What do you expect the person to do about it?

Dear Sir,

I am writing this letter to complain about the incorrect information provided in your advertisement because of which I bought a cell phone, which does not have all the features that your advertisement claims it has.

Last week, I saw your store's advertisement in the local newspaper about a cell phone which has a long battery life and a 20 megapixel camera. I went to your electronics store and bought the cell phone. I especially asked your salesman whether the cell phone was the same one, which was advertised in the paper and he replied in the affirmative. I realised very soon that the battery backup was very less and every few hours I had to recharge my cell phone. The camera was also 12 megapixel and not 20 as you had claimed in the advertisement.

I would like you to replace my cell phone with a different model, which has all the claimed features or give me a total refund. I would also suggest you not to put up such misleading ads just to lure customers.

Hoping for a prompt action from you regarding this matter! If you need to contact me, please feel free to call me at 98xxxxxxxx.

Yours faithfully,
Kiran

150. One of your friends has asked you to be a partner in his new start-up business. Write a letter to him and say
- What is your opinion on his new business idea?
- What have you decided on this matter?
- What are the reasons for your decision?

Dear Rohan,

Hope this letter finds you in radiant health and the best of spirits. Thanks for considering me as a partner for your new business venture. I am sure your idea of opening a restaurant on Banga Road is great because there are no other restaurants in that area.

Unfortunately, I will not be able to join you, as presently my financial situation is not good and I will not be able to contribute my share of the initial investment costs.

My mother has not been well lately and a lot of money has gone into her treatment. Also, I don't really want to leave my current job, and I think it will be impossible for me to commit to the restaurant project while I'm still working full time.

Best of luck with your new business and I am sure you will make a success of it without me.

Yours lovingly,
Kiran

---

151. A reporter complained about a new TV program that you like. Write a letter to the newspaper editor.
- Describe your point of view.
- Say what you like about the show and why.
- Ask the newspaper to take some action.

Dear Mr. Smith,

I am writing this letter to you regarding your article in the 'Times India' against the TV serial Satyamev Jayate, in which you unfairly criticized Aamir Khan as he reported a few things against malpractices done by some doctors. I believe that this programme is only meant to make the general public aware about all the things going on around them and is in no way aimed against any particular group of people.

Personally I feel that the show's presenters are honest and they have put in a lot of effort to collect authentic data on the basis of which they have made the show. All episodes of this serial have won the highest TRPs and this is only because people have liked it. This is unlike the modern TV shows which are bland and have nothing to pique our interest.

I will be very grateful if you could, in future editions of your newspaper, 'Times India' publish only positive articles about this programme since it has thrown light on various social evils and has changed the thinking of many for the better.

Hoping for a positive response from you regarding this matter.

Yours faithfully,
Kiran Makkar

---

152. Write a letter to the Airport Manager, about a flight that you missed for your business trip because of a problem that occurred at the airport. Please explain in your letter:

- What was the problem?
- What happened as a result of the missed flight?
- What would you like him/her to do about it?

Dear Sir,

I am writing this letter to inform you about a business trip that I could not go on because of an accident that occurred at the airport last Tuesday.

On Tuesday July 2, I had to board the flight BA143 at 11pm. I reached the airport well in time and completed all formalities in time. In the waiting lounge I went to use the rest rooms and there was some water spilled over there. I slipped and fell and sprained my ankle. Some helpful persons who were there helped me get up gave me some first aid. But, my foot started swelling and so I decided to cancel my trip.

I had a business meeting in Ilford London. It was a very important meeting. However, when I called and told them about my predicament, they were kind enough to postpone the meeting for one week.

Sir, will you be kind enough to accommodate me on the next Tuesday BA143 flight at 11 pm and also give me some concession on the ticket. I am also a member of your frequent flyer programme. I will be very grateful to you for this kind gesture.

Hoping to hear from you soon.

Yours faithfully,
Sanjeev Arora

153. You will have to undergo a minor surgical procedure and you won't be able to do your job in full. Write to your manager

- Explain about the operation.
- Say what part of the job you won't be able to do.
- Suggest a solution to this situation.

Dear Sir,

I am writing this letter to inform you that I have had to undergo a minor surgical procedure because of which I will be unable to carry out all my duties.

I had an ingrown toe nail on the big toe of my right foot because of which I was in extreme pain and so on the advice of my doctor I got my nail excised. It will take about a week to heal. My doctor has advised me to keep my foot raised and not do much walking for about a week. As you know, my duites require me to visit all departments everyday and address the problems of the junior employees. However, I will not be able to carry out my regular rounds for a week.

It will be very kind of you if you allot me some other duties for a week such as office work which does not require any walking.

Hoping for a kind consideration from you regarding this request.

Yours faithfully,
Indroop

154. You have just returned from a working trip overseas. Write your colleagues a letter thanking them for your experience. Please say:

- How do you feel about being home?
- Thank them for their time.
- Invite them to come and visit you.

Dear Richard and Elaine,

I hope this letter finds you in radiant health and the best of spirits. I am writing this letter to formally thank you both for the guidance and cooperation extended by you during my working holiday in your company.

It's good to be back home, but I still miss you all. Before coming to UK for my Holiday Work Maker visa, I was very nervous, but because of you, I enjoyed a lot. I can never forget how you spared your valuable time in guiding me step by step throughout my time there. It was a very interesting 6 months for me and I learned a lot, which I am sure I will apply in my job here.

I also take this opportunity to invite you to visit my country, India. It will be my pleasure to show you around and be your host for the period you stay here. There is so much to see in India. I am sure you will enjoy your stay here.

I hope to hear from you soon.

Yours truly,
Kiran

---

155. You are working in a very busy office. A particular piece of office equipment is not working properly. Write a letter to the manager and say

- What is wrong with the equipment?
- How does this affect your work?
- What do you suggest be done?

Dear Sir,

I am one of the office supervisors at Hargobind Nagar branch of Karur Vysya Bank. I am writing to inform you that our Canon printer-cum-copier is not working properly.

From the last month or so, I have been noticing that the prints are not upto the mark, and so I got a new toner cartridge. Even after that the problem was not resolved. Last week, I called the Canon after-sales service department. Their mechanic came and checked and said that the printer will have to be sent to their office as he was unable to diagnose the problem.

Sir, our office work has literally come to a standstill because of this problem. We have to send our clients outside to get photocopies done and it gives a very poor impression of our office. I have to copy most of the documents in my pen drive and then get them printed from elsewhere.

I seriously think this machine needs to be replaced. Even if this printer gets repaired, a new one is still needed as our office has become very busy lately. This matter needs your urgent attention.

Hoping for a prompt action from you regarding this matter.

Yours faithfully,
Kiran

156. As part of your study you have worked for a short period of time in a company. Write a letter to the manager of this company.

- Thank him/her for the opportunity.
- Explain how the experience gained there has helped you.
- Share your plans for the future.

Dear Mr. Phillips,

I am writing to express my thanks to you and your staff for the opportunity of working with you during the summer as part of my work experience for my undergraduate course. It was an amazing time and I learned a great deal while working there.

Interestingly, I am now involved in a project at my university and am applying some of the techniques and knowledge I gained while I was with you. It has made a big difference to my understanding of this area and I hope to continue to research it in more depth.

Hopefully, I will be graduating at the end of this academic year and would like to request you to consider me for any entry-level vacancy your company may have the following year. I thoroughly enjoyed my time with your company and will be interested in working on a full time basis.

Once again, thank you for the opportunity, it was extremely useful and I look forward to hearing from you soon.

Yours sincerely,
Kiran

157. You found a small object from the soil and you think that it has some historical value. Write to the museum to give some information about it

- Describe the object.
- Explain how you got it.
- Ask information about its value.

Dear Sir,

I recently found an interesting object while I was walking in the area near the famous historical Sukhchain Gurdwara. It appears to be some kind of utensil or maybe a tool, but it looks very old. We are all well aware of the historical significance of that particular area and was wondering if you, or someone else at the museum, might be able to help me in determining if the object is indeed from the ancient ruins of the village which was founded in this area many years ago.

The object is about 40cm in length, narrow, but with one end bigger than the other, it looks like it might have been some kind of spoon or tool for mixing, maybe. Oh, and it appears to be made of some hard kind of material, it isn't wood or metal.

Would it be possible for me to bring the object to the museum and let you examine it in further detail?

Thank you for your time, I look forward to your reply.

Yours faithfully,
Kiran Makkar

158. Write a letter to the cinema manager to inform him/her that you have lost your bag in the cinema. In your letter you should:
- Tell exactly what happened and when
- Explain where you think you left the bag
- Ask the manager to help find your bag

Dear Sir,

Last night my friend and I attended the late show of 'Queen', the Kangana Ranaut movie, in auditorium number 4 at the Sarab Multiplex. Unfortunately, I left my bag behind when I left.

I placed it on the floor, under the seat, during the movie and forgot to pick it up before leaving.

I wonder if you could let me know if any of your staff or anyone else has handed it in. I tried ringing the reception of the cinema but they couldn't help me, they didn't know anything about it and they suggested I should contact you, so I am writing to see if you could help locate my bag so that I may collect it from you.

This bag is black, made of leather and has two pockets or pouches on the outside. The maker is American Tourister and it looks like a small backpack.

Thank you for your cooperation in this matter, and I look forward to your reply.

Yours faithfully,
Kiran

159. Write a letter to friend to ask her to take care of your children while you are away for a business trip. Tell her:
- What food do they love to eat?
- What activities they like to do?
- What arrangements you have made to pick them?

Dear Elaine,

Hope this letter finds you in radiant health and in the best of spirits. I have heard that you have taken some time off-work nowadays. I hope you are making the most of your leisure time.

I am busy as usual. And now I have to go on a four day business trip next Monday. Do you think you could take care of my kids while I am away? I am not exactly comfortable about leaving them in a day care centre. That's why I am asking your help. If you think you could babysit, I will drop them at your place on Monday morning.

They are very easy-going and get on well with everybody –they are particularly fond of you. As for their food habits, well, they are not really into veggies, but they do eat fruits and cereals. So you should have no trouble keeping them full throughout the day. You also don't have to worry about keeping them busy. They will pass their time watching TV or playing video games. In the evenings, you could perhaps take them for a walk.

I will be back in town on Thursday evening and pick them up from your place on my way home from the airport. I hope you don't mind doing this for me.

Hope to hear from you soon.

Yours lovingly,
Kiran

160. Your friend has offered to sell you something. Write a letter to this friend. In your letter you have to include:
- What the item is?
- Questions requesting details of the item being sold.
- What price you think is fair?

Dear Amarjeet,

I hope this letter finds you in radiant health and in good spirits. I am writing regarding the Dell laptop you offered to sell to me. I am keen on buying this because I have always wanted to own a laptop. However, I will really appreciate it if you can clarify a few details regarding this transaction.

The last time that we spoke you told me that the laptop is in good shape and works well. I just want to know if it is I-5 or I-7. I would also like to know the RAM and the storage configuration. Another thing I am keen to know is whether it has Windows 7 or 8. Would you mind writing back to me with these details?

As for the price, well, I am willing to offer you $500 if the laptop is still covered by a warranty. If you accept this price, I will be happy to finalize our transaction as soon as possible.

Waiting to hear from you.

Yours lovingly,
Sahib

---

161. Write a letter to your college's administration department complaining about the college's facilities. In your letter include:

- What the problem is?
- How this problem has affected you?
- What the college should do to fix this problem?

Dear Sir,

I am a third year computer science student and I am writing to complain about the inadequate facilities available at our laboratory. There are 60 students in our batch, but only 20 computers are available in the lab. As a result of this each computer is shared by three students, which severely limits our access to the machine.

As you probably know, computer science is more about gaining practice than about learning theory. Unfortunately, this shortage of computers seriously limits our chances of getting good practical knowledge. Library facilities, too, are inadequate. Computer science text books become obsolete in a matter of months because the technology is developing at such a fast pace. Although the library has a fair number of computer books, they are not up-to-date. Needless to say, we are forced to buy these costly text books on our own.

On behalf of my batch mates, I am requesting you to buy more computers and latest edition textbooks for the lab and the library.

Look forward for a prompt action from you regarding this matter.

Yours faithfully,
Kiran

162. There is a swimming pool proposed to be built in your town. Write to the city council and say

- Why is this swimming pool important to you?
- Suggest where it should be built.
- Why is it a good idea to have a swimming pool in the town and not outside of town?

Dear Sir,

On behalf of the residents of Phagwara I am writing this letter to express my appreciation of the plan of opening a swimming pool in our town. Of the two sites you have proposed, the one in the centre of the town will be more suitable.

A swimming pool is just what the residents of the town need. We all know children today are leading sedentary lives and it is difficult to motivate them to play outdoor games when they have so many distractions at home. Swimming, however, is different. Children like swimming and it will give them the necessary exercise also.

The location in the centre of the town would be more suitable because children could go there on their own. If the swimming pool is outside the town then parents would have to take their children there. Parents are too busy these days and so most of the times they would not be able to accompany their children. Not only for the children, but also for the adults this site would be more approachable.

We appreciate your efforts in this area.

Yours faithfully,
Kiran Makkar

163. You organized the 90th birthday party for a relative in a hotel. Many elderly guests attended this party which was a great success. Write a letter to thank the hotel manager. In your letter:

- Give the details of the party.
- The reason why the party was so successful.
- Mention a staff who helped you a lot.

Dear Sir,

I celebrated my aunt's 90th birthday at your hotel on 6th April. It was a great success and it was all because of your excellent services. I am writing this letter to thank you for everything.

The party was on 6th April at 7.30pm. There were about 100 guests. I had invited all my relatives and family friends. There were many elderly people in the party. Three of my elderly guests were on wheelchairs. I had meant this party as a surprise for my aunt. We had some games like musical chairs which were enjoyed by all.

All your staff was very co-operative but I must specially thank Mr Rohit Bali for the special care and attention he gave to all my guests. Every guest was looked after. There was soft music in the background and a lot of snacks. The preparations were very delicious. The snacks reached each and every table and even the cake cutting ceremony was very nicely arranged.

Thank you once again for your co-operation due to which my party was a memorable one.

Yours faithfully,
Kiran Makkar

---

164. You want to volunteer to help the old people of your community. An organization in your area works for the benefit of old people. Write a letter to the in-charge of that organization explaining

- Why do you want to help?
- How can you help them?
- When will you be available?

Dear Sir,

My name is Amit Gaba and I am working with Bayer Pharmaceuticals. I have heard that your organisation works for the elderly people of the community. I am writing this letter to enquire whether it will be possible to offer my voluntary services for any kind of work in the evenings and on weekends.

I live alone and after my work hours, I have a lot of free time, which I would like to utilise productively. I have done a certificate course in Gerontology and would like to help the aged in the Old Age Home of this locality. The main problem of the elderly is social isolation and by spending time with them, I could help bring some cheer into their lives.. As it is, we belong to a greying society and the population of the elderly is growing by leaps and bounds. So, I feel there would be a lot for voluntary workers to do in this field. It would also be a win-win situation for me because I would be able to pass my time usefully.

Sir, I would be highly grateful if you give me the opportunity to work in this field in the evening hours and on weekends. I am busy Monday to Friday 9 am to 5 pm. (It is better to give the hours when one can do the Voluntary work rather than give the hours when one is not available).

Please feel free to call me for any further information. My contact number is 98xxxxxxxx.

Yours faithfully,
Amit Gaba

---

165. An international company is offering a temporary job (without pay) for work experience. Write a letter to apply for that job. You need to explain

-   Where did you find this information?
-   Why you want to apply this job?
-   What qualification you have?
-   What position you want to apply?

Dear Sir,

I have learnt from an ad in the Employment News Weekly that you need Sales Managers to work on a voluntary basis during evening hours. I wish to apply for this opportunity.

I have graduated from at the University of Texas. My major was International Marketing. It is very important for me to work so that I get some practical experience. Attached is a copy of my resume. I would be happy to provide references from members of the community.

My chances of finding permanent employment will improve substantially if I get this opportunity to work for your organization. I assure you, sir, I will provide excellent service to both the organization and its customers.

I am available to come for an interview at your convenience and look forward to hearing from you soon.

Yours faithfully,
Kiran

166. Your friend is asking for your advice. She is going to a university and can't decide whether to study music or business management. Write a letter

- How you felt when you got the letter?
- What the good points are for both sides and
- What your advice is?

Dear Sarah,

It was such a pleasant surprise to hear from you. I feel honoured that you have asked for my advice regarding the choice of subject.

Music and business management are very different subjects. Both have their own scope. Today, we live in a global village and doing any business in this era of globalisation will definitely need some degree in hand. If you do the course in business management, you will be able to start your own business or help a lot in your parents' existing business. However, I feel that there is a lot of saturation in the field of business management.

Considering your exceptional abilities in singing and playing instruments like the guitar, I would suggest you go for music. Music has a lot of scope today and people in this field are earning telephone-figure salaries. Nowadays there are many reality shows related to music and people are willing to pay anything to get their children the best coaching. You have innate abilities in the field of music and a degree will polish your skills further. Music holds a bright future for you.

Hope my advice satisfies you. Do convey my regards to your parents.

Yours lovingly,
Kiran

167. You are a member of a sports club located in an old building. The manager asked you to suggest some improvements to the building. Write a letter to your manager and say

- Why the club is important to you?
- What improvements should be made in the building and
- How these changes would benefits the members?

Dear Sir,

I am a life member of your Leo Sports Club. I am writing this letter in response to the notice you have sent to all the members to suggest improvements in the building.

This club is very important for me. I have been a member for the past ten years. I regularly come there with my family to play snooker and use the swimming pool. However, I do agree that the building is in a very bad state and needs extensive renovation.

The whole building needs a fresh coat of paint. The changing rooms too need a few changes. The bolts on the doors and windows are all broken as a result of which anyone can barge into the room while we are changing. To add to it, the curtains are so dirty that they smell. The urinals attached to the changing rooms also stink. The dust bins are also very dirty. The swimming pool also needs a new filtration system.

All these changes will benefit all the members. Many members are not renewing their membership because of the problems they face. If these renovations are done then this sports club could get back its original glory.

Hoping for a careful consideration of these suggestions.

Yours faithfully,
Kuldeep Singh

---

168. Write a letter to local council about the closure of playground and explain

- Why so few children are using the playground?
- How to increase the number of children using the playground?
- Why this is important?

Dear Sir,

I am writing this letter to apprise you with an important issue concerning the pitiable condition of the local playground located in Model town. It is being used by few children nowadays, whereas earlier it used to be the source of much fun and laughter, a safe meeting place for many children.

Nowadays the playground is very run-down and in bad condition. The seats on the swings are broken and the see-saw is also wobbly. There are some cracks on the slides, which could be very dangerous for children. There are also no shady trees for children to gather below and play. That is why parents are worried about children going to that playground and so few children are seen there nowadays.

If we are to encourage our children for outdoor activities then it is important to immediately improve the condition of the playground. As it is children today are suffering from childhood obesity and therefore beautiful and well-maintained playgrounds are a must to encourage children to engage in outdoor activities. It is my humble request to have new swings, see-saws and slides because the earlier ones are beyond repair. Shady trees need to be planted which in due course of time will be a big asset.

Hoping for a prompt action from you regarding this matter.

Yours faithfully,
Kiran Makkar

---

169. You received a letter from your friend informing you that his elderly parents are coming to visit in your area and he is asking for your advice on
- Which places they should visit?
- Where should they live?
- Invite them to do something with you.

Dear Simar,

It was a really pleasant surprise to receive your letter after such a long time. I am happy to know that your elderly parents are coming to visit Punjab in India. It is very nice to know that in your country even the retired people are so fond of tourism.

There is a lot to see in India. I would suggest they visit the Golden Temple in Amritsar, the Wagah border, the Durgiana Temple, Haveli, the Pushpa Gujral Science City at Kapurthala and many more places in this area. If you send me their itinerary, I could plan their time here nicely.

As far as stay is concerned, there are many good government hotels which are very reasonably priced and good but they have to be booked well in advance. However, it would be my great pleasure if they stay with me in my house. I would take great care of them and also show them around. My parents join me in inviting them to stay with us. We shall also enjoy holidaying with them.

Hoping to see your parents soon.

Yours lovingly,
Mohit

170. A telephone company made a mistake about sending your bill to a wrong address. Write a letter to the account manager to complain and explain

- what problems this caused?
- what you would like them to do?

Dear Sir,

I am writing this letter to complain about the problems I had to face because your company sent my bill to the wrong address.

Every month, I receive my telephone bill in the first week, but last month I did not receive my bill. After about 10 days, a person from the neighbouring block gave me the bill saying that it had been wrongly delivered at his address. My address is 341, Eastwood Avenue and his address is 341, Westwood Avenue. The next day, I went to pay the bill and I was charged a late fee of Rs.500/-. I argued a lot but they did not listen and I had to pay the fine.

Sir, I request you to refund the amount that I had to pay as fine or adjust it in the next bill because it was not my fault that I was late. If you need any more information from me regarding this matter, please feel free to contact me at 98xxxxxxxx.

Hoping for a positive response from you regarding this matter!

Yours faithfully,
Kiran Makkar

171. Your English teacher who taught you several years ago has invited you to have a meal at his house but you cannot go.

- Explain the reason that you cannot go.
- Suggest next arrangement.
- Tell him about yourself and your improvement in English learning.

Dear Sir,

Thank you so much for inviting me to dinner at your home this Thursday. Unfortunately, I will not be able to make it because I am leaving for Australia on Thursday morning.

You have not just been my English teacher but also my friend, philosopher and guide throughout my school days. It was you who motivated me to go abroad for my higher studies and it was because of your guidance that I cleared my IELTS with such good bands that I got into one of the best colleges of Australia. It is also very kind of you to invite me for dinner and it is my loss that I cannot come. Actually, my ticket has been already booked. My flight is leaving on Thursday night and I have to leave from here for Delhi that morning.

I will come home in my winter vacations. I will surely meet you then and share my experiences of the foreign country with you.

Sir, I take this opportunity to thank you once again for all that you have done for me and I shall keep in touch with you after going there through e-mail. My e-mail ID is kiran@yahoo.com.

Yours faithfully,
Kiran Makkar

---

172. You have just finished a trip booked through a travel agency, but you are not satisfied with it Write a letter to the travel agent. In your letter, you should say:

- Why you felt so unhappy?
- What happened?
- Make some recommendations about what the travel agent should do about it.

Dear Sir,

I am writing to complain about the 'Star Cruise' I recently went on with your company. I travelled on Victoria 203 from the 3rd. to the 17th.of April and I was shocked by the standard of food and accommodation offered on the cruise.

To begin with, I was disgusted by the size and condition of the cabin. It was very small and dirty unlike the 'large deluxe cabin' that your advertisement promises.

What is more, there was no private bathroom in the cabin. I was appalled to find that I had to share a bathroom with several other passengers, in spite of the fact that I specifically requested a private bathroom when I booked the trip.

To make matters worse, the food on board was very unsatisfactory. Although your advertisement promises a five star restaurant with gourmet food, the food was in fact of a very poor standard.

I feel I am entitled to a full refund for the cost of the cruise and a written apology for the misinformation contained in your advertisement. I hope to hear from you regarding this matter as soon as possible.

Yours faithfully,
Kiran Makkar

173. You are about to start social meetings in a particular area where people from different nationalities can take part. Write a letter to the editor of a local newspaper requesting him to publish information about this.

- What activities you have planned?
- When the first meeting takes place and where?

Dear Sir,

I am Mohit Sharma, the president of the local Rotaract Club. Our club is organising seminars in which delegates from different nationalities will be taking part. I am writing this letter to request you to give adequate space about our activities in the columns of your esteemed daily so that we get the maximum participation and support of local people.

We shall be touching upon various social issues in our meetings. Besides the cultural exchange, which shall automatically be there, we shall be discussing issues like environmental pollution, drug trafficking, child abuse, female feticide and so on. We have also planned a career counseling camp, which shall run for a whole week.

The first meeting is on 10th June 2011. The venue is Club Cabana and the theme is 'Global Culture versus Traditional Culture'. We would look forward to your presence in this meeting.

All the club members are working whole-heartedly for these meetings. It is a matter of great pride for a small town like ours to organise such a world-class events. Through the power of your pen, you can help us in spreading a word about our activities.

Thanking you in anticipation.

Yours faithfully,
Mohit Sharma.

Writing Task 2

Essays

1. Nowadays, many people have to work longer hours, and they feel more stressed out than before. What are the reasons? What can employers do to make their life easier?

Stress is a big problem in today's workplace. While some stress is a normal part of the workplace, excessive stress can interfere with employee productivity and adversely impact their physical and emotional health. This essay shall analyse some causes of stress at the workplace, and also suggest some steps that employers can take to reduce it.

There are a plethora of causes of stress in the workplace. To begin with, excessively high workloads, with unrealistic deadlines, makes people feel pressurized. Similarly, insufficient workloads, makes people feel that their skills are being underused and this too may cause stress. Then there may be a lack of interpersonal support or poor working relationships leading to a sense of isolation. Moreover, there may be times when people are asked to do a job for which they have insufficient experience or training.

Furthermore, stress can be caused by lack of job security, lack of career opportunities, or level of pay. It may also be caused by bullying, or harassment by management, which can leave employees feeling undervalued and affect their self-esteem. Last but not the least a poor physical working environment such as excessive heat, cold or noise, inadequate lighting, uncomfortable seating and malfunctioning equipment may also lead to stress.

Employers can take a lot of steps to cope with workplace-stress. To begin with, they should diagnose what is causing stress. If overwork is causing stress in the business, then they should try to reduce people's workload. They should ensure that their employees' targets are challenging, but realistic, and make sure that employees take their full holiday entitlement. They should check that individuals are well matched to the jobs they've got. From time to time they should review people's performance so that they know how they're doing. Then they would be able to get feedback from their staff about potential problems and identify any training they may need.

Employers should also consider whether the employee should work fewer hours, or otherwise vary their work. If any of the employees are sick, they should keep in touch. If their employee has experienced personal problems, such as a relationship break-up or an illness in the family, employers should take a sympathetic approach and if necessary, enable and encourage the employee to seek further help through their doctor or a counseling service.

To sum up, stress at the workplace is an issue of great concern. Unless the employers take some steps to reduce the problem, it can reduce the efficiency of workers, which ultimately is detrimental for the company.

Plan followed

Intro:

Para 1: Reasons - increased workload and lack of support

Para 2: More reasons, such as job security, poor working conditions

Para 3 & 4: Solutions – Steps employers could take

Conclusion:

2. Some companies and organizations require their employees to wear uniform. What are the advantages and disadvantages of wearing uniform?

Setting a dress code in the workplace is becoming increasingly common. In the following paragraphs, I intend to delve into the advantages and disadvantages of wearing uniforms at work.

One of the major benefits of a dress code within the office is that it establishes an atmosphere of discipline and uniformity. It ensures that inappropriate or dirty clothing is not worn to work. It is also a social leveller. If everyone is dressed to the same standard, there will be no judgments made about other employees on the basis of their clothes. Having an uniform also reduces employee confusion: a clear dress code means they don't have to wonder "what" to wear or whether something would be appropriate to wear to work.

A dress code is also very important in non-office environments, such as in factories, for keeping employees safe. For example, if the employees work around machinery that a tie could get caught in, ties are not appropriate. The same is true of jewellery, belts, scarves, and long hair. Therefore, a dress code keeps employees safe from injury and also allows them to look presentable if clients or visitors come on site. A dress code is also very beneficial for other places of service, such as fast food, or grocery stores. It portrays a feeling of cleanliness when you know that the staff is wearing their appropriate uniform, as opposed to if they were wearing their own clothing.

Furthermore, a dress code sets the "tone" of the company. For example, a law office with all the lawyers and associates wearing suits and formal business attire is viewed as being professional and able to handle court cases. How the public perceives a company is important to the type and amount of business it does.

The disadvantages are that it can become very boring to wear the same clothes daily. Secondly, the uniform may not be very comfortable to wear. These disadvantages can, however, be lessened by giving the employees a say in the choice of uniform.

To conclude, a dress code is very essential nowadays in the workplace. The disadvantages are negligible as compared to the advantages.

Plan followed

Intro: a balanced approach as it is a discuss essay.

Para 1: Advantages

Para 2: More advantages of uniform

Para 3: More advantages of uniform

Para 4: Disadvantages of uniform

Conclusion:

3. More and more people are working from home rather than at the workplace. Some people say this will bring benefits to the workers and their families, but others think it will bring stress to the home. Discuss both views and give your own opinion.

Working from home with the help of telephone lines, or, in other words, telecommuting has become very popular especially where Internet connections are fast and reliable. Some individuals are of the opinion that it is advantageous for the employees and their families where as others think it leads to tension at home. This essay shall discuss both sides of the issue.

There are many advantages of telecommuting to employees and their families. To begin with, it saves time as no time is wasted commuting to and from the office. It also saves money as no spending on private or public transport has to be done. Furthermore the worker can look after minor family commitments like dropping the child to school etc. Although most of the work done by tele-workers is monitored, still a few minutes can be snatched at times. Finally, the tele-worker can do some side business side by side because of the time saved.

On the other hand, there are some problems which telecommuters and their families face. Firstly, a corner of the house has to be reserved for office work and a good internet connection is needed. This is very important because a person working from home has to be connected with his colleagues and seniors at all times during the office hours.

What is more, the expectations from the family members also increase. They sometimes forget that the person working from home has to concentrate on his office work and is only physically there with them. This leads to stress as it has generally been seen that telecommuters try to put in their best at work so that they are not laid off and keep reaping the benefits of telecommuting.

To conclude, as every garden has weeds, similarly telecommuting too has its downside. On the whole, advantages are much more than the disadvantages and some amount of stress at the home is a small price to pay for the vast amount of benefits associated with telecommuting.

Plan followed
Intro: Discuss essay intro
Para 1: Advantages of telecommuting
Para 2: how it causes stress
Para 3: other cause of stress
Conclusion:

4. Nowadays, a lot of people are able to do their work from home. Discuss the advantages and disadvantages of this development.

The modern era is an era of the IT revolution and all those jobs, which are dependent on the Internet can be done from anywhere. This has enabled many companies to provide their employees with computers and a good internet connection to work from home. This is called telecommuting and has become very common in recent times. This is largely advantageous to both employees and employers but has a few disadvantages as well.

On the positive side it saves time and money of employees as they don't waste time commuting to and from office and also do not need to spend on fares of public transport or on petrol and diesel if they use their own vehicle. The time they save in this way can be given to personal or family needs, which is very much needed in the fast-paced hectic lifestyle of today. They can also look after minor family commitments such as dropping their child to school. They also save on the clothes, as they don't have to spend on formal office wear. Finally, they can work for anyone in any corner of the world sitting in their homes.

Telecommuting helps the employers also because they do not need to build and maintain big offices. We all know that land prices are exorbitant and even maintenance of offices is very expensive. Moreover, it has been seen that telecommuters don't take much sick leave or other leave, which in turn benefits the employers. Then, there are advantages to the environment. Less people going and coming from offices means less traffic on the roads which means less petrol and diesel being burnt and so less pollution.

Disadvantages of telecommuting to the employees are that they have to reserve a corner in their home for office as they have to sit there undisturbed during office hours. Secondly, they do not get the office atmosphere to work in and so it can get very boring at times. They can also be disturbed by the family, who fail to realise that the person sitting at home is not free. The employers also find it very difficult to supervise tele-commuters.

To sum up, telecommuting has pros as well as cons but definitely the advantages have an edge over the disadvantages.

Plan followed
Intro:
Para 1: Advantages of telecommuting
Para 2: More advantages
Para 3: Disadvantages
Conclusion:

5. Nowadays, many families move overseas for job opportunities. Some people think that this is beneficial for the children of these families, while others think children will find it difficult. Discuss both views and give your own opinion.

The opportunities to work abroad are more today than they have ever been in the history of mankind. The big planet Earth has become a small global village and sovereign barriers seem to have disappeared. While working in a foreign country, some individuals take their family with them. This situation has both merits as well as demerits but definitely the pros outweigh the cons.

There are many obvious benefits of going abroad to work along with family. To begin with, individuals have more bonding with family. The family relationship is not weakened by distance. Some families who do not go abroad together may end up in divorce, as one or both of them cannot endure the long-term separation. Secondly, many people feel homesick and lonely and therefore cannot adjust in the foreign country and return home, thereby missing the golden opportunity of working abroad.

The most important point is that children, especially who are young , need the care from both parents. Childhood is a crucial phase of life and comes only once. If children are deprived of one parents love, it may have a considerable impact on their psyche. Therefore, working abroad with family can provide complete love and care to the children.

On the other hand, there are some problems of working abroad with families. To begin with, living with family members abroad means more expenses. A single person can share a room with someone in the initial stages but a complete family needs a proper house. What is more, all the members face stress of adaptation to alien surroundings. Parents themselves feel culture shock and therefore cannot help their children.

To conclude, there are both advantages and disadvantages in any choice of this issue. Personally, I believe that people should decide according to their specific circumstances. If there are financial constraints, then it is better to go alone initially. However, the family should be called as early as possible.

Plan followed

Intro: advantages outweigh the disadvantages

Para 1: Benefits

Para 2: more benefits

Para 3: disadvantages

Conclusions: reiterate your opinion

6. Most people take interviews to select a person for job. What are the other ways? What do you think is the best way to recruit new employees?

Recruiting new employees can be a long and painful process. The success of any business or organisation depends on the quality of its staff. Some employers conduct interviews to select new workers. However, there are various other approaches. This essay intends to analyze methods of hiring new employees and pick out the best one.

Undoubtedly, an interview is an important method of recruitment. If selection has to be done merely on an interview, then the interview has to be well executed. It requires a detailed understanding of the organizational needs as well as a careful grasp of the prospective employees' responses. It is not an easy task. If the recruitment is on a small scale and only a few employees are needed, it can prove fruitful otherwise alternative methods to hire have to be taken into account.

There are many other methods, which can be employed to hire new personnel. These hiring methods are a combination of several step-by-step tests. Initially, job vacancies are advertised, after which the recruiters select resumes, which meet the basic requirements for that particular job position. Then a written test is conducted to judge the skills and knowledge of the person. This is followed by group discussions and some other skill tests. Then the shortlisted candidates are interviewed. After this, background checks and reference checks are done of those shortlisted after the interview. It is important to check the credit record and criminal record. The reference checks are done to ascertain the authenticity of what is written in the resume. Finally, the selected candidates are sent for a health check to rule out any communicable diseases.

Analyzing the above mentioned methods it can be seen that no single method is perfect. Each job has its own requirements. Some jobs require qualification and some require experience. Big companies have a department devoted to human resources, which takes care of the hiring issues, but for small businesses finding the right employees at the right times can be an especially time-consuming and frustrating struggle. External recruitment agencies can be assigned the task of searching suitable candidates for jobs, but it may be very expensive. However, I believe that spending on the recruitment of new employees can prove to be a good investment, as good employees can breathe new life into your business.

To sum up, finding suitable employees is an arduous task and has to be a combination of written tests, group discussions, interviews and reference checks.

Plan followed:

Intro:

Para 1: Importance of interviews   Para 2: Other methods,

Para 3: More methods and own opinion.

Conclusion:

7. Some people believe that no one should be allowed to continue working after the age of 65. However, others say there shouldn't be a limitation on age and anyone should be allowed to work regardless of their age. Discuss both views, give your own opinion and include relevant examples.

It is true that mandatory retirement age is being extended in many nations and this is causing some problems in society. Nonetheless, I disagree that such workers should be retired. A number of arguments surround my opinion.

To begin with, we have to face the reality that today we belong to a graying society and the latest demographic trends show that very soon one in four persons will be over the age of 60. Can we afford to retire such a huge population? The answer is a definite 'no'. If they don't work they are a liability on the government, as then the government has to provide pensions. But, if they work they remain independent and at the same time pay taxes.

Another reason for keeping such people working is that they have years of experience, which can go waste if they retire early. No doubt, young people are more energetic and work more enthusiastically, but the older employees know the ins and outs of the company. Someone has rightly said that 'a new broom sweeps clean but an old broom knows the corners'. What is more, these employees also do not job-hop and are more loyal to the company they work for. They are also prepared to work for less, which is ultimately beneficial to the company or organisation they work for.

Those who wish to see them retired soon have the problem of unemployed youth in their mind. Undoubtedly, youth unemployment also is a big problem as it leads to violence and crime in society. The young people are very energetic and if this energy is not channelized in the right direction then they can go astray and cause problems. Job openings should be created for them in some way or the other. However, if the elderly are retired earlier, we shall be adding more burden on these young shoulders to support a burgeoning dependent population.

To sum up, retiring people above 60 would be an unwise and unpractical decision, considering the changing demographic trends towards an ageing society.

Plan followed
Intro: I disagree that such workers should be retired.
Para 1: 1st reason why the older people should not be retired
Para 2: 2nd reason
Para 3: Opponents view and then refute it
Conclusion: reiterate opinion

8. Many people prefer to stay in the same type of work all their life, whereas others prefer to change the type of work. Discuss both sides and state your own opinion.

The world is changing rapidly. People today face numerous challenges in achieving a meaningful and fulfilling life. That is perhaps why some people change their job many times during their lifetime. However, there are still some who stick to the same job for life. This essay shall look into the benefits of both approaches.

There are many reasons why some people like sticking to one job. Firstly, the chances of promotion are much more because of longevity of service. Furthermore, they find greater depth of satisfaction from their working relationships. There is also much better work-life balance if a person's job is stable and secure.

On the other hand, there are some strong benefits that can come from job-hopping. One of the major reasons for changing jobs is a better pay package, which can help to lessen the financial burden of an individual or family. Secondly, the experience that is formed through a change in job can be beneficial in the future. Individuals with a wider range of job experiences and skill sets are seriously considered for new job openings. Moreover, those who have a wide range of careers under their belt also have more job security. If they lose their job, they can seek out jobs in different career fields, as opposed to one career field.

What is more, it is generally seen that earlier on in life people settle for whatever job they can get. Job satisfaction at that time is not given any priority. But, later on when the person is a bit comfortable, then changing the job and doing something, which the heart desires is better because it gives more personal fulfillment. By changing jobs a person may finally discover a job which gives him the maximum job satisfaction.

To sum up, it can be said that changing jobs several times during a lifetime, may bring some challenges in life, but overall it is a positive development.

Plan followed

Intro: Discuss essay intro
Para 1: reasons why some people like sticking to one job
Para 2: benefits that can come from job hopping
Para 3: More benefits
Conclusion: changing jobs is better

9. Some people prefer to be self-employed, whereas others like working for companies or institutions. Which is a better approach?

Many people prefer to work in a company or institution where as some choose to open their own business and be self-employed. It is necessary to look into the pros and cons of both before deciding which situation is more advantageous.

One of the main advantages of being self-employed is that you are completely self-reliant and can make decisions on your own. This can give you a great sense of freedom and allow you to do exactly what you want without any interference. What is more, your working day can be planned for your convenience allowing you to work when you want rather than when you have to. Moreover, if your business is successful, people will know that you alone should be given the credit. Finally, if you work for yourself, you decide your pay check. If you want more, you work more; that is the bottom line.

On the other hand, there are obvious advantages of working for companies or institutions. The main advantage is that you don't have to make any investment and so you have nothing to lose. You also get hands-on training in companies and the work environment is also very good. Additionally, if your company does well, you get bonuses and perks from time to time. Another important benefit is that you get your regular pay check even if the company is going in loss. Finally, working for a reputed company is a status symbol.

I believe, it is better to work for few months or a couple of years in a company to get the know-how before embarking on your own business. Being self-employed can be very gratifying but it can also be very challenging. Many self-employed people have said that in order to be successful in business you have to be prepared to work long hours and sacrifice your personal life. As B.C.Forbes once said," If you don't drive your business, you'll be driven out of business". A 1996 study found that over a quarter of businesses run by newly self-employed people failed within the first two years.

To conclude, being self-employed can be very fulfilling but not without difficulties, so working for a company would be a much safer option.

Plan followed:

Intro:

Para 1: Advantages of being self-employed

Para 2: Advantages of working for others

Para 3: Challenges of being self-employed

Conclusion: working for others is better

10. Many people strive to maintain a successful career and happy family life at the same time. What problems can this situation create? What are the possible solutions?

It is undeniable that everyone dreams to have both - a prosperous career and a contented family. However, there seem to be a lot of problems preventing people from achieving that goal. This essay shall discuss these problems and suggest some solutions.

The first problem is that today's world is ruled by money and so people devote a lot of time to their work or business. They have become workaholics. As a result, they fail to draw a line between work and family. The second reason is the cut-throat competition of today. Young people, new to their jobs, have to put in their time and effort to meet the expectations of their employers. Similarly, those who run their own businesses have to drive their business otherwise their business can drive them out. Another problem is that the family expectations are soaring higher and higher day by day. The earning hand is expected to fulfil all those expectations as well as give time to the family. Sometimes, it becomes difficult to live up to those expectations and this leads to stress.

The solutions are not simple. People have to learn to set their priorities. Some things have to be sacrificed for the sake of others. Effective time management is very important. The most severe problem existing among most people tends to be their unsuccessful time management. People should learn to switch the office button off once they come home. Practicing some exercise regime for a few minutes every day can keep a person physically fit enough to have a successful work-life balance.

The non-working members of the families too can help in this respect. They should try to support, to care and to understand the efforts that others are making. One meal of the day should be fixed which all members have to have together. A more practical way to be considered might be setting up family plans, for example, a monthly family trip or weekly picnic, to share some happy time and memories together.

Summing up, I believe that with a mutual understanding of each other and continuous efforts, people will eventually find the balance point of their life and work.

Plan followed

Intro: This essay shall discuss these problems and suggest some solutions.

Para 1: Problems

Para 2: Solutions

Para 3: More solutions

Conclusion:

11.Nowadays, some celebrities such as film stars, sportsmen and pop musicians are paid too much money. Do you agree or disagree? Which jobs should be highly paid?

The high incomes of celebs in the field of sports and entertainment have always been a matter of dispute. I agree that they are getting high remuneration for what they are doing but I also firmly believe that they well deserve it. In the following paragraphs I shall put my arguments to support my opinion, and also suggest some other jobs, which should be highly paid.

My first argument in favour of the high salaries of these celebrities is that they have a major contribution in the lives of people. They provide entertainment and inspiration and they also bring name and fame to our country. They are role models for the society and people follow them and listen to them. Secondly, they have a very short career span. Most of the people in the sports and entertainment field start their career at the age of 19-20 and retire by 33-35 years. Whatever these celebs earn is during these few years and after that they face struggles.

My final argument is that these celebs sacrifice their personal life completely and so they do deserve these high salaries. They cannot enjoy the common things of life like the normal folks do. They are always followed by the paparazzi and their children too always need security. This is a steep price to pay for the high salaries they receive.

There are many other professions, which deserve high salaries. Doctors, teachers and nurses also serve humanity and should be paid higher salaries. Then, there are people working in our defense services such as the army, navy and air force. Because of them, we are leading secure lives. That is why they deserve higher pay-packages. Furthermore, people working in high-risk professions such as fire-fighters and security guards should be paid more and finally people in administrative posts such as IAS and IPS officers should have higher salaries.

To sum up, people in the field of sports and entertainment well deserve their high incomes. However, there are many other professions, which also deserve high salaries.

Plan followed

Intro: agree
Para 1: Reasons
Para 2: More reasons
Para 3: Other professions, which require higher salaries
Conclusion:

12.Promotions to higher levels should be from within a company and not to a new hire from outside. Do you agree or disagree?

It is a highly debatable issue whether promotions should be given to employees from within or to a new hire. The given statement is in favour of in-house hiring. It is necessary to look at the pros and cons of promoting from within the company before forming an opinion.

There are many benefits of hiring from within. To begin with, the employee is familiar with the company. No special training needs to be given. The person knows about the general working of the business. Moreover, employees feel that they will be rewarded for their extra effort and hard work. So, an employee who has been tested and has excelled at a lower level can be shifted to an upper level.

On the other hand, there are some disadvantages of hiring from within. Sometimes, the established policy of hiring from within makes some employees feel that they are entitled to promotion just because they have spent time with the company. Secondly, this can hurt the feelings of other employees who are not promoted. They may feel that they deserved the position better.

In my opinion, a manager or business owner needs to remember that all the hiring decisions need to be made with the idea of strengthening the business. This means that sometimes a person from within can be moved up and sometimes a highly qualified person can be hired from outside.

To conclude, each promotion needs to be done on a case-to-case basis and at all times the HR manager needs to do what is in the best interest of the company.

Plan followed
Intro: It is necessary to look at the pros and cons of promoting from within the company before forming an opinion
Para 1: benefits to hiring from within
Para 2: disadvantages of hiring from within
Para 3: sometimes a person from within can be moved up and sometimes a highly qualified person can be hired from outside.
Conclusion: each promotion needs to be done on a case to case basis

13. Some people think that managers alone should make decisions in the company, while others think that employees should be involved in the decision-making process too. Discuss both views and give your own opinion.

A company may have the best product, the most competitive prices, the best workforce and the best managers, but if it lags in decision-making, it won't last long. People are divided on the issue of who should be the decision makers, whether it should be the managers alone or whether employees too should have a say. This essay intends to analyse both perspectives. I side with the latter view for trivial routine decisions and with the former view for the crucial top-level decisions

Managers are seasoned men. They manage. They are educated in management skills and are trained to handle crucial tasks. A well-trained manager, who is at the helm of affairs of any company, is obviously a better person for the job. Moreover, decision-making is an activity which requires only a selected few managers and owners. It can only happen when the owners and managers are well versed about the company's goals, aims, objectives, policies and conditions. Furthermore, confidential matters are shared only among the top brass of the organisation. Only the top managers know the loopholes and trade secrets of a company and can handle the challenges of the organization better.

On the other hand, the view to involve the employees in the decision making process is an evolving one. It has become the need of the hour to delegate and decentralize not just responsibility to the employees, but authority as well. An employee who does the same activity every day is a better judge and decision maker for that particular activity. He shouldn't be made to seek permissions for trivial matters. For example, if an operator is made responsible to assemble 50 motors, he should get a matching authority to decide for his activity too.

Moreover, when employees are involved in the decision-making connected to their respective activity, they feel motivated. They come up with better and newer ideas. They build a bond with the company and their job. They even perform better when their voices are heard.

To sum up, having discussed both views, the best approach would be to strike a subtle balance between the two. With authority should come responsibility and responsibility should be backed by authority. It would be best to involve the employees in the day-to-day decisions and keep the key level decisions to the managers alone.

Plan followed

Intro: Discuss essay

Para 1: Why managers are better

Para 2: Why employees should have a say

Para 3: More reasons in favour of employees, Conclusion

14. Many students take part-time jobs while studying in universities. Do you think it is a good idea or bad idea?

It is irrefutable that the cost of tertiary education has become very high and students have to work part time to fund their education. This situation has both positive and negative effects. In the following paragraphs, I shall discuss the issue in depth.

There are many reasons why working part-time is beneficial while studying in universities. Firstly, higher education is very costly and students need work part time to fund their education. Secondly, the habit of working hard right from early years makes students realise the dignity of labour and value of money and hence they are better placed in life later on.

What is more, students do not indulge in any violence and crime and drugs. This is because they don't have time for such activities. This also instills some discipline in their lives because they have to manage time effectively so that their studies don't suffer. Finally, while doing these jobs, they develop a network of friends doing different courses and from diverse backgrounds.

It is a negative development because it leads to stress and strain. Sometimes, students cannot strike a balance between work and study, which may result in stress. Consequently, when students face failures or can't cope with the pressures they can have depressive tendencies.

On balance, I believe that being pushed to hard work is a positive development. However, there should be a limit to the number of hours students are allowed part time work, otherwise their studies will suffer.

Plan followed

Intro: situation has both positive and negative effects
Para 1: Why it is positive
Para 2: How it is a positive
Para 3: How it is a negative development
Conclusion: reiterate opinion

15.In many places women are taking jobs which are traditionally done by men. What do you think make these changes happen? What's your opinion about it?

The physical and genetic differences between men and women equip them for different activities and skills. However, in today's scenario it has been seen that women are proving their mettle even in the traditionally male-dominated jobs. This essay shall delve into the reasons for this change.

The first and foremost reason is the opportunity today's women are getting. Nowadays, as more and more women in different countries have started working outside the home, it is clear that they are able to perform jobs that were traditionally only held by men. Secondly, today's woman is also going for higher education and because of this, even the highest positions in science, politics or law, for example, can be held successfully by women.

Another reason is that today anyone can be trained to do any type of job. There is also increasing scientific evidence that individual differences between people may be more important than gender differences. In other words, some women may be physically stronger than some men, while some male individuals may be more sensitive, or more caring than some women.

I believe that today societies are becoming more egalitarian. Earlier, women worked in the homes in most cultures. The girl child was even denied education in many places. Even if there were employed women, they tended to dominate the so-called 'caring professions' such as teaching, nursing or social work. But today, men and women are walking shoulder to shoulder in every field and the line of demarcation between them has faded.

To sum up, in the modern world individual men and women can be trained to develop similar abilities. Differences in aptitude and talents are greater at the individual level than at the gender level. That is why women are taking up jobs traditionally thought to be men's jobs.

Plan followed
Intro: This essay shall delve into the reasons for this change.
Para 1: Reasons
Para 2: more reasons
Para 3: your opinion
Conclusion

16.Some people believe that young people bring more profits to a company. Others say that older people actually bring more profits. Discuss both views and give your opinion.

In this world of ever-changing technology and fast-paced innovations in the business world, it has become a much-debated issue whether the younger employees are more productive or the older ones. Some people are of the opinion that the tech-savvy youth make an organization more profitable and others opine that the experienced older employees are more important. I, however, believe that a combination of the creativity and innovation of the younger workers along with the wisdom and experience of the older employees would lead to the success of any company.

There are many benefits of hiring young workers. They are energetic, creative and bring new and innovative ideas with them, all of which are very important factors in making any business successful in this age of competition. They are more efficient and productive because of their energy and enthusiasm. Younger people are also more suitable for the jobs which require more physical work and are labor-intensive, like construction work. Providing more job opportunities to the youth also helps in addressing the unemployment problem.

The importance of having older and experienced employees cannot be denied. They have knowledge and skills which the younger employees will take years to attain. There are certain work areas which deal with confidential information that cannot be shared with a newly hired person. A manager would be more comfortable dealing with an older, loyal employee, when it comes to sensitive or confidential work-related information. It has been rightly said, "a new broom sweeps clean, but an old broom knows all the corners". So, an older employee would know the ins and outs of the work, whereas, a company might need to spend resources on training and induction of a new inexperienced, younger employee.

In my opinion, for any business or company to be successful, both innovation and experience play an indispensable role. The loyalty, trust and experience of the older employees are as important as the new ideas, creativity and enthusiasm of the younger employees. The younger and older employees are like the wheels of a car. If even one of the wheels is missing, we cannot drive the car.

To recapitulate, it can be said that we cannot chose between youngsters and older employees. There should be a right balance of both for any work or business to be successful.

Plan followed

Intro: Discuss essay

Para 1: benefits of young workers

Para 2: Benefits of older workers

Para 3: Own opinion- combination of both

Conclusion

17.Which is more important - A high salary or job satisfaction?

Many people choose their jobs based on the size of the salary offered. Personally, I disagree with the idea that money is the key consideration when deciding on a career, because I believe that other factors such as job content and job satisfaction are equally important.

On the one hand, I agree that money is necessary in order for people to meet their basic needs. For example, we all need money to pay for housing, food, bills, health care, and education. Most people consider it a priority to at least earn a salary that allows them to cover these needs and have a reasonable quality of life. If people chose their jobs based on enjoyment or other non-financial factors, they might find it difficult to support themselves. Artists and musicians, for instance, are known for choosing a career path that they love, but that does not always provide them with enough money to live comfortably and raise a family.

Nevertheless, I believe that other considerations are just as important as what we earn in our jobs. Firstly, personal relationships and the atmosphere in a workplace are extremely important when choosing a job. On an average we spend a great deal of our time in the workplace, which means that if we are not happy with our job, we are also unhappy with our personal life. Having a good manager or friendly colleagues, for example, can make a huge difference to workers' levels of happiness and general quality of life.

Secondly, many people's feelings of job satisfaction come from their professional achievements, the skills they learn, and the position they reach, rather than the money they earn. Low job satisfaction often leads to low productivity levels and work stress. Finally, some people choose a career because they want to help others and contribute something positive to society.

In conclusion, it is clear that choosing a career that one loves has many advantages. If you love what you do, your chances of success are pretty high and money will follow. High salary is also important but job satisfaction is definitely more significant.

Plan followed:

Intro:

Para 1: Importance of high salary

Para 2: Importance of job satisfaction

Para 3: Importance of job satisfaction

Conclusion: Job satisfaction is more important

18. In many countries, teenagers are encouraged to do part-time jobs. What's the situation like in your country? What do you think are the advantages and disadvantages of doing part-time jobs?

Some countries such as the USA and UK encourage their secondary school students to do part time jobs. There are many pros and cons of this practice, which shall be discussed in this essay.

On the positive side, a teenager's job can teach work skills that will serve him well in college and prepare him for careers in adulthood. The right jobs may expose him to new work possibilities and set him on the path to a lifetime career. Teens also gain useful, marketable skills such as improving their communication, learning how to handle people, developing interview skills and filling out job applications.

To add to it, he can acquire confidence, develop a sense of responsibility and feel more independent. Earning money will enable him to buy the things he wants and will provide an opportunity for learning responsible money management. What is more, studies find that students who work a moderate amount—no more than 10 to 15 hours a week during the school years—tend to earn higher grades than those who don't work at all. Furthermore, if parents work outside the home, an after-school job can give the teenager adult supervision in those crucial afternoon hours.

On the other hand, working more than 13 to 20 hours a week is associated with lower grades. Teens who work too many hours find it difficult to keep up with their extracurricular activities and social relationships. Some studies have found that teens who work long hours are more likely to engage in such risky activities as using illegal drugs or alcohol - in part because they are exposed to older co-workers who lead them astray. Finally, early entry into a negative or harsh work environment may foster negative views of work. This would depend greatly on the maturity level of the teenager and the type of job obtained.

In India, teenagers generally do not work part time. This practice has recently started in big cities but is not very popular yet.

Summing up, teenagers are definitely benefited by working part time. However, the type of work should be carefully chosen and they should not be allowed to work more than 10-15 hours a week.

Plan followed

Intro: Discuss essay intro
Para 1: Advantages
Para 2: More advantages
Para 3: Disadvantages
Para 4: Situation in India | Conclusion: Advantages more than disadvantages

19. Nowadays doctors can become very rich. Maybe they should not focus on profitable activities such as plastic surgery or looking after rich patients and concentrate more on patient's health, no matter how rich they are. Do you agree or disagree?

It is irrefutable that the medical profession is a very lucrative field, but I disagree that doctors should not delve into money-making plastic surgeries and treatment of rich patients and focus on patients' health instead of looking at his pocket. A number of arguments surround my opinion.

To begin with, I would like to say that it takes years to become a doctor and medical education is also very expensive nowadays. No doubt, doctors must serve the society, but to serve the poor or needy, first they have to generate their own sources of income. For a doctor the status of the patient is not important and he has to treat anyone who comes to him. By rendering his services to the rich, he can provide help to the weaker sections and thus help society.

Secondly, I would like to add here that cosmetic surgeries are also part of people's health. They are part of mental health, which is also very important. It is not just the celebrities who go in for such surgeries. People having accidents in which facial features are affected, also need to go in for such surgeries. Can you imagine the mental status of a woman who has lost her external ear or has disfigured her nose in an accident?

Finally, there are children born with cleft lip or palate, who also need plastic surgery. Therefore, it would be wrong to say that doctors should not focus on such surgeries. There are doctors who are doing plastic surgeries absolutely free for children suffering from cleft lip and palate. They charge their rich patients but they never say no to a poor and needy one. Also, it is a well-known fact that as in any other profession, it is not all who earn very high.

To sum up, a doctor's duty is to treat patients; there is nothing wrong if he charges money from those who can afford to pay, as long as he is looking after the poor ones too. It would also be wrong to label all cosmetic surgeries as unnecessary and money-making activities as they are also a part of the intrinsic health of patients.

Plan followed

Intro: I disagree

Para 1: it takes years to become a doctor and medical education is also very expensive nowadays.

Para 2: cosmetic surgeries are also part of people's health – mental health

Para 3: children born with cleft lip or palate, who also need plastic surgery

Conclusion: reiterate opinion

20.According to a survey, people involved in certain occupations and professions are seen to be honest. What is the situation in your country? Why?

It is well known that some professions require people to demonstrate extra levels of honesty than other professions. For instance, those working in the medical and the teaching profession are seen to be more honest than advertisers and insurance agents. The situation is the same all over the world and my country is no exception. In the following paragraphs, I shall put forth some reasons for this phenomenon.

In some professions being honest is the best way to maximize profits in the long run. Let us take the example of a businessman. The most effective way for a businessperson to maximize profits over a long period of time is to follow the highest standards of ethics. Ethical conduct will gain a company the kind of good reputation that earns repeat business. Treating suppliers, customers and others fairly is likely to result in their reciprocating.

Moreover, in some professions there is no room for dishonesty. For instance, in the medical profession you have to tell the correct diagnosis to the patients. A lawyer has to stick to facts and cannot afford to distort them based on his judgments. Similarly, journalists must provide news based on facts and cannot afford to present ill-founded news.

On the other hand, there are some professions such as insurance agents and advertisers, who are seen to be less honest than others. This dishonesty may not be apparent, as they may not be lying about their products or services; they may just be hiding facts. Thus, focusing on complete honesty in these cases might result in lower profits and perhaps ultimate business failure.

However, it is difficult to generalize professions based on honesty. For instance, in the medical profession, some doctors may be prescribing an un-necessary battery of tests just for their personal benefit and some insurance agents may be telling all the positive and negative points of their insurance plans to their clients.

To conclude, some occupations seem to be more honest than the others. The situation is the same all over the world. To survive in the long run, honesty always pays. Mary Kay Ash has rightly said that, "Honesty is the cornerstone of all success, without which confidence and ability to perform shall cease to exist."

Plan followed in the essay

Intro: Start with a quotation. Acknowledge the statement and tell about the situation in your country.

Para 1: One reason for honesty – beneficial in the long run

Para 2: Another reason – some professions have no room for dishonesty

Para 3: Reason for dishonesty in some professions with example

Para 4: Difficult to generalize honesty – individual variation

Conclusion:

21.Although there are more and more women police officers in reality, are they really suitable for this job?

Increasing numbers of women are choosing to work in the police force nowadays and have showed their mettle in this field. The issue raised is whether women are actually suited for such jobs. I believe that not only are women suited for such jobs, they are in fact better than men in many areas of police jobs.

In many areas of police activity, women are especially adaptable and can even perform better than men. For example, policewomen are especially suitable for working for special police prostitution groups, dealing with trafficking in women within the larger cities. They are also better in dealing with domestic violence and juvenile affairs. Policewomen are generally more acceptable to women and children who have been the victims of the misdeeds of men. Girls and young children have more confidence in women.

What is more, the field of crime prevention is becoming more important to police agencies and here policewomen play their greatest role. They are gifted in gaining the confidence of small children and in determining whether behaviour is normal or antisocial. The employment of policewomen offers the best method of finding out the real problem, and then determining the best course of action to pursue.

Research conducted internationally clearly demonstrates that women officers use less physical force and are therefore better at dealing with violent confrontations with citizens. Additionally, women officers often possess better communication skills than their male counterparts and are better in obtaining the cooperation and trust required in their job. They are considered at least equal to male officers in most areas of police work. They have shown no differences in the quality of their performance in street patrolling. Those skeptical about their role of police officers base their argument on women's lack of physical strength. However, with proper training even this factor can be overcome.

To conclude, female officers are equally capable as their male counterparts. In some situations they have even proved themselves better than men. No wonder, we are seeing more and more women in police force.

Plan followed in the essay

Intro: Give your opinion and write a thesis statement. I have said women are suitable for these jobs and are even better at places.

Para 1: Give examples where women are better than men – Prostitution, juvenile crime

Para 2: More examples of where they are better – crime prevention

Para 3: Better communication skills – as good in street patrolling. Opponents view – less physical strength – negate it | Conclusion: Reiterate your views.

22. Nowadays some professionals such as doctors, lawyers and engineers are paid much higher salaries than ordinary workers. What do you think of this trend? Are there any jobs, which you think should offer higher salaries?

It is irrefutable that doctors, lawyers and engineers are paid much higher salaries than ordinary workers. In the following paragraphs, I shall discuss this issue at length and also suggest some other occupations, which deserve higher salaries.

To begin with, professions, such as medical, engineering and law, require far more years of study than what ordinary workers have to do. For example, for a basic M.B,B.S. degree, more than 5 years of study is required, and after that to specialize in any specific field another three to five years are required. A person with a simple M.B:B.S degree does not earn all that high. Similar is the case with engineering and law professions. They have to undergo many years of struggle and training to finally reach their telephone-figure salaries.

Secondly, it requires a lot of financial input to attain these degrees. Many students have to take loans to study, which they have to repay later on. They may remain in debt for many years while they pay off their student loans. Therefore, their higher salaries are justified. Ordinary workers, on the other hand, do not have to spend huge amounts on their college and university fees. What is more, some of these higher paid professions are round-the-clock professions and very challenging physically as well as emotionally. Finally, it would not be wrong to say that not all such professionals are highly paid. Many of them keep struggling throughout their lives.

There are many other jobs, which merit higher salaries. I believe that teachers and nurses are doing commendable jobs for the society. They should be paid lucrative salaries so that people want to join these occupations. Then, there are people working in our defense services such as the army, navy and air force. Because of them, we are leading secure lives. That is why they deserve higher pay-packages. Furthermore, people working in high-risk professions such as fire-fighters and security guards should be paid more and finally people in administrative posts such as IAS and IPS officers should have higher salaries.

To sum up, there is no doubt that doctors, lawyers are receiving high salaries, but they rightly deserve them; there are several professions which should to be paid more.

Plan followed

Intro: agree

Para 1: 1st reason

Para 2: 2nd reason

Para 3: Other professions, which need higher pay

Conclusion: Reiterate what you have already said

23.In some countries, it is common for women to participate in the workforce when their children are young. What are the advantages and disadvantages of this?

The mother's employment status does affect families and children. These effects can be both – positive and negative which shall be discussed in this essay.

On the positive side, two family incomes are very important to make both ends meet. So women work and add to the financial security of the family. This additional income helps to provide better education and other facilities to the children. What is more, it has been seen that the children of working mothers do better academically, have better behaviour and adjust themselves better socially. Another advantage is that most families accommodate to the mother's employment and in doing so provide a family environment that works well. In two-parent families, the fathers take on a larger share of the household tasks including child-care and this seems to have benefits for the children.

Furthermore, employed mothers have a higher level of well-being than those who stay at home and this, in turn, affects their parenting in positive ways. Therefore, the mother's employment itself does not seem to have any negative effects on the children. The society also has changed and today we have affordable and quality day care centres, which are a blessing for working mothers. Finally, women have proved their mettle in many fields and the modern workplaces need their services more than anything else.

The disadvantages, on the other hand, are that children need the loving and affectionate care of mothers in the early years of their lives and if mothers go to work then they are deprived of this to some extent. Women also need some rest after child birth as it is a physically and emotionally challenging time for them. Some people also opine that juvenile delinquency is on the rise because mothers do not give time to their children because of going to work.

To sum up, it can be said that there are both advantages and disadvantages of women going to work when their children are young. However, the pros far outweigh the cons.

Plan followed

Intro: Balanced intro as it is a discuss essay

Para 1: advantages

Para 2: more advantages

Para 3: Disadvantages

Conclusion: advantages outweigh disadvantages

24. Some employers want to be able to contact their staff at all times, even on holidays. Does this development have more advantages than the disadvantages?

Technological innovations have revolutionized every aspect of our lives, especially the workplaces. One of the developments of these advancements is the way the employers and employees communicate. At some workplaces, the managers or bosses expect their employees to be available to take work related requests at all times, even on weekends and on holidays. I believe that such expectations of the employers have more negative effects than positive.

Admittedly there are some benefits of the 24/7 connectivity between the employer and the employee. The first is that it leads to better relations between them, if used wisely. If they are well connected through the mobile phones or emails, then there will be fewer misunderstandings, better rapport and a certain amount of comfort level, even for the employee. This further helps the employee being more creative and productive. To add to it, in some emergency situations, requiring immediate attention, critical decisions can be taken without any delays.

Having looked at the benefits, undoubtedly the drawbacks of this development are many and worrisome. It is one of the leading causes of the work-life imbalance. The employee is not able to give time to the family or sometimes has to leave a family outing or a meal or an important family occasion to deal with the work related issue. This leads to many problems in their personal lives. Furthermore, the employee may always be stressed about the fact that the employer can call them anytime and so, they are not able to enjoy anything fully. This may also create a rift in the employee-employer relationship.

To add to the above mentioned points, the employee may not be able to cope up with the stress, which not only affects the productivity and efficiency at work, but also leads to many health related problems, like hypertension, cardiovascular diseases and so on. Moreover, such employees are more likely to be resented by others at the workplace and again this will add to the pressures and anxieties they are already dealing with.

To conclude, it can be reiterated that if used prudently, the communication technology can be a boon for both the employees and employers. However, the detrimental effects can be quite grave, if the employer doesn't respect the staff's personal and family time.

Plan followed
Intro:
Para 1: Advantages of the 24/7/employer employee relation
Para 2: Disadvantages of the 24/7/employer employee relation
Para 3: More disadvantages of the 24/7/employer employee relation
Conclusion:

25.Some developed countries have reduced the number of school hours. Is this a positive or a negative development?

Shortening of the school day is a topic that has been debated a lot recently. There are advantages and disadvantages associated with shortening the school day, which shall be analysed in this essay. I believe it is largely a negative development.

On the downside, a shortened school day would reduce the amount of instructional time. For some laboratory classes reducing the number of minutes in class each day could have a detrimental impact. Shorter segments of instructional time might diminish the quality of instruction. Biology, chemistry, art, physical education and music classes all have the potential to be detrimentally affected.

Secondly, if the school day were shortened, the system might have to reduce the number of vacation days or add days at the beginning or end of the school year in order to satisfy the hours requirement. Finally, it would add to the stress of finding day care for after school hours for those parents who are working full time.

On the positive side, reducing the number of hours would allow extra time for students to participate in additional educational or vocational experiences. Students from lower income families would have more time for an after-school job to provide supplemental income to their parents. Students might also have the opportunity to participate in internships, perform community service, take advanced classes or investigate another activity that might broaden their intellectual horizons.

Furthermore, there may be some financial savings to the school as teachers would work fewer hours and therefore, would get less pay. The utilities, such as heating, air conditioning, electricity, of the actual school buildings would be used less and contribute to the savings. For example, the potential savings of shortening a school day by 1.5 hours might result in a savings of 6 percent to 20 percent of the overall budget, depending upon buildings and staffing.

To sum up, shortening the school hours would have pros and cons, but the disadvantages far outweigh the advantages.

Plan followed

Intro:

Para 1: Negative effects

Para 2:More disadvantages

Para 3: Advantages

Para 4: Advantages

Conclusion:

26.In many countries, children spend long hours on homework. Some people think less homework can reduce student's stress and give them a chance to develop other skills. What is your opinion about this?

People have been deeply divided over the homework issue for a long time. On one hand there are the proponents of homework who talk of its benefits and efficacy, and on the other hand we have some individuals, who would like schools to adopt a no homework policy for students. The given statement, however, raises a concern about too much homework and says that homework should be light and non-stressful. I completely agree with the given notion.

On the one hand homework gives the chance for a student to learn lessons in a more comfortable environment. It helps to consolidate and clarify what was learned during the school day. It is an extension of classwork that allows students to achieve mastery of the content or skills to be learned. It reduces time for TV and video games and promotes good study habits. It teaches self-discipline and time management and above all, it lets parents see what their children are doing at school.

But, when the children are overburdened with homework, all the advantages of homework seem to fade away and the dark side becomes prominent. Too much homework reduces family time. Most parents have to work full time in order to support their family today. When they come home, they want to spend time with their children, but the children are too busy in homework. It also prevents students from helping parents in household chores.

Moreover, students need time to relax, play and pursue sports and hobbies. Too much homework can make students very tired after a long day at school. It may also keep them up too late at night. What is more, homework is often meaningless busywork, which does not promote real learning. Therefore, care must be taken to ensure that homework is relevant and linked to vital learning objectives at all times. It must be designed to deepen students' understanding, and facilitate mastery of the material to be learned. Teachers should not overburden students with homework. There should always be reasonable homework timetables or schedules and homework should be age appropriate. It can range from one hour or a little less per night in the lower school, to three hours or a little more per night in the upper school.

To sum up, homework should be there, as it has many benefits, but it should be within reasonable limits and should promote real learning.

Plan followed:
Intro: Agree
Para 1: Advantages of homework
Para 2: Disadvantages of too much homework
Para 3: More disadvantages   Conclusion: Reiterate opinion

27.Some people think that children should receive formal training at school on how to be good parents in the future. Do you agree or disagree with this statement?

Children represent both the present and the future. In recent years, childcare has gained as much importance as any other subject of academic studies. Traditional childcare skills, which are passed on from one generation to another through oral and informal instruction, are not sufficient to guarantee quality care, so some people opine that childcare should be added as a subject in schools. I, however, do not agree with this notion.

Those who advocate childcare courses in schools say that childcare is not a simple process of feeding children, changing diapers and making them sleep regularly. Contemporary childcare is much more than all this. Childcare is a complex science that goes beyond nutrition. It involves the physical and emotional well-being of children. Given our changing times and family structures, childcare-training courses should be the norm for all.

However, adding childcare as a subject in schools would add to the burden of children as well as schools. The children of today are already burdened with tough academic competition. Their school bags are at times heavier than their own weight. Moreover, teaching childcare would not register in their minds at that tender age, when they themselvesare children. I believe that would be taking away some of their childhood.

Another argument which goes against childcare as a subject is that nowadays, youngsters are very career conscious and are marrying late and having children late in life. They plan to have children when they are prepared for the added responsibility. At that time they are mature enough to face the challenges of parenthood. Finally, what may be a good parenting strategy today, may not seem right by the time they become parents. Times are changing very fast, as we all know. So such classes are not needed.

To summarise, successful childcare is a challenge. The healthy development of children is measured not only by physical wellbeing but also by growth in other dimensions. However, adding this as a subject is not a practical idea.

Plan followed

Intro: Disagree

Para 1: Arguments of those who advocate such courses in schools

Para 2: Arguments against

Para 3: More arguments against

Conclusion

28. Some people think that uniformsin schools is unnecessary and should be banned. To what extent do you agree or disagree? Give your opinion and examples from your own experience.

Schools uniforms are mandatory in most schools, but some students dislike wearing uniforms. Therefore some people opine that uniforms should not be there in schools. I, however, oppose such a notion. I firmly believe that uniforms should be compulsory in schools.

To begin with, uniforms give a sense of identity to the school. It instills a sense of discipline in school children. The students feel that they belong to the school. Every student of the school feels like part of a bigger group. Secondly, uniform is a social leveler, where pupils are drawn from a wide cross-section of society. A uniform erases these differences and thus reduces the gap between the rich and the poor. The teachers also tend to treat all students equally when they are in the same uniform.

Another big advantage is that if students play truant and bunk school, they can be easily identified. Finally, the uniform provides security. For example, if some miscreants come in the school, they can be easily spotted from afar. Even on school excursions, it is easier for the teachers to manage if all students are in same uniform.

There are people who oppose having a school uniform. They say that uniform is unattractive and old fashioned. They believe that students can express themselves better through their clothes and should be given the chance to show their individuality. Wearing a uniform creates an opposite effect. I still believe that if schools started running without a school uniform, there would be utter chaos in the classrooms.

To sum up, school uniforms should be retained in all circumstances. Students should not be given the liberty to wear clothes of their own choice. Uniforms can be modernized and changed according to circumstances but an uniform is a critical aspect of education.

Plan followed

Intro: uniforms should be compulsory

Para 1: Advantages of uniforms

Para 2: More advantages of uniforms

Para 3: Why some people oppose uniform

Conclusion: reiterate opinion

29.Many people believe that cooking is an essential life skill and should be taught to boys and girls in schools. Others disagree and believe it is a waste of school time. Discuss both views and give your opinion.

People are divided on the issue of teaching cooking in schools. Some say that cooking is a valuable skill and should be taught as a subject in schools. Others are opposed to it. This essay intends to analyse both perspectives. I, however, side with the latter view.

To begin with, today children are already burdened with many academic subjects. Today's child does not have to compete with children of his country, but with children of this shrunken planet, this global village. Adding another subject like cooking is not at all wise. What is more, cooking is something which children can learn as and when the need arises. Today, technology is so advanced that if you need any recipe, just search on the Internet and even the detailed videos are available. There is no need to waste precious schooldays on this skill.

Secondly, cooking is not a theoretical subject; it has more of a practical component. It would, therefore, be a big burden on the infrastructure of the schools to provide kitchen laboratories. What is more, children could suffer injuries while working in these school kitchens. Finally cooking is something which one keeps learning while doing throughout life. Therefore, there is no need to incorporate this subject in the school curricula.

Proponents of having cooking as a subject say that today children belong to nuclear families and in most cases both parents are working. If children know cooking, they can cook for themselves in times of need. Secondly, today many students go abroad for their higher education. There they would not face any food problem if they have culinary skills. Another big advantage would be that children would also know the value of healthy ingredients of food. Definitely, they would refrain from eating too much fast food.

To conclude, although there is no doubt that home cooking is a disappearing skill in many countries, it would not be advisable to add it as a subject in schools.

Plan followed
Intro: Discuss essay intro
Para 1: Why not have it as a subject
Para 2: More reasons
Para 3: Reasons for having it as a subject
Conclusion:

30.Some people think students in primary school / secondary school should be taught how to manage money because it is an important life skill. Do you agree or disagree?

It is irrefutable that in today's complex life, monetary skills are essential for people of all ages. I agree that financial management is a vital life skill and hence should be taught to primary and secondary school students. A number of arguments surround my opinion.

The main advantage of incorporating financial planning at school level is that students have the opportunity to enter adulthood armed with a better understanding of how money works, and how to make it work for them. For example, individuals who start a business or even start a family require certain level of financial know-how to function efficiently. In addition, such proficiencies learned in school make young adults acquainted with superior budget planning strategies, thus increasing the chances of success by taking judicious decisions. Thus, it is understandable how knowledge about money can contribute to studentsleading an erudite adult life.

As well as providing a basis for future learning, early financial education can also be of benefit to primary school pupils in the shorter term. Young people are encountering money earlier and earlier in life. A survey conducted found that the average age at which children first have their own mobile phone is eight years, while the average age that children borrow a debit or credit card to purchase items online is just 10. So, today's children need to be money-savvy very soon and primary and secondary school years are the best to teach them all that. Moreover, this encourages them to wisely spend their funds, while making them realize the worth of all the facilities provided to them by their parents.

To conclude, financial planning classes at school level can help a lot in the short term as well as long term. Therefore these classes are an absolute must in school.

Plan followed
Intro: Agree
Para 1: Advantages
Para 2: advantages
Conclusion: Reiterate opinion

31.Some people think that schools do not do enough to teach young people about how to look after their health. To what extent do you agree or disagree?

"Health is Wealth" is a well-known saying. The home, the school and the community should share the task of helping each child to be healthy. Unfortunately, health education is not given any place in most schools. Wherever it has been started, it has brought enormous benefits. This essay shall delve into the advantages that can be brought about by school health programmes.

To begin with, it has been seen that schools that provide health services and education not only benefit school-aged children, but also the entire community. This is because school children can act as messengers for other out-of-school children and members of their communities to communicate better practices in hygiene and overall health. It has also been demonstrated that de-worming programs in schools benefit out-of-school children by reducing disease transmission in the community as a whole.

Furthermore, healthier children are more likely to attend school, and absenteeism is reduced. Education and good health offer children the power of choice and opportunity, as well as optimism for a better life. In this way, health education in childhood can help establish lifelong positive behaviors. What is more, health education can help protect individuals, particularly young women, from HIV infection and pregnancy. It is widely recognized that school health and nutrition programs are essential to prevent further HIV/AIDS pandemic.

Finally, we all know that today childhood obesity is a big problem because of the trend of fast foods. Obesity is not just one problem; it can lead to many other problems such as hypertension and diabetes at a young age. If health education is incorporated in the school curricula, this problem can be tackled to a large extent.

To conclude, it can be said that health education should be a mandatory part of all school curricula. It would bring many benefits in times to come, not only for children but for entire communities.

Plan followed
Intro: This essay shall delve into the advantages that can be brought about by school health programmes.
Para 1: advantages
Para 2: more advantage
Para 3: more advantage
Conclusion:

32.Some people say that the study of Science should be mandatory in schools, whereas others argue that it is unnecessary. Discuss both views and give your opinion.

Science is a very important subject, just like many other subjects. However, people are divided on the issue about it being a part of school studies. Some people are of the opinion that it is a very important subject and must be taught in the school years. Others opine that it shouldn't be a compulsory subject at schools. I will discuss both these perspectives in this essay. I, however, side with the former view.

Science should be taught in the early years, as a part of the elementary education. This is the one subject that provides answers to all the questions that children are curious about and about how things work. For instance, why the moon looks different on different days of the month or why do we have different seasons? This increases their knowledge and understanding. It also makes children think logically, solve problems and also makes them understand the other subjects better. It makes children question everything and not accept anything as it is. This develops critical thinking among children.

Some other benefits of teaching science in schools are that it increases awareness about technology and various issues like pollution, conservation of natural resources, endangered wild animals, different weather conditions and so on. It is a practical subject and students can learn easily by performing experiments in laboratories. Furthermore, it cannot be denied that the countries that support more science programs are more progressive than those, which don't give importance to science.

Those who say that science should not be taught to schoolchildren say so because they think that science is ever changing. They say that keeping up with the advances made in science every day and new discoveries made is very difficult for children to cope with. They shouldn't be burdened with difficult concepts like the big-bang theory, sub-atomic particles, neurotransmission and so on. If they have an interest in science, students can take it up as a specialization in high school or secondary education.

In conclusion, study of science subjects clearly has more benefits than cons. It may be difficult to understand concepts; however, if taught in an engaging and interesting way, it will help with the holistic development of children.

Plan Followed
Intro: Discuss essay intro
Para 1: Why science should be compulsory
Para 2: More advantages of teaching science
Para 3: Other view
Conclusion:

33. Do you think that physical activities should be introduced to schoolchildren on a regular basis? Explain. What kind of sports are the most useful?

It is very important that for the holistic development of a child that regular physical activity be a part of their routine. The best way to do that for children is to include it in their school time. There are a number of sports that children can play to stay both physically and mentally fit. The numerous benefits of physical exercise for children are discussed in the upcoming paragraphs.

Regular physical exercise is needed for a healthy body and a healthy mind. It helps with proper growth and builds strong bones and muscles. Including sports or any other exercises in a child's daily schedule helps set a good habit very early, and this helps them remain fit and active throughout their lives. Research has proved that exercising during early childhood years helps prevent many diseases later in life, like obesity, diabetes, cardiovascular diseases and so on.

Sports and any other form of physical exercise also help reduce stress and anxiety. This in turn helps the children do well academically, as they are able to concentrate better, do their tasks on time and achieve better grades. This is the reason why most schools have physical education as a part of their curriculum. It is as important as any other academic subject taught at schools.

Another very important benefit of including such activities at schools is that students learn some very important life skills, like teamwork, co-operation, discipline, sportsmanship spirit, punctuality etc. These skills have become the need of the hour, with the ever-growing competition, in every field. Children also learn about different cultures when they play sports, as they come across other participants from different regions and backgrounds. This helps broaden their horizons and inculcates a sense of equality.

There are many sports that can be easily incorporated by schools. If there is sufficient open area available at a school, sports like basketball, volleyball, cricket, football etc. can be easily included. If a school premises doesn't have enough open area, then many indoor games can be taught to the students, like table tennis, badminton, basketball and so on. Many other indoor games like chess can also be included, which can help students develop strategy-related skills. Games like scrabble can help students build their vocabulary in an interesting way and help them academically as well.

To conclude, I would reiterate that it is very essential that physical activity be a part of every child's daily routine, so that they develop skills and good health, which helps them throughout their lives.

Plan followed

Intro: Yes

Para 1: advantages of sports   Para 2: More advantages

Para 3: Even more advantages   Para 4: What physical activities could be there

Conclusion

34.Some people believe teenagers should concentrate on all school subjects, even ones they do not enjoy. Others, however, believe that teenagers should only focus on the subjects they are best at or find most interesting. Discuss both views and give your own opinion.

In today's competitive world, a broad knowledge is needed to succeed in any field. However, some people some people say that it is a waste of time if students study subjects which are not of their interest. This essay intends to analyse both perspectives. Personally, I side with the former view.

Let us first examine the reasons why some people hold the opinion that students should not have to study all the subjects and should be allowed to choose the subjects they want to study. They opine that in this case the students will probably be more enthusiastic about their study. In addition, if students are forced to study all subjects, they can easily lose interest in education. What is more, if all subjects are compulsory, students will not have enough time to learn all of them properly therefore they will be constantly under a lot of pressure.

However, I believe all subjects are of great importance and for the holistic development of the students they need to study all subjects equally at school level. Later on, during admission to the colleges, students can select the subjects of their choice and can explore them further. At that age they are mature enough to decide their subjects for themselves. At school level the student may not know what his real interests are.

Furthermore, nowadays, the job market is very demanding and the recruiters select students who are skilled in various fields. Acquiring basic knowledge of varied subjects during school definitely widens the horizons for the students. To add to it, it is a well-known fact that most subjects are related to each other in some way or the other. For example, a basic knowledge of mathematics is needed to excel in computer languages. Finally, I believe that it is up to the teachers to develop interest of the students in any subject. For instance, during my school days, my history teacher was so good that a boring subject like history was the favourite subject of the whole class.

To conclude, students should learn all subjects at school level as they are not mature enough to know their real interests at school level and a broad knowledge is also needed for their holistic development.

Plan followed

Intro: Disagree

Para 1: reasons why students should be allowed to choose the subjects they want to study.

Para 2: Why all subjects are important

Para 3: More reasons to study all subjects

Conclusion: reiterate opinion

35. Nowadays, as a part of the educational process, students work at a company for a short period of time without pay. Do the advantages of this outweigh the disadvantages?

Unpaid internships are a part of many degree programs nowadays. I believe the advantages of this trend fairly outweigh the disadvantages.

The main advantage of working in companies for free as part of course accrue to the students themselves. Students gain valuable experience, which can help them in deciding the career of their choice. An internship can also give them the possibility of securing a job upon graduation or shortly thereafter. Former interns have a competitive advantage over other job seekers since the company knows them.

These internships also benefit the employers in several ways. They get services at no cost. They can screen trainees and get acquainted with their quality of work. They can always hire employees who show good progress when performing duties assigned by them. In this way employers can convert interns to full-time employees seamlessly, which reduces or eliminates any training-related costs.

There are benefits to the educational institutes also. Their student interns tend to bring their real-world experience back to the classroom, which helps keep courses relevant and curriculum up-to-date with the current trends. This results in a richer learning experience for everyone.

On the other hand, unpaid internships also have a downside. Those who do unpaid internships can be exploited and made to work longer hours, which may affect the current employees. They may find these younger counterparts a threat. Secondly, many students can't afford to take an internship if it doesn't pay anything, which can contribute to social inequality. Finally, it has been seen that doing a free internship does not actually increase employability. Employers start thinking that such unpaid interns may also be willing to work for lesser money than their regular employees.

To sum up, unpaid internships have advantages to interns, employers and educational institutes. There are a few disadvantages, but the advantages out-weigh them.

Plan followed
Intro:
Para 1: Advantages to students
Para 2: Advantages to employers
Para 3: Advantages to educational institutes
Para 4: Disadvantages
Conclusion:

36. Some people say that in our modern age it is unnecessary to teach children about the skills of handwriting. To what extent do you agree or disagree?

A common opinion is that with the increasing role that computers play in our society; handwriting is no longer an important skill to learn at an early age. Unfortunately this opinion is misguided. I firmly believe that handwriting is very important even in today's era of technology. A number of arguments surround my opinion.

Handwriting is important because research shows that when children learn how to do it, they also learn how to express themselves. Handwriting is so much more than simply putting letters on a page; it is a key part of learning to communicate. Writing is almost as important as speaking, as a medium for communicating thought. For this reason it is said that "Writing is a secondary power of speech, and they who cannot write are in part dumb." Scrawls that cannot be read may be compared to talking that cannot be understood; and writing difficult to decipher, to stammering speech.

Handwriting is also important because children are required to use it daily in school from kindergarten onwards. Children who struggle with the mechanics of handwriting may have trouble taking notes or tests or completing their schoolwork. This can affect both their self-esteem and their attitude toward school. Good handwriting can mean better grades. Studies show that the same mediocre paper is graded much higher if the handwriting is neat and much lower if the writing is not.

What is more, handwriting proficiency inspires confidence. The more children practice a skill such as handwriting, the stronger the motor pathways become until the skill becomes automatic. Once it's mastered, children can move on to focus on the subject, rather than worry about how to form letters. Furthermore, handwriting aids memory. For example, if a person writes a list or a note — then loses it — he is much more likely to remember what he wrote than if he just tried to memorize it.

In summary, handwriting skills are very essential even today. Apart from being a tool of communication, it helps the brain develop, it can improve grades and confidence and also aids memory.

Plan followed

Intro: Disagree
Para 1: Writing is a method of communication
Para2: Handwriting improves grades
Para3: Improves confidence and memory
Conclusion: reiterate opinion

37.Some people say subjects like arts, music, drama and creative writing are more beneficial to children, and therefore they need more of these subjects to be included in their timetable. Do you agree or disagree?

Arts have little or no place in the educational curriculum so far because we have a feeling that time spent on these things is time wasted. Recent studies, however, have shown that a good curriculum that includes arts education can have multiple benefits, which I shall highlight in this essay.

The most important benefit of arts in schools is that it contributes to making a well-rounded student. Certain forms of arts instructions enhance and complement academic skills such as basic reading skills, language development and writing skills. So, children do well in other subjects also.

Another big advantage is that it encourages the pursuit of extra-curricular activities. Children get a chance to show their creative expression. When such hidden abilities are exposed in school time then those with exceptional talent can be encouraged to adopt it as a profession later-on in life. It is a well-known fact that people in such professions are earning telephone figure salaries nowadays.

Last but not least, such subjects are stress-busters. In the highly competitive era of today, pressure of academic subjects is too high. Arts like music, drama and creative writing break the monotony of tough academic studies.

To conclude, our educational curriculum needs a serious revision and more of such subjects need to be added to the school curriculum. They complement academic study, bring out hidden talent and break the ennui of tough academic studies.

Plan followed

Intro: a good curriculum that includes arts education can have multiple benefits, which I shall highlight in this essay
Para 1: advantage
Para 2: another advantage
Para 3: another advantage
Conclusion:

38.Some people who failed at school can be highly successful in their adult life. Discuss why does this happen? And what are the main factors to get a successful life?

It is often seen that some students who are not very brilliant in school become very successful in their adult life. There could be many reasons for this phenomenon, a few of which I shall put forth in this essay along with some factors which contribute to a successful life.

To begin with it could be said that some students may not be good at studies, but may have some talent in them, which could make them reach the pinnacle of their careers and they could become rich and successful. For example, one of my class fellows always used to fail at school, but he was a born singer. He took part in a reality show of singing and reached the third last elimination round. Although he did not win the show, ever since then he has his evenings booked for shows and he is earning handsomely. Here the main factor for success is inborn talent.

Another reason can be attributed to the education system, which relies on rote learning and in which too much emphasis is given to theory and very little to practical. Because of this some intelligent students may be left behind in studies and those with good rote learning capability could pass with flying colours. Later on in life, when they enter the world of work, they may succeed in life because of their practical skills. Furthermore, some students may be very good at some sports or other extracurricular activities. They may succeed in life because they work hard in those sports and excel in them. Who has not heard of the famous cricketer Sachin Tendulkar. He was a school dropout and failed his board exams. Here the factor for success is the hard work and perseverance later on in life.

Some children are born with a silver spoon in their mouth. They may take school very non-seriously but may be very successful in life because they may learn businessstrategies from their parents, which may make life smooth sailing for them. The son of the biggest cloth merchant of my hometown is a school dropout but he has got a very good business acumen and today he is earning much more than the highly educated elite of my home town. Here the factor for success is family support.

To conclude, there are many reasons why many, who fail at school, succeed in adult life but such examples are not very common and many school failures have to struggle throughout their lives.

Plan followed

Intro: There could be many reasons for this phenomenon, a few of which I shall put forth in this essay.
Para 1: The main reason and factor for success is inborn talent.
Para 2: Another reason could be attributed to the education system,
Para 3: Another factor for success is family support. | Conclusion

39.Some people think if students are afraid of the teacher it is better. Others say that having a friendly relationship is better. Discuss both points and give your opinion.

Young children are buildings under construction and teachers are the builders. It is a highly debatable issue whether teachers should be friendly or strict. In my opinion, extremes of both approaches are bad. A good teacher should know when to be friendly and when to be strict and also know the extent of friendliness and strictness required.

There are many advantages if teachers are strict. To begin with, discipline can only be maintained if teachers are strict. For example, if students are afraid of the teacher, they will attend classes regularly and complete their work in time. But, if the teacher is too strict, then the students may lose interest in the subject and may not come to the teacher with their problems.

On the other hand, a friendly teacher is like a good mentor with whom students can share their problems. Students also take more interest in the subject. Students bloom under the guidance of such a teacher. The disadvantage, however, is that a too friendly or partial attitude results in diversion from studies.

In my opinion, a good teacher should be like a friend, philosopher and guide for his students. But, from time to time, he should pull the reins so that the students do not go out of hand. After all, he is shaping the future of the nation. There is a well-known saying in Sanskrit that 'Acharya Devo Bhava' which means that a teacher is like a God.

To conclude, it has to be decided by the teacher when to be friendly or strict and also the degree of friendliness or strictness. Extremes of both approaches are detrimental to the future of a student and ultimately for the future of a nation.

Plan followed

Intro - highly debatable issue whether teachers should be friendly or strict. In my opinion, extremes of both approaches are bad.

Para 1: Adv of teacher being strict and disadvantages of being too strict

Discipline

Students attend classes regularly and complete their work in time

Para 2: Advantages of teachers being lenient and disadvantages of being too lenient

a friendly teacher is like a good mentor with whom students can share their problems

Students also take more interest in the subject

Para 3: Teacher should know when to be strict and when to be lenient

Conclusion:

40.Some people say that to become a good teacher, you should acquire enough training, while others say that teaching capabilities can be developed with experience. Discuss both views and give your opinion.

It is a matter of intense debate whether training is required to become a good teacher or if one can become a good teacher just with experience. This essay shall look into both arguments before reaching a conclusion.

There are many reasons why teacher training is considered necessary. To begin with, it can be said that mere knowledge of the subject is not enough to be a good teacher. Teachers have to fight against pressures from multiple fronts. They have to cope with unending parental expectations, pressures from the management of the school, handling studentswho misbehave, etc. in class of at least 40 students. Above all since they are teachers, the children's future is in their hands so they have to do their best in making children learn. Teacher training ensures that teachers are well prepared to cope with all such challenges.

It is easy to understand why some believe that teaching capabilities can be developed with experience alone and therefore teacher training is not needed. They have a point because in most of the teacher training schools, teachers are given training at the end of the session just to complete a formality. The trainers provide stray bits of advice, which actually are of no use to teachers but wastage of time. Such training is futile and therefore majority of the teachers learn through their own experience or through the experience and guidance of their senior colleagues.

In my opinion, teachers are the backbone of education. They play an important role in moulding our country's future. Therefore, teacher's training should be regarded as a serious issue and should be given preference. It goes without saying that experience does matter, but teachers are expected to perform right from day one and unless they have gone through some training, they are unable to do so. If they have to rely on experience alone, it may take them ages to become a good teacher.

To conclude, I would like to say that both teacher training and experience are needed to be really good teachers. Teacher training is very important in the early stages of a teacher's career. However, this training should be really good and not just a formality.

Plan followed

Intro: Balanced view as it is a discuss essay
Para1: Why teacher training is considered necessary
Para 2: Why some believe that teaching capabilities can be developed with experience
Para 3: Own opinion
Conclusion: Teacher training should be there

41.People find it very difficult to speak in public or to give a presentation before an audience. Do you think public speaking skill is really important? Give reasons. Some people say public speaking should be taught at school. Do you agree or disagree?

Public speaking and oration are the most valued skills that an individual can possess. These skills can be used for almost anything. The most influential prophets and leaders were those who could sway their audiences verbally. The powerful oratory skills of many leaders have won wars, averted mass panic and saved companies from financial disaster. Unfortunately, speaking in public is one of the most feared activities today. In the following paragraphs, I shall delve into the importance of the skill of public speaking. I believe that it should definitely be a part of the school curricula.

To begin with, public speaking is interrelated with communication skills and can be described as a form of communication. Public speaking does not always mean that you have to give a speech to a large audience. When you go for an interview, and speak to a group of interviewers or when you are giving a class presentation: all these are also a form of public speaking. In such situations, if you have the ability to communicate properly, it can help you shape up your future. Secondly, it helps to overcome fear. Surveys have revealed that most people are afraid of public speaking more than their fear of death. The major reason is that one has to gather a thorough knowledge of the subject matter on which one has to speak. Once a person goes into the depth of any topic, he realizes that his anxieties and fears associated with it go down quite remarkably.

Furthermore, this skill helps in personality development. When a person successfully delivers a good speech, it gives a sense of self-worthiness. A positive response from the audience can help a person feel more confident. Thus, it can bring about a lot of improvement in one's overall personality. Last but not the least, the art of public speaking improves relationships. Once a person develops good public speaking skills, a marked improvement can be seen in his interpersonal skills, which in turn, will help him maintain a healthy relationship with his friends and family. Even in one's professional life, an effective interaction with one's boss, clients or subordinates can help a person enhance the possibility of advancement in his chosen profession.

In our present teaching system, writing and reading seems to be the main focus of literacy, and oratory skills are not stressed. The system needs to change, so that it can focus more of its resources on teaching how to interact in the world. Almost all jobs require an interview, and if one doesn't know the workings of a job interview, he will probably do poorly. But if the schools teach the skills of public speaking, appearing for an interview would be a piece of cake.

To conclude, the art of public speaking is very important in today's scenario. If today's children overcome glossophobia or the fear of speaking in public, they would stand a much better chance in the highly competitive global village of today

---

Plan followed

Intro: Agree   Para 1: Advantages of public speaking   Para 2:More advantages
Para 3: Why schools should teach public speaking   Conclusion:

42.Some think that children should start school as early as possible, while others believe that they should start school at the age of seven. Discuss both views and give your own opinion.

Education is very important for everyone. Some people think that children should begin their formal education at a very early age (4 years), whereas others opine that the age of seven years is the best for young people to commence educational studies. This essay intends to analyse both perspectives before reaching a conclusion as to which approach is better.

Advocates of sending the child to school at the age of 4, cite a host of benefits. They say that children who begin to study at a very early age have more chances to succeed in the future. It is a well-known fact that the younger the individual, the easier it is for him to acquire new knowledge and information. Such children get a head start in learning, which definitely gives them an advantage in their later school years. Secondly, if children remain at home till 7 years, they while away time in unproductive activities. But, when children attend school, they are purposefully engaged in activities that stimulate their minds and encourage them to develop and improve.

On the other hand, there are myriad reasons for sending children to school at around 7 years of age. Every child must have his or her childhood, during which playing and communication with friends and parents is very important. Childhood comes but once in life and should be spent as much as possible with parents. Basic qualities, such as kindness, self-confidence and a good sense of humour cannot be gained from studying. This interaction with parents decreases after children start school, because they get busy in homework and other activities.

Another important aspect of sending children to school at a later age is that in their early ages children need more exercise, because at this age the development of their body is a very essential aspect. The stress of school and homework stifles the growth of many children. As it is, there are many years of schooling for children even if they start at seven.

To conclude, both approaches have their own sets of merits. Parents have to see what suits them best. If both parents are working, and the family is nuclear, then early age would be better. Otherwise, it would be better to send children to school at the age of seven.

Plan followed

Intro: Discuss essay intro

Para 1: why some people say that a very early age is better to start school

Para 2: Advantages of later age (7 years)

Para 3: More advantages of starting school late

Conclusion: Give opinion

43.Some people think children should attend extra classes after school, while others disagree. Discuss both opinions and give your own view.

Today, we belong to an era of cutthroat competition. Parents want their children to excel in everything. That is why some parents arrange for tuitions outside class hours. Other people, however, are opposed to tuitions. This essay shall discuss the advantages and disadvantages of tuitions.

Private tuitions can be advantageous in many ways. To begin with, private tutors can re-explain the topics learnt in the class and reiterate key points and help to solve problems students find difficult to tackle. Secondly, allocating times for private tuition reduces their time spent in useless pursuits such as chatting with friends and watching TV.

Furthermore, private tutors also help to motivate the students to study hard. Sometimes students may lose their motivation to work hard. A private tutor can keep the students on the right track when they stray off course. For example, private tutors can help parents to reprimand their children if they become too playful. Private tutors can assign homework to them, so that they can spend their time in a more meaningful way. A private tutor can thus enact the role of disciplinarian. What is more, sometimes students have personal problems that they find hard to confide in their parents. At that time tutors can act as a 'listening ear' and help them resolve some of their problems.

On the other hand, having private tuition also has its disadvantages. Sometimes tutors prescribe additional homework in addition to those given by teachers in school. The extra homework from tutor is an added burden to the students. Moreover, private tuition can be a financial burden to parents who are poor. Additionally, some students just use these extra tuitions to finish their homework given by schools with the help of tutors without thinking through the solutions by themselves.

On balance, I believe that when student is a slow learner who needs a tutor outside school, tuition is very necessary. However, there are some parents who have unreasonable expectations. They insist that their children engage a private tutor even though their children perform well academically. This is not good at all because children need time for other activities also.

In conclusion, it is good to have private tuition provided the student really needs one and the parents can afford it. However, if the student is already doing well in school, then he should be allowed to follow other pursuits. The benefits are also plentiful if parents manage to find a good tutor who can play various roles to help his students to achieve academic success.

Plan followed

Intro: Discuss essay intro

Para 1: Advantages   Para 2: Advantages   Para 3: Disadvantages

Para 4: own view

Conclusion:

44.Some people think that young children benefit from going to nursery school before starting primary school. Others think it is better for young children to stay all day with their families. Discuss both views and give your opinion.

The appropriateness of preschools and nursery schools has always been a debated issue. It should be left to the parents to weigh the pros and cons of nursery schools before deciding on one.

On the positive side, social interaction is probably the most important skill children learn in preschool. School is not just about academic learning. It is also about developing the skills needed to get along with others, learning how to share, taking turns, handling conflicts, and listening to one another. Interacting with other children teaches them these social skills and generally improves their communication skills. Secondly, a good preschool program also teaches children pre-literacy skills such as learning all the letters of the alphabet and basic concepts of mathematics such as number and quantity.

Additionally, preschool also helps to prepare children for school by helping them learn appropriate classroom behavior, how to interact with adults other than their parents, and gives them an opportunity to build their independence. What is more, exposure to different types of activities such as playing with blocks and listening to poetry and songs are just a few of the many experiences children benefit from in a fun learning environment. While most children may have access to do these activities with their parents, it is a completely different experience for them when they have the opportunity to play with their peers.

On the other hand, there can be some disadvantages of preschools. Firstly, if the children are not monitored properly, they will also learn negative social skills such as teasing, bullying, and fighting. Secondly, children do not get enough quality time with their parents. Moreover, children in preschool programs are exposed to a number of illnesses, so they get sick more often than kids who stay at home. Finally, good quality nursery schools may be very expensive.

To sum up, quality nursery schools can enrich kids' lives, build socialization skills and enhance their development. But these types of programs can also be expensive, expose kids to a plethora of illnesses and cause missed quality time with parents. After weighing the advantages and disadvantages of preschool programs, parents can decide for themselves what's best for their child.

Plan followed

Intro: Discuss essay intro

Para 1: Advantages

Para 2: Advantages

Para 3: Disadvantages

Conclusion: Choice of parents

45.In some countries, schools are open till late so that children can be looked after when parents are at work. Discuss the advantages and disadvantages.

In nuclear families, where both parents are working, there has been a growing trend of schools, which keep open till the late hours. This essay shall look into the pros and cons of such schools.

There are many advantages of such schools. The main advantage is that attendance in such schools can provide children with supervision during this crucial time. When the dismissal bell rings, many children go home to empty houses and many others hang out on the streets until their parents return home. Children left unsupervised after school often fall prey to deviant behaviors that are harmful to them, to their schools, and to their communities. They are more likely to be involved in delinquent acts during these hours. Numerous reports have documented that a high proportion of juvenile crimes are committed between the hours of 3:00 p.m. and 6:00 p.m. each day. Such extended school hours occupy students productively during these hours.

In addition to providing supervision, after-school and extended school-day programs are now being seen as a means of improving academic achievement of students who are notperforming as well as they need to during regular school hours. These schools are also affording opportunities for providing social, cultural, and recreational activities. In this way they provide enriching experiences that broaden children's perspectives and improve their socialization.

On the other hand, such schools also have their demerits. The most important is that these are generally very costly. They may be hard on the pockets of many parents. Another disadvantage is that once the child gets home there is very little time left to interact with the parents. The child is so tired that after coming home he takes his meals and goes to bed.

To conclude, the benefits derived from the use of such schools definitely outweigh the demerits. They are the best option when both parents are working and there is no one at home to care for them. As far as the cost factor is concerned, parents can weigh the advantages according to their needs and take decisions accordingly.

Plan followed

Intro: This essay shall look into the pros and cons of such schools

Para 1: Advantage

Para 2: more advantages

Para 3: Demerits

Conclusion:

46.In modern society, many people think that primary schools should teach science and technology rather than history and geography, which are useless and boring. Do you agree or disagree with this statement?

Some people opine that traditional subjects such as history and geography should not be taught in primary schools as they are boring and just add to the burden on primary school students. They believe that science and technology should be there in primary schools. I agree that arts subjects should be axed from the primary school curricula. A number of arguments surround my opinion.

To begin with, it has to be made clear that removing history and geography from the primary school syllabus does not mean these subjects are less important. These subjects are as important as science and technology. The main concern is to lessen some burden off the primary school children. These subjects must be incorporated in middle and high school curricula. At the primary school level, children need to be introduced to science and technology because today's children belong to an era of science and technology.

Secondly, if teachers have to teach fewer subjects, they will be able to do so in greater depth. If there is curriculum overload, then all subjects will be taught superficially and the foundation of the child will not be strong. If all subjects are taught, then children usually resort to rote learning which is definitely inferior to meaningful learning. What is more, science and technology are more interesting than history and geography, so in early years, children will develop interest in studying which will continue into later years.

Finally, schools should give priority to science and technology skills, with a greater focus on children's health, wellbeing and personal development. What is generally seen is that the weight of the primary school student's bag is heavier than the weight of the student himself. So the child is physically unhealthy and cannot bloom properly. Their individuality is snubbed. At the primary stage the child should be engaged in joyfully exploring the world around and harmonizing with it. The objectives at this stage are to nurture the curiosity of the child about the world and not to overburden him.

To conclude, the demands of society on primary schools have risen and continue to rise but if we are to establish a 'world class' high quality curriculum, we must face the reality of prescribing less so that teachers can teachbetter and children can learn better. Science and technology must be started early and the arts subjects can be started after primary school years.

Plan followed
Intro: Agree. Arts subjects should be axed from the primary school curricula
Para 1: main concern is to lessen some burden off the primary school children
Para 2: if teachers have to teach less, they would be able to do so in greater depth
Para 3: greater focus on children's health, well-being and personal development
Conclusion: reiterate opinion

47. Some people think that secondary school students should study academic subjects (such as history and physics), while others believe they should study practical subjects (such as car machinery and cookery). Discuss both views and give your own opinion.

Some individuals are of the opinion that secondary school curricula should have academic subjects such as history and physics where as others opine that students should study practical subjects like car machinery and cookery. This essay shall look at both arguments before forming a conclusion.

Those who wish academic subjects in the school syllabus say that academic subjects have withstood the test of time. They represent the accumulated wisdom of our ancestors down through the ages, and equip us with the knowledge and confidence to make sound judgments about any problem, which may crop up. Secondly, they say that it is the duty of parents, not teachers, to prepare their children to deal with the practical affairs of life. The home, not the classroom, is the ideal place to learn about cookery and car machinery. Finally, schooldays devoted solely to instruction of practical matters would be dull indeed. Lessons in diverse subjects such as literature, science, geography and mathematics add flavor to school life.

Those in favour of practical subjects such as car machinery and cookery opine that the subjects taught in schools tend to be too academic, and contribute little to preparing a young person for the real-life tasks he or she will have to perform after graduation. They say that academic subjects are rooted in the past, and are not useful for solving modern problems.

On balance, I believe that we need to provide young people the best possible chance of doing well at school. In traditional curriculum there should be a wide variety of subjects with a mix of academic and non-academic subjects. In this way a young person grows up with a well-rounded education. Car machinery, however, is not needed at school level. Non-academic subjects should include sports, cooking and music. I believe this is the best form of education. A young person should also learn things other than academic subjects.

To conclude, secondary school curriculum with only academic or only practical subjects is not good. It should be a combination of both for the holistic development of the student.

Plan followed

Intro: Discuss essay intro
Para 1: Why some people are in favour of purely academic subjects
Para 2: Why some people are in favour of practical subjects
Para 3: Own view
Conclusion

48.Students in schools should learn practical skills like car maintenance and managing a bank account in addition to academic subjects. Do you agree or disagree?

It is true that children learn academic subjects at school, but not many practical skills. However, I disagree that schools should teach skills like bank account management and car maintenance.

To begin with, there is a lot of importance of academic subjects like mathematics, science, languages etc. Academic subjects have withstood the test of time. They represent the accumulated wisdom of our ancestors down through the ages, and equip us with the knowledge and confidence to make sound judgments about any problems which may crop up. We live in a knowledge-based economy where independent thinking and problem solving are the most important skills. With timetables already full, schools do not have time to teach children anything else.

There are also non-academic subjects such as sports and music, which are taught in schools. These are very important along with the academic subjects. They bring out the hidden talent and stimulate the creative ability of students. These subjects are as important as academic subjects as they act as stress-busters and give the students much-needed relaxation.

On the other hand, bank account management is a 'life skill' that anyone can learn by simply opening a bank account. Most adults have no problem managing their finances without being taught accounting lessons at school. Other skills like car maintenance are not really necessary. Most people take their cars to a qualified mechanic. Therefore, these practical skills do not need to be added to the school curricula.

To conclude, schools are already doing a good job teaching the traditional academic subjects along with the non-academic subjects. If they start to teach practical skills, the study of important academic subjects will suffer.

Plan followed

Intro: disagree

Para 1: Importance of academic subjects

Para 2: Importance of non-academic subjects such as music and sports

Para 3: Why practical skills such as car maintenance and opening a bank account not needed.

Conclusion

49.Some say that secondary schools should spend less time on traditional subjects such as history and should spend more time on teaching communication skills and business courses. To what extent do you agree or disagree with it?

At the secondary education level, students are taught a variety of subjects that are supposed to help and guide them in their future career and personal choices. It is irrefutable that in today's global era communication skills and business courses are very important. However, I disagree that subjects such as history should be given lesser importance than these subjects in the secondary school curricula. A number of arguments surround my opinion.

On the one hand, there is no doubt that today we belong to a global era, in which there is cut-throat competition in every field. To be successful, the most important skills needed today are communication skills. The study of business courses is also invaluable today. Eventually, all students will encounter the world of business, whether they work in urban or rural areas. They must be prepared to engage in business activities with confidence and competence. Young people need to understand how business functions, the role it plays in our society, the opportunities it generates, the skills it requires, and the impact it can have on their own lives and on society, today and in the future.

On the other hand, the field of history is important for many educational, as well as practical, reasons. Through historical study, one can pursue a career in a wide array of fields. A student of history can go on to law school or delve into politics, because he will possess knowledge that will help him make invaluable choices that affect society. Although the practical side of it may not be noticeable to the student, it is true that every subject deals with history, and every inanimate object and every enjoyable pastime has a history behind it. For example, a student of medicine can't become a doctor without studying the history behind the profession, and most legends of Hollywood have studied the history of acting and film before obtaining their stardom in this field.

Regardless of whether or not a 17-year old will ever take another history course outside of high school, teaching history to that student will help him or her acquire the skills necessary to continue with education at the college level. History will also make that student a better prepared citizen in society, capable of making informed choices about current issues and being able to follow up on events by using basic research techniques.

To conclude, although business and communication skills are important subjects in today's scenario, it is also important for people to have a basic understanding of what has driven, and what drives, the world in which we live in. That is perhaps why it has been rightly said that, "If you don't know history, then you don't know anything."

Plan followed

Intro: disagree that subjects such as history should be given lesser importance
Para 1: Importance of the study of business and communication skills
Para 2: Importance of the study of history
Para 3: More importance   Conclusion: Reiterate your opinion

50. Some think the subject of music is not necessary in primary school, and other practical subjects like science should replace it. What is your opinion?

I disagree with the notion that music as a subject is not essential in elementary school and should be replaced by other practical subjects such as math and science. I firmly believe that music is a more potent instrument than any other for education and it is even more important than other subjects in the early years of life. Music uses both sides of the brain as a result of which the child's brain develops academically, emotionally, physically and spiritually.

The most important advantage of music in primary classes is that music trains the brain for higher forms of thinking. It was seen in a research that second graders who were given music lessons scored 27% higher in math than children who received no music lessons. This means that children who learn music in schools are better problem-solvers and are better at analysis and overall critical thinking. Because studying or playing music uses the same part of the brain that is used in mathematical thinking, music education can help promote better math students. Additionally, exposing children to music in the early and primary years increases listening and concentration skills also.

Moreover, music is an art form. We are emotional beings and every child requires an artistic outlet. Music may be the child's vehicle of expression. Music helps the child to open up and improve his communication skills. It helps him to express his ideas and thoughts in a better manner. What is more, music education can open doors for children who can later adopt it as a hobby or even profession in later years. Young children can experience camaraderie and teamwork by participating in music activities done in groups. Involvement in a music group, chorus or band gives the young child a sense of importance and belonging.

Those against promoting music in primary schools say that children are already overburdened with so many subjects. They feel that children of today belong to an era of cut-throat competition and they should be well versed with practical subjects, which they will need for a successful career in later years. They opine that those interested in music may take it as an optional subject in later years, but primary school children need not learn music. However, their reasoning does not hold much water.

To sum up, music is very important for children especially those in primary schools because it helps the brain develop fast and is needed for the holistic development of children.

Plan followed

Intro: Disagree

Para 1: importance of music

Para 2: More importance of music

Para 3: opponents view

Conclusion: reiterate opinion

51.Schools should teach children good behavior and introduce ideas of 'right' and 'wrong'. It should not only be left to parents. To what extent do you agree or disagree?

Families and schools are the two institutions, which impart moral education and virtuous qualities in children. I disagree that it is solely the onus of the schools to teach such things to children. I believe it should be a joint responsibility of both, schools as well as parents.

It is understandable why parents should be responsible for inculcating good habits in children. They are responsible for bringing their children into the world and it is their responsibility to teach them social values. First of all, they can act as role models and children are their copycats. Secondly, as children spend a huge amount of time with parents, they get more time to build up good behavioral patterns in children.

On the other hand, schools can play a pivotal role to mould a child's character. To begin with, peer group interaction at schools makes a child highly social and he learns a lot of what is right or wrong from his fellow students. Tenderhearted children do not accept wrongdoings. Furthermore, many competitions held at school teach a child to accept defeat and to appreciate success, which makes him a well-behaved person later on. Finally, teachers are observed very intently by the students and inadvertently children learn a lot of social values from them. Teachers can also admonish children for wrong doings and pat their back for good gestures.

I believe that children are our future and they have to be groomed to be well behaved and respectable citizens of tomorrow. Therefore, both parents and schools should play their role in shaping their behaviour and teach them good manners and etiquettes.

To sum up, schools are the temples of learning and this learning should not be restricted to only academic learning. Social learning is as important as academic learning.

Plan followed
Intro: Disagree
Para 1: Role of parents
Para 2: Role of schools
Para 3: Own view
Conclusion: reiterate opinion

52.Some people think young people are suitable for learning foreign languages. Some people think adults are more suitable. Discuss both and give your opinion.

Learning a new language is an activity which is very useful and takes a considerable amount of time. Some people opine that children learn a foreign language quicker than adults. Others believe that adults are better equipped to learn a new language. This essay shall look into both sides of the argument before forming an opinion.

There is no doubt that a young mind readily absorbs new information. Child psychologists often mention that the most formative years of learning happen in the first few years of life. Therefore, what children are exposed to is very often retained and remembered. In this way, a child is in a good position to learn new information associated with a new language. What is more, children also don't have any hesitations while learning; they are not afraid that others will laugh at them if they speak wrongly.

However, there are a number of significant advantages for the adult language learner. Firstly, the adult learner has his or her first language to compare with the new language. In this way, new terms or concepts are very quickly understood by comparing them with concepts or ideas that are already known.

In addition, adults often have a strong motivation to learn a new language. When learning a language is connected to an employment opportunity, the learner is typically very focused and motivated. Also, because most adult learners are educated, they are usually aware of what has worked best in their learning experience and therefore can approach the new language with more mature and realistic expectations.

To conclude, in learning a new language, adults and children, both are good, but adults definitely have an edge

---

Plan followed

Intro: This essay shall look into both sides of the argument before forming an opinion
Para1: why young learn better
Para 2: why adults learn better
Para 3: why adults learn better
Conclusion: adults are better at learning

53. An increasing number of people decide to learn a foreign language. What is the most difficult part when learning a foreign language? How can the learner overcome these difficulties?

If you talk to a man in a language he understands, that goes to his head. If you talk to him in his language, that goes to his heart.   (Nelson Mandela)

In this era of globalization, it is often beneficial to be bilingual or multilingual. Learning a foreign language may be a piece of cake for some while others may take years to master it. There are many components of language learning. This essay shall outline the toughest part of learning a foreign language and also suggest some solutions to overcome these problems.

One of the challenges in learning a foreign language is phonological difference. No language makes use of all the many sounds the human speech organs can produce, and no two languages use exactly the same set. In other words, the student should be aware of the differences in the system of sounds between the mother tongue and the new language. There are some sounds that do exist in one language but not in the other language. For instance, Hindi has approximately half as many vowels and twice as many consonants than English. This leads to several problems of pronunciation.

Moreover, vocabulary, grammar and the sentence structure of the new language have to be learnt which may be a daunting task for many. For example, the standard word order in Hindi is Subject-Object-Verb as against Subject-Verb-Object in English. Thus it can be very difficult for a person to obey the grammar rules and the sentence structure of the new language every time. What is more, while learning a foreign language one needs a partner with whom to practice. This could be the most difficult part in learning a foreign language.

However, if a person is determined he can overcome all these hurdles and become proficient in learning the new language. One should join a language course if available in the propinquity of one's residence or join an online course. Learning a new language is an ongoing process and one should be willing to give it time every single day. Practice is the key to success. Reading newspapers in that language would also be useful. Adding a few new words to one's vocabulary would definitely help and last but not least, one should listen to the native speakers as often as possible. This can be done by watching movies in that particular language. If a person can afford the time and money, he should stay for some time in the country where that language is spoken to learn the language better.

To conclude, learning a foreign language is a challenge. Learning accurate pronunciation is the most difficult task. But, all these difficulties can be overcome with determination and practice.

Plan followed

Intro: Problem and solution intro

Para 1: Problems   Para 2: more problems

Para 3: Solutions   Conclusion:

54.In some countries students are required to learn a foreign language, but in other countries it is not necessary to do so. Discuss the benefits of each case and give your own opinion.

In some countries, more than one language is compulsory. Sometimes pupils have to start learning a language at primary school. Foreign languages are less often compulsory in English-speaking countries. This is probably because English is widely understood worldwide. This essay shall delve into the advantages of having to study a foreign language as well as the advantages of no such compulsion.

Foreign languages are important for the economy. The more languages one can speak the more places one can work in. Employers value people who are able to speak more than one language. Learning a language will therefore help students get good jobs when they are older. It will also increase their understanding of other cultures. Moreover, foreign language skills help companies do business with other countries. It is especially important that children whose native language is not widely spoken (e.g. Hindi, Danish) learn other languages. It is also important for English-speakers to learn foreign languages, since not everyone speaks English. What is more, it is polite to be able to speak some of another person's language. Governments should try to promote economic growth. Since languages are important for the economy, governments should make all young people learn them.

On the other hand, there are obvious advantages of not forcing a foreign language on students. To begin with, many young people are hardly able to do simple sums or read and write in their own language. Therefore, more time can be spent on these basic skills, not foreign languages. Cultural understanding can be gained by the study of other subjects such as History and Geography. Foreign language should be an optional subject and not obligatory. Young people have to learn to make choices. If they do not realize the benefits of learning languages, these benefits should be explained to them. If pupils choose to study a language, they are more likely to be keen and interested than if it is something they are forced to do. In any case, many adults do successfully learn new languages through evening classes or distance-learning courses if they feel the need to learn one later on in life.

On balance, there are more advantages of being bilingual or multilingual than being monolingual. In India English is taught as a second language right from primary school. That is why Indian economy has picked up very fast as many MNCs have opened their offices here. Even countries like Canada have begun to realize the importance of a second language and French or Punjabi is taught in many areas as a second language. It has also been proved by researches that bilingual students do better in other subjects too.

Summing up, although there are advantages of having a mandatory foreign language and not having any such obligation, it is better to study a foreign language than not study one.

Plan followed

Intro: Discuss essay intro
Para 1: Advantages of a compulsory foreign language
Para 2: advantages of not forcing a foreign language on students
Para 3: On balance
Conclusion: opinion

55. Nowadays it is possible to use computers and mobile phones for automatic language translation, and there is no need for human translators and interpreters. Do you agree or disagree with this statement?

Advancements in technology have given us many benefits and the translation of languages is an important use of this technology. It may be thought that since we have machine translators now, which can translate one language to another, there is no need to have human interpreters and translators. I completely disagree with this notion and a number of arguments support my perspective, which I will elaborate on in the forthcoming paragraphs.

To begin with, translating a language is not a simple process. It is rather complex, involving the structure, meaning, nuances, culture, tone of the expression and many more such details need to be kept in mind. The machine translation is mostly direct word-to-word translation and usually doesn't take into account the grammatical differences in different languages, leading to errors in syntax. So human interpretation cannot be undermined as people can gauge the underlying tone or emotion of the text, change the structure depending on the language and take care of the subtleties of the language. For instance, the meaning of one word can be changed in terms of the context it is used in.

Another reason why human interpreters are better than automatic machine translators is because a language is directly related to the culture it is spoken in. A machine translation cannot be designed to include this aspect. The machines cannot capture these nuances and thus, the machine-translated text will be literal and the actual message of the expression will be lost. For instance, there are idioms and proverbs in every language that have an underlying message and do not have a direct translation.

Admittedly, in this fast paced contemporary world, we need to get our work done quickly and machine translators are quick and mostly available for free. We can easily look for information about any topic and if it is available in a different language, it can be quickly translated and understood. The 'Google translate' tool is a very good example for this use. Even though there might be some sentence structure errors, we can mostly use such translators for personal use or internal use in offices. However, when sending official emails, formal letters, writing assignments, etc. it is best to have a professional human translator, so that the exact message can be conveyed, keeping in mind the differences in the culture of the audience.

To sum up, it can be reiterated that even though technology has revolutionized and eased our work, however, in areas like language translation, machines can't surpass human ingenuity.

Plan followed

Intro:

Para 1: How human translators have an edge over machine translation

Para 2: More advantages of human translators

Para 3: Advantages of machine translation

Conclusion

56.Some languages spoken by very few people are losing their importance and may become extinct completely. Is it a good or a bad development? What are the reasons for this?

Today, we do not belong to a big planet called Earth. We are part of a global village and there is more interaction among people of different parts of the globe than ever before. Therefore, for easing communication, only those languages are surviving which are spoken by more number of people. This essay intends to analyze the reasons behind this phenomenon. This is both – a negative as well as a positive development.

On the positive side, the increasing use of some languages is easing communication among people. For example, English is now spoken in more than 86 countries of the world and French in around 33 countries. In fact, English has become the lingua franca in many parts of the world. Because of this people do not face difficulty when they travel from one country to the other. What is more, if people speak the same language then they also find it easy to do business with each other. Global trade is based on good communication. Businesses cannot flourish if for every small communication an interpreter is required.

Nowadays, we belong to a 24/7 society. Many multinational companies have opened offices in different parts of the world. These MNCs provide jobs to millions of people worldwide. Naturally, a person who knows their language is better placed in these companies. The pay package is also better and chances to work abroad also go up. In a way the widespread use of a few languages also helps to decrease the gap between the rich and the poor.

On the other hand, the decline in use of some languages is also something to be concerned about. It is a well-known fact that language and culture are inter-related. If languages die out then culture also fades away. Moreover, we all enjoy life on this planet because of its diversity. If diversity decreases, then boredom sets in and the earth becomes a dull and boring place to live in.

To conclude, it could be said that, the increase in use of a few languages and the decline of others is both a positive as well as a negative development. This situation is an inevitable sequel of globalization. If the governments take steps to protect the endangered languages, then the negative effects can be minimized.

Plan followed

Intro: It is both – a positive as well as a negative development

Para 1 – Advantages of the increasing use of a few languages

Para 2 – More advantages

Para 3 – Disadvantages

Conclusion: restate your opinion

57.Schools have a limited amount of money to spend. Some people suggest that it should be spent on good teachers, while others say it should be used for buying equipment like computers. Discuss both views and give your own opinion.

In situations where schools are facing crunch situations, they have an option either to spend on good teachers or on technology such as computers. This essay intends to look into both choices. However, I firmly believe that there are no technology shortcuts to good education, and even with limited resources, blended learning is the answer.

Spending on hiring the best teachers is better because children require the ongoing guidance and encouragement to persevere in the school years. Caring supervision from human teachers is the only known way of generating motivation for the hours of a school day. While computers appear to engage students, the engagement is usually fleeting and children are soon distracted. No technology can provide the tailored attention for students that dedicated teachers can, and thus, attempts to use technology as a stand-in for capable teachers are bound to fail.

There are some technology enthusiasts who claim that it is advantageous to spend on computers. They argue that computers are becoming better at providing customized direct instruction and in assessing student's knowledge. They also say that computers are better at repetitive tasks like vocabulary drills. Teachers find these jobs very monotonous. Therefore, they opine that computers are better.

I believe that even though the resources of schools are limited, the focus should be on blended learning. Both teachers and technology are important. Resources should be equally spent on both. Blended learning allows much of the work of basic instruction to be done by computers so that teachers can keep students focused on studies and assess them from time to time. Blended learning does not eliminate teachers, but instead eliminates some of the job functions that teachers find most onerous. Technology will not improve our education system if we marginalize or eliminate teachers. Likewise, our education system will not meet modern needs until we incorporate technology.

To sum up, primary and secondary schools that are underperforming or limited in resources, should allocate resources equally on both in their efforts to improve their education standards. We should focus on finding ways to let technology do what it does best so that we can allow teachers to do what they do best.

Plan followed

Intro: Discuss essay with opinion

Para 1: Why teachers   Para 2: Why computers

Para 3: Why spend equally on both   Conclusion

58. Some people think that schools are more effective if students are allowed to participate in running the school. State whether you agree or disagree. Give reasons for your answer using personal experiences or other examples.

Today, education is student-centered and there are many sources from where students can get information. Students of the contemporary world know what and how they want to learn. Therefore, I agree with the given statement that schools can run more effectively, if students have a say in their working. In the following paragraphs, I intend to discuss the ways in which students can be involved and the benefits of such methods.

To begin with, student involvement can help school administration in maintaining discipline in schools. Student participation in school administration through student councils gives them a voice and makes them feel important. It has been seen in many places, where such practices have been implemented, that violence and other harmful behaviours have reduced, both among teachers and students. Teachers have become more respectful and responsive to student rights. Such involvement helps the school management hold students accountable for their actions, which encourages transparency and responsiveness.

Secondly, student involvement can improve the overall results of the school. Student participation in teaching can result in better learning for the students. When students teach other students, they start actively thinking about the topics. They become active drivers of learning and do not just remain passive recipients of learning. For example, my biology teacher in class 10 used to identify some good students and give them small groups of 4-5 students to discuss what had been taught in class and also discuss some new topics. We used to enjoy those group sessions and our concepts became very clear. As a result, the biology result was always cent percent.

Furthermore, when students are given a voice in the school operations, such as by making them evaluate teachers, the administrators can retain better teachers and shunt out the bad ones, which would definitely improve the schools' overall performance. Finally, it is well known that the schools' main role is in making students into better citizens for the future. Students who are involved in school administration become better citizens later on. Students, who participate in student councils, learn about the democratic process, civic responsibility, leadership, problem solving and teamwork. All these traits make them better citizens.

To sum up, I reiterate that students have a big role in effective running of schools, and their involvement should become the norm in modern schools.

Plan followed:
Intro: Agree
Para 1: It would help in maintaining discipline   Para 2: It would help in overall results
Para 3: It would help in hiring the best faculty and make better citizens for the future
Conclusion: Reiterate opinion

59. Road transport is taking over rail services. Discuss the positive and negative effects of this development. Is this situation true for your country?

Transport refers to the activity that facilitates movements of goods and individuals from one place to another. So, it removes the distance barrier. Roadways and railways are the two means of land transport. It is true that in many countries road transport is becoming more popular. It is both a negative as well as a positive development which I shall discuss in this essay.

There are many advantages of road transport over rail transport. To begin with, it is a relatively cheaper mode of transport than rail transport. Secondly, perishable goods can be transported at a faster speed by road carriers over a short distance. Moreover, it provides door-to-door service. So, loading and unloading is possible at any destination. Finally, it is the only mode of transport in hilly areas, which are not connected by other modes of transport.

On the downside, road transport has its limitations, which are indirectly the plus points of rail transport. Firstly, due to limited carrying capacity, road transport is not economical for long distances. Secondly, road transport is affected by adverse weather conditions like floods, rains, landslides etc. On the other hand rail transport is hardly affected by such situations. Finally, road transport leads to too much congestion on roads, which in turn may cause accidents and increase pollution.

In India, over the years, more and more inland freight traffic has been shifting from rail to road. In 1951, 88% of the country's freight was moving on rail and 10% on road. But today, about 60% of the freight moves on road and 38% on rail.

To conclude, road transport definitely has an edge over rail transport. That is why it is becoming more popular. This situation has both pros and cons which I have explained in the above paragraphs.

Plan followed

Intro: a balanced approach as it is a discuss essay.

Para 1: Advantages of road over rail

Para 2: Disadvantages of road transport / advantages of rail transport

Para 3: Situation in India – road transport is gaining popularity

Conclusion: Road transport has both advantages and disadvantages.

60.More and more people use private cars instead of taking public transport. What are the reasons for this trend? How can the government encourage people to take public transport?

Someone has rightly said that – "The car has become an article of dress without which we feel uncertain, unclad, and incomplete". It is irrefutable that many individuals are using their own cars instead of travelling by buses and trains. In this essay, I shall discuss the reasons for this phenomenon and also suggest ways by which the government can motivate people to use public transport.

There are many reasons for the increasing popularity of cars. The first and foremost reason is that the car is the most convenient mode of transport. It takes you from destination to destination and you do not have to waste time to go to the bus stand or railway station to wait for public transport, which runs at specific times. Secondly, families can go out together and enjoy their outings more. What is more, you can halt anywhere you need for some refreshments. The car is also a blessing in times of emergencies when a sick family member has to be rushed to the hospital. Finally, because of the increased competition among the automobile companies, cars have become affordable by the vast majority of people. For example, the basic model of Maruti 800 and the Nano by Tata Company are called the poor man's cars.

This increased number of cars on the roads is causing many problems such as traffic congestion and pollution. To reduce these problems, the government can encourage people to use public transport. This can be done in many ways. Firstly, the comfort of the public transport could be made better. Secondly, the fares could be reduced and the frequency of public transport increased. Definitely, if all these improvements are made in buses and trains, then people would prefer them over cars in many situations.

Another way to stimulate public transport use is to make private car use more expensive and inconvenient. The introduction of tolls along urban motorways has been successfully employed in many cities. Other such measures such as high parking rates in urban areas couldalso help a lot. Faced with high costs or no place to park, people would perhaps be more willing to abandon their cars in favour of buses or trains. Construction of metro rail networks has also resulted in taking a substantial number of cars off the roads.

To conclude, it can be said that there is no doubt that the private vehicle is gaining a lot of popularity but if the government takes some steps to encourage public transport then definitely the use of cars can reduce substantially.

Plan followed:
Intro: write the intro suitably to answer the question
Para 1: Why people are using cars more
Para 2: How government can encourage people to use public transport
Para 3 More measures
Conclusion:

61.Some people say that cars should be banned from the centers of cities. Do you agree or disagree?

Someone has rightly said that – "The car has become an article of dress without which we feel uncertain, unclad, and incomplete". The increased use of cars has created many problems. Therefore, I strongly believe that cars should not be allowed in city centres. A number of arguments surround my opinion.

The most important reason is pollution from car exhausts, which damages people's health causing respiratory diseases such as asthma and bronchitis. At the same time, traffic fumes attack the stonework of historic monuments and buildings, while the vibrations from passing vehicles damage their foundations. This, for instance, has happened to the Taj Mahal in Agra because of which private vehicles are not allowed in the vicinity of the Taj.

A second reason why I am in favour of cars being banned is in order to reduce the noise pollution from traffic, which forces people to keep their windows permanently closed and may cause psychological problems including stress and depression among people living in busy streets.

A further reason is that most cities were not designed for motor traffic. A good example of this is the old part of Ludhiana city in Punjab, which has narrow streets and few facilities for parking. As a result, traffic moves at a snail's pace and there are frequent traffic jams. Beautiful buildings are spoilt by always having cars parked in front of them and pretty streets become unpleasant due to permanent traffic congestion and exhaust fumes.

Finally, I am sure that if cars were banned, people would find other more pleasant ways to move around cities. For example, they would walk or use bicycles as these would once more become safe and enjoyable activities within the city. This in turn would bring about a general improvement in people's health.

In conclusion, therefore, I strongly support the idea that traffic should be banned from city centres, as this would enable people to rediscover cities as pleasant and healthy places to live.

Plan followed
Intro: agree
Para 1: First reason
Para 2: Second reason
Para 3: Final reason
Conclusion: Reiterate opinion

62. Airline companies in many countries have reduced the cost of tickets. Discuss whether this is a positive or negative development. Give some examples based on your own experience.

In today's world, we are now in a position to enjoy cheaper air flights than in the past. It is both – a positive as well as negative development. It is advantageous in terms of freedom and the opportunities to learn from other countries. It is detrimental in terms of the pollution it creates.

Cheap air flights can be beneficial in many ways. One of them is the opportunity to go overseas. Earlier, only the affluent could afford it, but now it is within the pocket of the ordinary man. Some of the discounted tickets are fairly cheap and flying abroad is no longer a dream for many. Moreover, small businesses have prospered because of the ease of travel because of these flights.

In addition to this, cheap air flights enable intercultural exchanges between countries. The advent of cheap air-fare makes it possible for people the world over to travel regularly, regardless of the purpose of the trip. Therefore, people have opportunities to learn from different cultures and have a better understanding of countries they were unfamiliar with. This, in turn, enhances cultural communications between countries.

On the other hand, it is generally known that airplanesconsume vast amounts of fuel and the gas emission generated by an airplane is enormous. Therefore, the environmental impacts would only get worse in the long run. Besides, cheap air tickets have stringent terms and conditions attached. One of them is that changing the date and time of travel is very expensive once the ticket is purchased. As a result, people find it inconvenient and frustrating if they have to reschedule their travel due to an emergency.

To conclude, cheap air fares have both pros and cons. I am convinced that giving people the freedom to travel is essential, but at the same time people should be made aware of avoiding un-necessary travel.

Plan followed

Intro: Discuss essay intro

Para 1: Advantages

Para 2: more benefits

Para 3: Disadvantages

Conclusion:

63.These days many countries face excessive traffic. Describe the situation in your country? Describe some possible ways to overcome traffic congestion.

It is irrefutable that the increasing traffic has become a grave problem worldwide. My own country, India, is no exception. This essay intends to suggest measures, which can be taken to ameliorate the situation.

The rising traffic is a global problem. India too is facing a boom in the number of cars on the roads. With developing economy, people's buying capacity has risen and so everyone is having his/her own vehicle. On top of that, the road system is not so good, and traffic jams and gridlocks have become very common. Although the government is expanding the roads and constructing more motorways, the situation is not improving because the number of private vehicles is also rising at an unprecedented rate.

One effective method to reduce traffic congestion is using public transportation. Since most car trips are by a single person driving alone, a bus substituted for driving can take 20, 30 or more cars off the road while a train has the potential to reduce congestion by hundreds of cars. A rail line can carry substantially more passengers using less physical space than a highway. Public transportation not only reduces congestion on the roads, but also helps eliminate the necessity of building additional roads and benefits those who continue to travel by automobile, whether by choice or necessity.

Additionally, the government could levy toll tax and increase the price of fuel to discourage people from using their own cars. Media could be used to make people aware about simple measures like car-pooling. For instance if five people from one block of flats have to go to the same office, they could each take out their car for one day a week. Technology is also enabling car-pooling. One of the aggregators, OLA, has an option where the customer can choose to share his ride with other customers to his destination and pay lesser. In Houston, Texas, there are special HOV (High Occupancy Vehicles) lanes for those vehicles, which have three or more people. Cars move faster on these lanes because of fewer cars on these lanes. This is a step by the authorities to encourage car-pooling.

To conclude, building more roads is not the solution for traffic congestion. It is essential that people use public transport and do car-pooling to decrease the traffic on roads.

Plan followed

Intro:

Para 1: Measures to address the problem

Para 2: Other measures

Para 3: steps at individual level

Conclusion:

64.In many countries, there are an increasing number of private cars. What are the advantages and disadvantages of this trend?

Someone has rightly said that – "The car has become an article of dress without which we feel uncertain, unclad, and incomplete". It is irrefutable that nowadays, the number of cars has increased at an unprecedented rate. This situation has both - advantages as well as disadvantages.

There are many advantages of the car. The most important advantage is that it has given people freedom of movement. The ease of transportation which a car brings is more than any other form of transportation. For instance, you can go from destination to destination and no time is wasted waiting for the bus or train. Therefore, time and distance are not a barrier any more. What is more, families can go out together. This becomes especially helpful when there are elderly or disabledor sick members in the family.

Furthermore, the automobile industry provides jobs to millions of workers. Filling stations, restaurants, and other businesses that serve automobile travelers are of major importance to a country's economy. In addition, many developing nations have begun making automobiles to boost their economy. That is why India has promoted many automobile manufacturing industries such as Maruti, Tata and Mahindra. Further, global brands such as Ford, Volkswagen, Hyundai etc. have their manufacturing hubs in India providing jobs to thousands of workers.

On the other hand the disadvantages of the car cannot be overlooked. The increase in pollution, traffic jams and accidents are the natural sequel to the burgeoning population of cars. Moreover, our overdependence on cars can lead to decrease in healthy practices such as walking and cycling, leading to a number of diseases such as obesity.

On balance, the advantages to people's lives and the economic impact created by the car definitely outweigh the disadvantages. However, we must know when and how-much to use the car so that we can minimize the demerits to some extent

---

Plan followed

Intro: Balanced intro as it is a discuss essay

Para 1: Advantages of car

Para 2: More advantages

Para 3: Disadvantages

Conclusion: Advantages more than disadvantages

65.Some people think that there will be decrease in international travel in future. Do you think the less amount of international travel is a positive or a negative development?

Because of economic reasons in some areas, international travel is becoming less common. I believe that it is largely a negative development. International travel has more positive than negative effects.

International travel has many benefits, the most important being related to the upliftment of the local economy due to tourism. Incoming tourists spend money for their stay in hotels, food and drinks in restaurants, coffee shops and bars, local travel on cabs; they alsomake use of tourist guides. All this generates gainful employment for the local populace. Further, tourists always buy locally made handicrafts as souvenirs, which keeps alive the traditional arts and crafts.

A third reason is that in order for tourists to be able to visit remote areas, roads, airports and hotels have to be built and local people also benefit by being able to use these new facilities. Construction of these facilities provides employment to a large number of people. Furthermore, when communications improve, it becomes possible for other industries to move into the area, bringing with them more employment opportunities and increased prosperity. A final reason why I am in favour of tourism is that visitors from outside bring fresh ideas and different ways of doing things to the local community. Consequently, local people may learn from tourists. Likewise, visitors learn about the local people and culture, and return home with a deeper understanding of the host country.

On the other hand, that there are some problems associated with international travel. Firstly, there is the increasing crime rate. Some locals see tourists as easy prey because, not only are they in unfamiliar territory and therefore less able to take care of themselves, but also they carry visible items of wealth, such as cameras and jewellery which can be disposed of quickly for a profit. Another major problem is health. With greater mobility comes greater danger of spreading contagious diseases around the world. Also to be considered is the natural environment, which can be seriously threatened by too many visitors. Australia's Great Barrier Reef, for example, is in danger of being destroyed by tourists and there are plans to restrict visitors to some of the more delicate coral reefs.

To conclude, international travel has both advantages and disadvantages. However, the advantages outweigh the disadvantages. Therefore if international travel decreases, it is largely a negative development.

Plan followed

Intro: it is largely a negative development   Para 1: advantages of international travel
Para 2: more advantages   Para 3: Disadvantages
Conclusion:

66. Young people say that traveling to different countries benefits them and the society. Do you agree or disagree? Give your opinion.

Youth travel is one of the fastest growing and most dynamic markets of the global tourism sector. Some individuals believe that travelling abroad is beneficial for the youth where as others opine thatit is wastage of time and money. This essay shall discuss both views before forming an opinion.

Some people consider it a waste of time and money because of several reasons. They believe that in today's era of cut-throat competition, young people should concentrate on their studies and careers. They do not earn yet and if they travel at a young age they are wasting their time as well as their parent's hard-earned money. What is more, they are not mature enough and may face problems while travelling such as food and language problems. Finally, they believe that today, the satellite TV and the internet has brought the whole world into their bedroom, so they should be doing other useful work instead of travelling.

On the other hand, travelling in young age has enormous benefits. It provides tremendous opportunities for fun, adventure and discovery. When young people visit places in other countries, they gain a better understanding of the people living there. They learn their cultures, history and background. They discover the similarities and differences. It is interesting to learn from people with diverse backgrounds.

Furthermore, research suggests that traveling overseas at a young age leads to successful careers. It helps them decide what they want in life. Traveling when young can be a great platform to diversify one's experience early in life and to discover one's purpose in life. Each country, each city, even each restaurant a person visits is an opportunity to experience something different. It is better to realize one's true desires and potential early in life than when it is too late.

To conclude, it can be said that although travelling at a young age involves time and money it is worthwhile and has a lot of benefits for the youth. So if the young people get the chance to broaden their horizons and go and experience new places it may make a world of difference to them.

Plan followed

Intro: Discuss essay intro

Para 1: Why some people say it is a waste of time and money

Para 2: Why it is useful

Para 3:

Conclusion:

67.Some people believe that travelling alone really benefits in learning a country's culture and experience, while others believe it is better to travel with someone you know. Discuss both these views and share your opinion.

Nowadays there is a significant increase in global tourism. While some people argue that solo travel is good for learning the host country's culture and enriching your experience, many others believe that travelling with partners is better. This essay intends to discuss both perspectives. I side with the latter view.

On the one hand, some people believe that travelling alone can enable a person to learn different customs and gain more experience. This is because you are alone in an alien environment and all your focus is on absorbing your surroundings and noticing the people around you. For instance, you will discover how the local residents talk, dress and even walk. If you need any help, you will have to ask the natives of that place and by interacting with them you will be able to understand their nature also. If you are with your friends or family, you will be engrossed among them and may miss a lot of these observations. Thus, it is clear that why some people hold this point of view.

On the other hand, many argue that it is better to travel with friends as this can have many benefits. First of all, it would substantially lower the cost of travelling. To illustrate, you will share the cost of the hotel and food and at times you may get discounts for certain group activities. Thus, you can enjoy the journey with your friends and save money.

Furthermore, when you are with someone you know, you feel secure. After all, you are in unknown surroundings and there is always security in numbers. You can also learn the country's culture when you are with friends. You can discuss your observations with those of your fellow travelers and you may get to see things from a different perspective. After analyzing these points of view, it is easy to see why many support this claim.

In conclusion, travelling alone is good to understand the local culture and experience, but definitely travelling with friends or family has an edge over travelling alone as you lower your cost of travelling, feel secure and share your experiences.

Plan followed:

Intro: Discuss essay intro
Para 1: Advantages of travelling alone
Para 2: Advantages of travelling with friends
Para 3: More advantages of travelling with friends
Conclusion:

68.Many people agree that free public transportation should be available in most major cities. What are the advantages and disadvantages of this idea?

Some people opine that the finest solution to urban traffic congestion is to provide free public transport round-the-clock. This essay intends to analyze the pros and cons of this approach.

Undoubtedly many people, especially daily commuters, would benefit from free public transport. But such a service would be a big burden on the governments, as it would require a lot of funds to maintain such free services. Moreover, a considerable proportion of these services would be wasted, as it would be underused on weekends and midnights. Therefore, it would not be practical on economical grounds to run free public transport.

There area plethora of means to solve the traffic problems. The most effective would be to encourage people to use public transport. This could be done by decreasing the fare, increasing the comfort and increasing the frequency of public transport. Obviously, if people do not have to waste time waiting for the bus or train, get comfortable seats and have to pay far less than what they would have to spend on their own personal vehicle, then they would willingly choose public transport and would not mind paying for it. So this step would prove better than giving a totally free public transport.

Additionally, the government could levy toll tax and increase the price of fuel to discourage people to use their own cars. Media could be used to make people aware about simple measures like car-pooling. For instance if five people from one block of flats have to go to the same office, they could each take out their car for one day a week. This would be a win-win situation for the environment and the people.

To sum up, having a totally free public transport would not be practical to implement, as it would not be economically viable for the people. Therefore, it would not be the best method. A better approach would be to encourage people to use public transport by making it better.

Plan followed

Intro: Discuss essay intro
Para 1: Points for free public transport
Para 2: Points against and other better methods
Para 3: Better methods
Conclusion: reiterate opinion

69.Some people think visitors to others countries should imitate local customs and behaviours. Some people disagree; they think the host country should welcome cultural differences. Discuss the two views and give your opinion.

Today, with the passage of time each and every country is on the path of development, and with this development, there is a growing trend of visiting different places in different countries. It is a highly debated issue whether tourists should behave as the people of the host country or should the host country accept visitors as they are. Both situations have their own pros and cons, which I shall discuss in this essay.

There are many benefits of adopting the customs of the host country. Firstly, it decreases chances of misunderstanding and embarrassment. For e.g. in the UK it is offensive to ask someone what their salary is, which is common in India. Secondly, a nation's customs and traditions are fascinating and offer a deep insight into that country. People visit other countries to broaden their horizon. So, if tourists copy the customs of host country, they learn more about them and that too in an interesting way. Finally, visitors establish a rapport with local people because people feel respected when their customs are understood and imitated. The visitors become a member of the host country and so they don't suffer any culture shock.

On the other hand, there are many reasons why a host country should tolerate and embrace foreign culture. To begin with, no country should cling to its own customs and traditions and not accept the new customs and traditions brought by visitors. Secondly, there should be no binding on the visitors to adopt the customs and traditions of the hosts. For example, if the visitors are pure vegetarians, they should not be forced to eat non-vegetarian food just because the host country's people eat that.

On balance, I feel that someone who is moving to another country should respect the customs, culture, traditions etc. of that country. This is necessary because a newcomer is like a guest in someone else's home. So he is expected to follow the rules of that country. However, it is not reasonable to compel a believer of a certain religion to ignore his religion in order to comply with the local customs.

Summing up, mutual understanding between both the visitor and the host is necessary to maintain harmony. A cosmopolitan society in which everyone is tolerant of each other's customs and traditions is the need of the day. After all, today, we are part of a small global village and not a big planet Earth.

Plan followed
Intro: Discuss essay intro
Para 1: benefits of adopting host countries customs
Para 2: reasons why a host country should tolerate and embrace foreign culture
Para 3: Own view
Conclusion:

70. The level of noise around us is constantly increasing, and is affecting the quality of our lives. What causes this noise? What should be done about it?

Displeasing sounds that upsets the balance of human or animal life is known as "Noise pollution." It has harmful effects on the physiological and psychological health of human beings. It can cause heart problems, hearing problems, sleeplessness and mental health problems. This essay shall discuss the causes and possible solutions to reduce noise problems.

There are a plethora of causes of noise pollution. One of the major sources of noise pollution is the traffic noise. Transportation systems create noise pollution. The number of vehicles on the road is increasing day by day and hence the sound produced by them is no less than a nuisance and is chiefly responsible for the noise pollution. To add to it, industrial noise also leads to noise pollution. Machinery and motors used in the industries create a lot of noise.

Furthermore, the construction of buildings, highways and city streets also cause a lot of noise and hence lead to noise pollution. People living beside railway stations also have to put up with a lot of noise from engines, horns and whistles. Other causes are the loudspeakers usually used in marriages, social and religious functions. The noise is just jarring and harmful for the ears. It can cause sleep disruption. It can also cause deafening.

Because of the harmful effects, it becomes quite necessary to curb noise pollution and take measures and steps to control it. Roadside plantations are one of the great solutions to help in reducing noise pollution. Vegetation buffer zones must be created in different parts of the city. Changing the design and operation of machines like sound proof cabins and sound-absorbing materials can greatly help in reducing noise pollution. Residential buildings should be as far as possible from noise sources. To block unwanted noise from outside soundproof doors and windows can be installed. The major cause of noise pollution in public areas is the loudspeaker. For the welfare of the people it should be banned at any cost. Thereshould be strict laws imposed against those who use loudspeakers in crowded areas and public places. .

To conclude, there are various sources of noise pollution but many steps can be taken to reduce it.

Plan followed

Intro: Problem solution essay intro.

Para 1: Causes

Para 2: More causes

Para 3: Solutions

Conclusion:

71.Some people say that popular tourist destinations are being affected negatively by travellers. Why does this happen and what can be done to resolve this.

These days the pollution produced by tourists has threatened the natural environment of some tourist attractions, making it a big problem to be addressed before those places are completely damaged. This essay shall try to highlight some reasons why people litter these places and also suggest some ways forward.

The most important reason why people litter these tourist places is that they have little awareness of environmental conservation. People think that their one plastic bottle or one wrapper of chips does not matter. What they don't realize is that if each tourist has the same thought then very soon these natural scenic spots would turn into mountains of such litter. People also don't know that this rubbish is mostly of non-biodegradable material and will stay like that forever.

Another reason why people don't care is that they think it is not their responsibility. They think the onus of keeping these places clean rests on the authorities. They have to realize that the environment is everyone's responsibility. Finally, the environmental protection facilities are not enough in many tourist attractions. People would not litter these places if trashcans were placed there at regular intervals.

The first step towards sustainable tourism would be that the governments and tourist companies could educate the tourists about their responsibilities. Tourists should be made aware through the media and tour operators about responsible tourism. They should be made to realise that their careless attitude could kill future tourism and nothing would be left for the gen-next. Additionally, the authorities should have proper facilities at such places and if facilities are not enough according to the number of tourists then the number of tourists should be limited.

To conclude, it can be said that irresponsible tourism has led to the damage of the natural environment and at many places the tourist places have been so much littered that they have ceased being a tourist attraction any more. The responsibility of saving these spots rests on both – the tourists and the government. One should remember the saying, "A good tourist is one who leaves behind nothing but footprints and takes away nothing but photographs".

Plan followed

Intro: This essay shall try to highlight some reasons why people litter these places and also suggest some ways forward
Para 1: they have little awareness of environmental conservation
Para 2: they think it is not their responsibility
the environmental protection facilities are not enough
Para 3: Solutions
Conclusion: The responsibility of saving these spots rests on both – the tourists and the government

72.Tourism has caused environmental problems in many parts of the world. What sort of problems has been caused and what can be done about them?

Tourism and the environment have a very complex and interdependent relationship. Negative impacts from tourism occur when the number of tourists is greater than the environment's ability to cope with them. This essay intends to analyze the damage to environment caused by tourism and suggest ways to alleviate the problem.

To begin with, development of tourism can put pressure on natural resources when it increases consumption in areas where resources are already scarce. For example, water, and especially fresh water, is one of the most critical natural resources. The tourism industry generally overuses water resources for hotels, swimming pools, golf courses and personal use of water by tourists. To cite another example of forest resource, one trekking tourist in Nepal - an area already suffering the effects of deforestation - can use four to five kilograms of wood a day.

Secondly, tourism can cause many forms of pollution such as air, noise and even visual pollution. Tourism now accounts for more than 60% of air travel. One study estimated that a single transatlantic return flight emits almost half the CO2 emissions produced by all other sources (lighting, heating, car use, etc.) consumed by an average person yearly. Noise pollution from airplanes, cars, and buses is an ever-growing problem of modern life. In areas with high concentrations of tourists, waste disposal is a serious problem and improper disposal can be a major despoiler of the natural environment - rivers, scenic areas, and roadsides. For example, some trails in the Peruvian Andes and in Nepal frequently visited by tourists have been nicknamed "Coca-Cola trail" and "Toilet paper trail". Visual pollution occurs when large dominating resorts are built in any natural environment and may look out of place there.

Many steps could be taken to ameliorate the negative effects of tourism. The attainment of sustainable tourism is an urgent need. It implies balanced commercialization, resource conservation, waste disposal management and pollution control. Eco-tourism is the need of the day. Depending on the resources, only a fixed number of tourists should be allowed in any place. Tourists should be cautioned against littering and spoiling natural places. Sustained active role of firms and governments is considered vital for the future of tourism development.

In conclusion, it can be reiterated that environmental issues have become pivotal in the economics of tourism. Many steps can be taken to mitigate the negative effects of tourism.

Plan followed

Intro:

Para 1: Effects on environment   Para 2: More effects

Para 3: Solutions   Conclusion:

73.Some people believe that tourists do not learn anything during their holidays, while others believe they learn a lot. Discuss both views and opine.

The world has become smaller and we can now travel to even the remotest parts of the world easily. Some individuals opine that travellers don't learn anything new when they visit a new place. Others are of the view that travelling teaches a myriad of things to the tourists. I intend to delve into both the perspectives in this essay. I side with the latter view.

Some people reckon that travelling is not a learning experience. The main reason for that is that most people travel in groups with their family or friends. They do not mingle with the local people and do not try the local foods. Tourists usually look for their own cuisine or international food brands like McDonalds or KFC. Another reason is that people go on holidays to relax, rejuvenate and take a break from their routines. So, people mostly do not want to learn anything new when they travel to a new place. For instance, many tourists today simply check into resorts and don't move out of the resort for the entire duration of their stay.

On the other hand, it cannot be denied that travelling brings a lot of learning with it. We not only get to experience a new way of life, but also learn about different cultures, history, food and languages. Furthermore, it makes us more responsible, independent and confident. We learn to plan and organize better. We come across different situations that help improve our decision-making and resource planning skills. Moreover, when we travel to a new place, we meet new people, make new friends and it helps build our social network. It also gives us an opportunity to get a different perspective on things, which broadens our horizons.

I believe that travelling is the best way to learn about a new culture, language, or history among many other things. I think that it is always an enriching experience and we become more aware about the world around us when we visit new places. Even if people do not go out of the resorts, it will still be a learning experience in terms of the social interaction with the staff of the resort or with other guests at the resort.

To conclude, I will reiterate that tourism offers tremendous opportunities for travellers to discover, learn and grow. It will be wrong to say that tourists do not learn anything at all when they travel.

Plan followed

Intro: Discuss essay

Para 1: Why some say that tourists don't learn anything

Para 2: Why some say that tourists learn a lot

Para 3: Own view

Conclusion

74.Nowadays, more people are travelling to other countries. Why is this the case? Is it a positive or negative impact for the countries they travel to?

International tourism has become a huge industry as more and more people are travelling to other countries. This essay intends to delve into the reasons why people travel overseas, and also the positive and negative effects on the host country. I believe that the effects are largely positive.

There are many reasons for international travel nowadays. The main purpose is for holidaying. People like to see new places and meet new people and thus widen their horizons. Besides vacationing, tourism today has expanded to include many other reasons to travel. People are medical tourists when they go abroad for treatments of various illnesses. For example, our famous cricketer went abroad for getting treatment of lung cancer. Many people now come to India for complex surgeries. Secondly, people do business tourism to expand their business network. Then we have religious tourism, sports tourism, education tourism, political tourism, adventure tourism and many more types of tourism. The names are self-explanatory.

On the positive side, the host country's economy is boosted. Many people get jobs in the tourism sector. Tourists spend on various things and everyone benefits. Secondly, people of the host country get a chance of culture exchange. They get to know foreign cultures and get to share their cultural norms. Moreover, when the government sees the influx of tourists, it develops the infrastructure of the country, which also benefits the natives.

On the negative side, sometimes tourists destroy the beauty of the place when they throw litter here and there. Secondly, there is air pollution because of air travel. In addition, diseases such as swine flu and bird flu can spread like wildfires. Last but not least, terrorists can come in the guise of tourists. Incidents of petty crimes also increase in areas frequented by tourists.

To sum up, people travel abroad for many reasons and the effects on the host country are largely positive.

Plan followed
Intro:
Para 1: Reasons
Para 2: Positive effects
Para 3: Negative effects
Conclusion

75.Some people think it is better to travel by cars in the city. Others, however, think traveling by bicycles is better. Discuss both views and give your own opinion.

Travelling by bicycle is fun, healthy, environment friendly and an economical means of travelling within a city. However, some people opine that it is better to travel by a car in cities, than by bicycles. This essay intends to analyse both perspectives. I personally side with the view in favour of bicycles.

Undoubtedly, in today's world where global warming and climate change have become burning issues, bicycles can greatly help reduce pollution. Studies have shown that cycling 10 km each way to work would save 1500 kg of greenhouse gas emissions.

Secondly, the bicycle is an affordable and independent means of transport as well, especially for those who have restricted travel options, like the unemployed, those under 18 and people with lower incomes who cannot afford a car. Besides all these advantages, riding a bicycle for short distances within the city would keep people physically fit, which is very necessary in today's times, where people have sedentary lifestyles.

The proponents of car travel within the city say that in this fast-paced life, time is of the utmost importance. They think that the faster means of transport is what is needed in today's world to get to work, schools, business meetings, etc. However, the use of bicycles in the city would rather save time of people than waste their time. The cars move at a snail's pace especially during peak hours, which literally increases the commuting time two or three fold. Bicycles have actually reduced the commute time, which has been seen in Denmark, where the government has made 19000 km of bicycle tracks all over the country for the convenience of the people.

The supporters of car travel within the urban areas also opine that if the numbers of vehicles are reduced, it will have an adverse effect on the economy of the city and subsequently the country. This may be true to an extent, however, it will only be a short-term issue. In the long run, it will be very beneficial to any country's economy, if more and more people start using bicycles for travelling short distances and to and from work every day. It will drastically decrease the hidden motor vehicle costs, such as accidents, congestion, pollution, road maintenance and so forth. This would be immensely beneficial at an individual level as well.

We cannot ignore the great advantages of travelling by a car and other motorized vehicles, especially when travelling long distances. However, for travel within the city people should be encouraged to use the eco-friendly and economical means of transport.

Plan followed

Intro:

Para 1: Advantages of bicycles

Para 2: More advantages of bicycles

Para 3: Advantages of car with refuting arguments

Para 4: Advantages of car with refuting arguments

Conclusion

76.Some people believe that taxing companies, which cause it, is the best way to reduce industrial pollution while some suggest that there are several other ways to solve this trouble. Discuss both the views and give your opinion.

Some individuals are of the opinion that industries which cause pollution should be taxed heavily so as to reduce pollution, whereas others opine that pollution should be controlled by other means. This essay intends to discuss both perspectives. I, however, side with the latter view.

Those who are in favour of taxing companies say so because it is these companies which cause pollution and they should pay for cleaning it up. The ordinary people should not have to pay for it through taxes. Obviously, if government pays for it, it would be through the common man's pocket.

On the other hand, other methods to deal with the situation would be better. This is because it would be very difficult to judge which industries are causing how much pollution. They would all shrug off their shoulders and that would make matters worse. Secondly, these companies would claim that they are already paying a lot of taxes and so it becomes the governments' responsibility.

Other methods should be used to tackle this problem. To begin with, the government can make it mandatory for these industries to set up effluent-treatment plants. Government can also give them subsidies for such projects. This would ensure that these effluents don't contaminate the underground water. These industries should also be encouragedto plant trees. They should have a green belt all around them so that the trees absorb all the carbon dioxide liberated.

To conclude, taxing the industries would not work as a good solution for reducing pollution and other methods should be looked into.

Plan followed

Intro:

Para 1: advantages of taxing the companies

Para 2: Why, taxing companies would not work-out.

Para 3: Other methods

Conclusion:

77.People generally know that the environment is important. However, most individuals still don't take responsibility to protect the environment. Why is this? What should be done to encourage people to protect the environment?

It is irrefutable that environmental damage is occurring at a very fast pace and people know that it is a global priority today to save the environment. However, when it comes to doing something, no one steps forward. This essay intends to delve into the causes of this phenomenon and suggest simple measures to encourage people to think about the environment.

There are many reasons behind the indifferent attitude of people. The main reason is that we people don't know that we are also the cause of environmental damage. We don't realize that global warming is the result of billions of decisions. We are cutting down trees for our needs; we are using too many luxuries in the home; we are driving too many cars and we are wasting resources like fresh water. If only awareness is brought about these things then many people would take a step forward in this direction.

People are also not doing anything because they think that it is a global problem and only government action can solve it. What has to be made clear is that small measures taken at the individual level will add up to mammoth dimensions when mounted up. For example, in a country like India with a population of more than one billion, if each person plants a tree and nurtures it for the first few months, the result would be un-imaginable. We can all take simple steps like recycling things such as newspapers, plastics and glass. We could also walk for short distances instead of using our vehicles and for long distances we could use the public transport.

Another reason why people do little about the environment is that people have become very busy in their pursuit of wealth and fame that they have no time to think about the environment. What they don't realize that if nothing is done today, it might be too late tomorrow. The rate at which global warming is occurring would soon transform the Earth into a boiling pot and it would be un-inhabitable for us one day.

Summing up, the onus of saving the environment is not just on the shoulders of the governments and big industries. We all must come forward and do our bit to save the environment before it is too late. It has rightly been said —"little drops of water, little grains of sand, make the mighty ocean and the vast land"

Plan followed

Intro:

Para 1: People don't do anything because they don't realize that they are the cause of this damage

Para 2: People don't do anything because they think it is a big problem and can only be tackled by the government

Para 3: People don't do anything because they have no time

Conclusion:

78.Nowadays people are using more consumer goods like refrigerators or washing machines. Does this have more advantages or disadvantages?

Today we belong to an era of materialism and everyone wants to have more and more in life. Things like a fridge, TV and washing machine were the luxuries of yesteryears, but have become the necessities of today. There are many advantages and disadvantages of this phenomenon but the disadvantages definitely outweigh the advantages.

On the positive side, the quest for material possessions is what keeps the society going. People work hard to fulfil their needs and achieve their goals. It is people's right to own the comforts of life. Secondly, because of the demand for such things, the national economy is boosted. Manufacturing units provide round-the-clock employment to thousands of people to produce things in bulk. Someone has rightly said that, "Be glad that you're greedy; the national economy would collapse if you weren't." What is more, when demand is more and mass production is done, then the cost of the appliances comes down and the consumer is ultimately benefitted.

On the downside, this is leading to stress and strain in the lives of people. People have become workaholics and are missing out on the joys of family and social life. Sometimes, people even adopt unethical means to get these things and this leads to crime and violence. There is no harm in owning things such as a car, TV or fridge, but things turn bad when this simple materialism turns into over-materialism and people start wanting a TV in each and every room of the house and a car per person of the family. Our neighbours have a triple storey house and there is a refrigerator on every floor just for their comfort. People fail to draw the line between necessity and indulgence and this creates all problems. They fail to realize that - "If you live for having it all, what you have is never going to be enough."

The most significant impact of excessive materialism is on the environment. Manufacturers promote their products through ads and people are lured into buying new things even without need. It is a bitter truth that a society in which consumption is artificially stimulated in order to keep production going is a society founded on trash and waste, and such a society is a house built upon sand. For example, new models of TVs and refrigerators are introduced every other day and people just go and buy them regardless of whether they need those things or not. The disposal of old ones is adding to the global litter and is destroying our environment.

To sum up, there is no harm if everyone wants to own a fridge and a washing machine, but it would be much better if we were satisfied with one fridge and one TV per family instead of having a TV in every room.

Plan followed

Intro: the disadvantages definitely outweigh the advantages

Para 1: Advantages of materialism

Para 2: Disadvantages of materialism

Para 3: Disadvantages of materialism

Conclusion:

79. In many countries there is a lot of rubbish (garbage) because more and more people are buying more and more things. What are the causes? Does your country have the same problem?

Environmentalists today are campaigning for "reduce, recycle and re-use" in a bid to save the world, but thepopulace of many countries have adopted "replace" as their mantra. My country, India, is no exception. This and many other factors are leading to a highly consumerist society. In this essay, I shall discuss the causes of this consumerism and some steps that can be taken to solve this problem.

To begin with, modern lifestyle has contributed greatly to the increasing amount of waste and garbage we produce every day. In other words, we have turned into a materialistic and mass-consumption society where we use more and throw away more than ever before. Once new things are acquired, we dispose-off these "unwanted" things to second hand shops or just in the trash cans. The solution lies in changing our attitude. We should get old things repaired and try to use them as long as possible.

Secondly, the markets today are flooded with cheap, single-use-only things that are more in demand than high priced quality items. Our houses and closets seem to be overflowing with goods that are more in quantity and less in value. Then, there is too much packaging done by the companies in a bid to make their things more attractive. Here too, the onus lies with us. We should not buy things with excessive packaging. This will deter companies from doing too much packaging. We can also bring our own personal shopping bags instead of using plastic bags provided by stores and shops. Besides, the government can enforce stricter laws on companies to use biodegradable packaging.

Furthermore, plastics, waste metal, and glass can be recycled. Companies can also contribute by developing new raw material, which is recyclable and will ultimately lead to less garbage.

To sum up, individuals, business and the government can share the responsibility to reduce the amount of waste material and to save the earth. If we do not take steps to tackle this problem on a war footing, our Earth will become un-inhabitable.

Plan followed

Intro: In this essay, I shall discuss the factors which are leading to consumerism and some steps that can be taken to solve this problem
Para 1: reason and solution
Para 2: reason and solution
Para 3: The answer lies in recycling
Conclusion –

80.The amount of garbage produced by our cities is a big problem for governments around the world. How can this problem be fixed?

Cities are producing more garbage than ever before and the amount is likely to double by 2025. This essay intends to study the ways to tackle this global garbage crises.

Most contemporary waste management efforts are focused at local government level and based on high-energy waste disposal by methods such as landfill and incineration or burning. However these methods are becoming increasingly expensive and energy inefficient. Therefore we have to focus on other sustainable methods for waste disposal.

The first way to deal with waste is waste minimization. This is an approach that aims to reduce the production of waste through education and the adoption of improved production processes and less wasteful practices. Ultimately, by discarding less and preferring durable goods and through appropriate handling methods, consumers can lessen the waste generated. We should reflect on what we really need and what we can do without.

Secondly, we should focus on the mantra of 'reuse'. Most materials are made from nature, such as trees, minerals, oil, gas and metals. The waste we create is really a resource that is thrown away sometimes after a single use. Reusing and then recycling these materials helps limit resource use, keeps valuable materials out of landfills, and prevents pollution. When we reuse things, fewer materials are wasted and non-renewable resources are conserved.

Thirdly, we should recycle things. As much as 80 percent of everyday waste materials can be recycled and given a new life when broken down and used again and again. Recycling still uses energy and resources, but it's much better than making things from scratch. For example, every ton of newspapers recycled saves approximately 17 to 19 trees and over 70 percent less energy is needed to produce aluminum from recycled cans than from raw materials.

Another important step we can all take at a household level is composting. Organic materials (food scraps, coffee grounds, egg shells, yard waste, etc.) make up about 30 percent of the garbage going to landfills. Instead of wasting this valuable material by throwing it in the garbage, it can be composted. Composting waste has two key benefits: it reduces the amount of waste going to landfills and it produces a free natural fertilizer that helps build healthy soil and plants, achieving a healthier environment.

To sum up, solid waste generation is becoming a colossal problem, but we can deal with it in many ways. The time has come to stop waste before it stops us.

Plan followed:

Intro:

Para1: Contemporary methods being used

Para 2: Reduce

Para 3: Reuse

Para 4: Recycle

Para 5: Composting

Conclusion:

81.In spite of technological developments in transportation, many people believe that a bicycle is the best way to reach any destination. What are the advantages and disadvantages of using a bicycle nowadays?

A bicycle is a mechanism that has transported man for many decades. Nowadays, many people use bicycles to move from one place to another for short distances. I believe that by riding a bicycle, people can decrease gasoline consumption, improve the quality of their lives, and protect the environment. This essay shall discuss the pros and cons of riding a bicycle in today's scenario.

The first benefit of using a bicycle for short distances is that it decreases pollution levels in the atmosphere. When many people use their cars to move short distances, the increased emissions impacts the pollution levels negatively, degrading the environment. That is why the use of a bicycle for short distances is a really good idea to help lower the rates of pollution.

The second benefit of using a bicycle for short distances is that you can help lower petrol or diesel consumption. If you use a bicycle togo to a place that is near your home, you will decrease the petrol or diesel consumption of your car. This can save you a lot of money because the price of these fossil fuels is expensive. Maybe, it is the laziness of some people who use their cars to drive to places that are near their homes. However, this habit of driving everywhere causes an increase of gasoline consumption.

Finally, the most important benefit of riding a bicycle on short trips is that it can help you have good health. When you ride a bicycle, you use your legs to move, and this physical exercise is aerobic which means that your heart is pumping blood throughout your body, so it fortifies your heart, lungs, and other important parts of your body.

On the other hand, the disadvantages of riding a bicycle in the contemporary world cannot be denied. Heavy traffic has become the norm of the day and the bicycle has become unsafe, especially where there are no separate lanes for bicycles. Moreover, it is more time consuming as compared to cars or other forms of transport. Finally, if the weather is not favourable, it is impossible to ride a bicycle.

To sum up, there are some excellent reasons to ride a bicycle. I think that we need to make a distinction when it is better to use a car or a bicycle. We need to keep in mind that riding a bicycle will provide us with health and other benefits. That is why if one uses a bicycle, it can improve the quality of life of the person who owns it.

Plan followed

Intro:

Para 1: First benefit - decrease of pollution

Para 3: Final benefit – help you have good health

Para 2: Second benefit - save you a lot of money

Para 4: Disadvantages   Conclusion:

82.Most countries allow 18 year olds to start driving a car. Some say it is good to allow driving at that age. Others think that the age to start driving should be at least 25 years. Discuss both views and opine.

People are divided on the legal age of starting to drive a car. Many countries issue a licence at the age of 18. However, some believe that this age should be raised to 25. This essay intends to analyze both perspectives. I side with the latter view.

There are convincing arguments to support that the age of 18 is good enough to be officially allowed to drive. This is the official age of adulthood in many countries, including my country, India. So, if a person is considered mature enough to be given voting rights, then he is mature enough to be given driving rights. Another argument, which goes in favour of the younger age for getting driving licence, is that most of the accidents are because of inexperience and not age. A 25 year old may also cause the same accidents. So, raising the age of getting a licence would not prove beneficial in reducing accidents.

On the other hand, if the legal age of driving is raised to 25, then the number of road accidents would definitely come down. This is because many youngsters indulge in fast and rash driving just to show off and get attention. In doing so, they are harming not only themselves, but also other innocent people who come in their way. Another very important benefit would be to the environment. The use of public transport would increase, as people would be forced to use the public transport till they are 25 years old. This might promote the use of public transport in general, even after they get their own rights to drive.

I believe that the age of driving should be raised to 25, because maturity to understand the rules of driving is definitely more at 25 than it is at 18. Secondly, it would be a big saving for those parents, who have to buy independent vehicles for their 18 year olds, and then give them money every month for fuel. All this expenditure could be deferred for 7 years. The cost of public transport would definitely be less. The use of bicycles, which do not need any licence, would also go up.

To sum up, getting a driving licence at 18 or 25, both have their pros and cons, but keeping the environment and health into consideration, I believe that the age of 25 has an edge over the age of 18.

Plan followed

Intro: Discuss essay

Para 1: Why 18 is a good age for getting driving licence

Para 2: why 25 is considered a good age

Para 3: Own view

Conclusion

83. Some people say that giving a small amount of money weekly to children will help them become more capable as they grow older. Do you agree or disagree?

I definitely agree that providing children with a little amount of pocket money on a weekly basis is helpful to their development. In the following paragraphs, I shall put forth my arguments to support my views.

Firstly, giving children a small amount of money instills in them a sense of independence and responsibility towards spending the money the right way. They learn and understand that the amount of money is limited and they need to always choose between their various desires to ensure correct use of their pocket money. Children get into the habit of planned income and expenditure. They also learn about saving and budgeting. For e.g. if they want to buy a present for their mother's birthday, they will need to put aside some amount of money every month to collect the commensurate amount and buy the gift.

Secondly, parents who issue their children a minute weekly allowance encourage the development of their child's sense of responsibility. It makes them feel an important part of the family since they know that they get a part of the family's monthly income. Furthermore, giving your child a set amount every week can work out much cheaper in the long run provided you don't top it up with more money if your child runs out of money. Parents who don't give pocket money but buy children whatever they need would be surprised if they just total the amount they spend on their children's desires every week.

What is more, when children are given the independence to buy things themselves they become more aware of how much things cost, therefore they begin to see the value in the things they already have and other household items more clearly. They may start to treat the DVD player or PlayStation with a bit more respect, for example, and realize that with their limited money, they can't just run out to the shops and buy a new games console if the other one breaks. Giving pocket money to their kids saves a lot of time for grownups to buy small things for their children. They can utilize this time for other important tasks.

After analyzing how giving children a little cash on a weekly basis develops their financial comprehension and level of responsibility, it has been proven that this practice is more positive than negative. Thus, parents are encouraged to consider adopting this regime.

Plan followed:

Intro: Agree

Para1: 1st reason – learn and understand the value of money

Para 2: 2nd reason – encourage the development of a child's sense of responsibility.

3rd reason – can work out cheaper in the long run

Para 3: they begin to see the value of things they already have

Conclusion: reiterate opinion

84.Nowadays plastic money replacements such as credit and debit cards are extremely popular, even more than banknotes and coins. Discuss the advantages and disadvantages of this. Include your personal opinion and examples based on your own experience.

The ease in swiping a credit card for a purchase has made it very popular nowadays. Therefore, many opine that this plastic money will replace the coins and paper money in future. I believe that it is both a positive as well as a negative development. The weight of the merits and demerits of credit card is in the hands of the user.

There are many benefits of credit cards. Firstly, people can use them practically everywhere, even overseas. Credit cards can also boost peoples' purchasing power because they can be used to buy goods and services over the phone, through the mail and online. To add to it, they provide financial backup in the event of an emergency, such as an unexpected healthcare cost, job loss or auto repair. For instance, if a person is on a holiday and has a medical emergency, he will have no problem in paying the hospital bills through credit card.

Furthermore, credit cards allow you to purchase items and pay them off in monthly installments. They also offer discounts and rewards at stores. For instance, when you make purchases using the credit card you can collect points, which accumulate and can be used to get free items, such as airline tickets. Some cards may offer cash back as an incentive to use the card. They can help build your credit history. A person with a good credit history does not face problems when applying for a loan for any reason. Credit cards also keep a record of your expenses, helping you to monitor your financial activities.

On the other hand, credit cards can have their disadvantages. The most dangerous part of credit cards is not paying off their dues on time, and once a person falls behind by one payment, then late fees, interest, and penalties build very fast, because of which many people find themselves sunk in credit card debt with no way out. The other big disadvantage is the hidden costs. There is the start-up fee, the processing fee and also the annual fee, which is quite an amount. Additionally, one of the most overlooked negative aspects to credit cards is the ease with which cardholders overspend. The psychology behind this is simple. Cardholders purchase items without ever exchanging actual money, so they don't get the feel of spending. Finally, people have to be cautious when they use their credit card for online transactions. It can be hacked and misused, if the site is not secure. Misuse can also happen if they lose their credit card. They have to report promptly if such a thing happens.

Summing up, as with anything, there are advantages and disadvantages of using credit cards. It is in the hands of the person using the card to make its advantages outstrip the disadvantages.

Plan followed

Intro: Advantages or disadvantages lie in the hands of the holder

Para 1: Advantages   Para 2: More advantages

Para 3: Disadvantages   Para 4: More disadvantages

Conclusion:

85.Many people believe money is a very important factor for achieving happiness. Others, however, believe that money has nothing to do with happiness. Discuss both views and give your own opinion.

It is irrefutable that money can bring ease and comfort in a person's life. However, the negative side of having too much money cannot be overlooked. This essay shall look into the advantages and disadvantages of having too much money.

It is easy to see how money can enrich our lives and make us happy. The world runs on money. The basic amenities of life such as food, clothing and shelter can be got only with money. You can trade money for almost anything. With money one can buy all the comforts and luxuries of life. One can study in the best schools and colleges and can also enjoy the best health services. Money is needed to enjoy holidays with family and with money one can bring smiles on the lips of one's nears and dears.

On the other hand, there are many reasons why people say that having a lot of money has no relationship with happiness. To begin with, the richer you are the more taxes you have to pay. You will also have to keep track of what you have. You may have to pay people to keep accounts of all of your holdings. Money may become an obsession; it can alter your perception of life; you may stop trusting even your true friends. In this way, it can alter your social behaviour. Too much money won't let you see every day's little pleasures.

It can be said that the excess of money is as bad as the lack of money. The poor person is certainly not happy, nor can happiness be seen in a very rich person. Happiness is in contentment. There are many things which money can't do. For example, money can buy you a pretty good dog, but it cannot buy the wag of his tail. Money can buy books, but not knowledge; money can buy medicines, but not health and money can buy a bed but not sleep.

To conclude, definitely money is needed for everything in life. However, excess of money has its downside. Therefore, one should be satisfied with just enough. However, how much is 'enough' is a very difficult question to answer.

Plan followed

Intro: Agree with both halves of the statement
Para 1: Advantages of having money and too much money
Para 2: Disadvantages of too much money
Para 3: Comparison of advantages and disadvantages of too much money. The excess of money is as bad as the lack of money
Conclusion: Reiterate opinion

86. Many people spend a lot of money on clothes, haircuts, and beauty products to enhance their appearance. Some people think that it is a good way to spend money, while others think that there is a better way to spend it. Discuss both views and give your opinion.

For centuries, men and women have beautified their eyes, lips and bodies. However, in today's contemporary society, people are spending excessively on their looks. Some people opine that this expenditure is justified, but others are opposed to this overspending. This essay shall discuss both perspectives. I side with the latter view.

This disproportionate spending on their façade appeals to many because it is a general perception that when you look good, you feel better; when you feel better, you behave better; when you behave better, the people around you tend to respond to you positively. There is no doubt that fashionable clothes, stylish haircuts and high quality beauty products can turn any ugly duckling into a beautiful swan.

Secondly, in today's competitive era, looks are very important, so much so that some professions are totally dependent on looks. Many film stars have got face-lifts and other cosmetic surgeries done on their faces to look younger and thus be in the job for longer. Even in some other professions, such as receptionists in offices and air-hostesses, looks are given weightage over other things.

On the other hand, some people opine that such extravagant expenditure on looks is unreasonable. They say that one should save or invest money to build a bright future. That money can also be spent on quality education in a reputed university. Some money should also be donated for charity.

I believe that looks are important and it is everyone's right to look their best. However, one must remember that ultimately what matters is the inner 'you'. It is more important to be beautiful from within. What is more, these products are not without their side effects. Too many products used on the hair and face may damage the hair and skin permanently. Therefore, one must not overspend on these things.

To conclude, outrageous spending on improving looks is bad. The outer appearance may have a temporary appeal but what ultimately matters is the person within.

Plan followed
Intro: Discuss
Para 1: Why spend
Para 2: Why not spend
Para 3: Why not spend – own opinion
Conclusion

87. Some people think spending a lot on birthdays and marriage celebrations is a waste of money but others think it is important to the young people and the society. Discuss both views and give your opinion.

Celebrations such as birthdays and marriages are an important part of everyone's life. However, it is a matter of intense dispute whether spending a lot on such events is a waste of money or whether it is significant for the youth and society as a whole. This essay shall look into both sides of the argument before coming to a conclusion.

There are many reasons why some people opine that having big weddings and birthdays is good for the youth and the society. They believe that such events are very special should be celebrated with great pomp and show. As it is the youth of today are forgetting their culture and tradition under the influence of the global culture and such events provide opportunities to revive such traditions in the minds of the youth. Secondly, in the fast paced life of today, it is only on such occasions that friend and relatives take time off to be together. Therefore, to make these days special, people spend lavishly on them. They believe that spending on such events is good to revive the community spirit among people.

On the other hand, there are those who are against such ostentatious spending. They say that such days can be celebrated in a simple way with only a few relatives and friends. There is so much poverty in the world and rather than frittering away a lot of money on such events it is better to donate some to charity to make such days special and meaningful. To cite an example, our great celebrity, Amitabh Bachchan celebrated his daughter's and son's wedding very simply with only a few friends and relatives.

Another reason, which goes against overspending on such events is that many a time people go into debt in order to keep up with their affluent friends and relatives. This one day of celebration may well become the cause of stress for many days or even months later on. What is more, if we want to be rid of the dowry system and female foeticide then it is very essential that we keep these celebrations simple and easy on our pockets so that there is no financial strain on anyone.

In my opinion, those who overspend on such days merely want to show their status in society. It is essential to celebrate such days. Celebrations bring a break from the routine and give us "milestones" for our life. Celebrations reminds us that we belong to a larger community, be it a family, a nation, or anything in between. However, it is not necessary to make them pretentious.

To sum up, it can be said that celebrating such events is important for the youth and society but it is not necessary to overspend on them.

Plan followed

Intro: Balanced view as it is a discuss essay

Para 1: For spending on these events

Para 2: Against such frivolous spending

Para 3: My opinion

Conclusion:

88.There are an increasing number of serious crimes committed each year. While some people say that the best way would be to use death penalty as a deterrent, many people say that other measures will be needed. Discuss both sides and opine.

Death penalty is based on the principle of retributive justice. Supporters of capital punishment argue that it is morally justified in cases of heinous crimes such as murders and mass killings. Others opine that other measures to curb crime should be employed. This essay intends to analyse both views. I personally oppose capital punishment with some concessions for the heinous criminals.

Supporters of death penalty believe people who commit murder, have taken the life of another, have forfeited their own right to life. Furthermore, life imprisonment is a drain on public finances. Maintaining a secure prison system for high-risk, violent offenders acts as a drain on government resources. Then it has a deterrent effect on potentially violent offenders for whom the threat of imprisonment is insufficient restraint. Finally, in many countries with capital punishment, a vast majority of citizens are in favor of retaining capital punishment. A survey held after the Delhi rape incident of Dec 2012, found that nearly 70% of Indians favored the continuance of capital punishment.

On the other hand, there are many arguments, which go against capital punishment. Firstly, innocent people get killed, because of mistakes or flaws in the justice system. For example, in 2012, 13 convicts had been erroneously sentenced to death (according to the Supreme Court's own admission) and were facing the threat of imminent execution. They were found innocent and were pardoned on the appeal of 14 former judges of various high courts.

Secondly, the death penalty doesn't seem to deter people from committing serious violent crimes. According to a survey conducted by the UN, executions do not have a greater deterrent effect than life imprisonment. Moreover, in countries with costly and lengthy appeals procedure like India, capital punishment becomes a more expensive option than long-term imprisonment. It is also argued that it is used more often against perpetrators from racial and ethnic minorities and from lower socioeconomic backgrounds, than those coming from a privileged background.

To sum up, the death penalty should be there only for the very serious crimes, such as mass killings and murders, but in all other cases life-imprisonment is better. Every person should be given a chance to reform. Oscar Wilde has rightly said that, "Every saint has a past, and every sinner a future."

Plan followed
Intro: Discuss essay
Para 1: Points for
Para 3: Points against

Para 2: Points against
Conclusion:

89.Most of the people in the society enjoy watching crime movies and crime based TV programmes. Why do you think people have more interest to watch them? What is the impact to the society due to this?

It is irrefutable that crime and violent world events are among the most frequently watched topics on TV and in films. This essay intends to analyse the reasons of this phenomenon and also discuss the effects of this on society.

The most important reason for this is obviously that such shows and movies make people aware about the crime and violence happening in the society, and they can thus avoid landing into such situations. For example, through the television shows such as 'Crime Patrol' and 'Savdhan India', which are based on true stories, people can be alerted of the kind of crimes happening around them.

Secondly, people watch such movies and TV programs purely for entertainment. They get the thrill out of watching such shows and movies. The TV channels also telecast more and more of such shows as they want to increase their TRPs (television rating points). If any channel has a high TRP, it gets more adverts and hence more revenue.

There are many positive and negative effects on individuals and society. On the positive side, the people are abreast of the crime around them and can take protective steps, as and when needed. On the other hand, the most disturbing effect is on the children and youth. Depiction of violence in media can stimulate fear in some children as it frightens them, making the effects long lasting. This can become traumatic in our children as they see it more and more. Children are starting to grow and are shaping their personality, values and beliefs. Such programs can affect their psyche.

Furthermore, young people imitate what they see, and it is logical that they see glamour in what they do when they commit violence. Consequently, the society suffers, as the streets are full of violence. Too much portrayal of these also leads to immunity among the people, and they are not affected by the disasters any more. Disasters like Tsunami and earthquakes also don't make people shed a tear any more.

Summing up, there are many reasons why people love to see too much violence on TV and in movies. These have a lot of detrimental effects on the individuals and society.

Plan followed

Intro: I shall discuss the reasons of this phenomenon and discuss its effects on society..

Para 1: Reasons for this phenomenon

Para 2: One useful effect and harmful effects on the individuals and society

Para 3: More harmful effects

Para4: Solutions   Conclusion:

90.Sending criminals to prison is not the best method of dealing with them. Education and job training are better ways to help them. Do you agree or disagree?

There are many different opinions on the best way to reduce crime. The traditional solution is to punish the criminals by putting them in prison. Some hold the view that education and job training are the long-term solutions to cut crime. In my opinion, prison is the only answer in a few situations, but in most cases education, vocational training and rehabilitation are better.

Prison is the only answer in case of criminals who are a risk to the society, such as murderers. They cannot be allowed to mix with society. Some people also say that people would not be afraid of committing a crime if fear of imprisonment is not there. But I still feel that in majority of cases, we can do without prisons.

In traditional prisons, people learn a lot about crime and so when they leave prison they will commit even more crime. In other words prisons act as universities of crime. So petty offenders like shop-lifters and pick-pockets should be given some vocational training and education. It is a well known fact that the basic causes of crime are poverty, illiteracy and unemployment. So, if we provide education and job training then we would be removing the causes of crime. If criminals are rehabilitated by some form of employment then they are likely not to indulge in criminal activities on their release from prison.

Furthermore, prisons are expensive to maintain. The government can spend that money on other important areas such as education and healthcare. This would ease some burden from the government's shoulders. The petty and minor criminals can also be employed in some community service projects after providing education and vocational training.

Summing up, we should hate the crime and not the criminal. To fight crime we should focus on the causes of crime. Education and job training help to rehabilitate the criminals. So, people who commit less serious crimes should not be sent to prison. Focus should be on reforming them.

Plan followed

Intro: partially agree

Para 1: Enumerate those crimes for which prison is the only answer -

Para 2: Why prison is not the answer -

Para 3: Maintaining prisons is a burden on the govt.

Conclusion:

91.Some people say that the main purpose of television should be education, while other says it should be for entertainment only. Discuss both sides and give your opinion.

People are divided on the purposefulness of television. Some believe that TV should primarily be for education, whereas others opine that TV should be for entertainment. This essay intends to analyse both perspectives. I, however, believe that television should equally fulfil the role of educator and entertainer.

Television has been given considerable importance in many countries as a source and a tool of teaching. Television is used for formal and non-formal education. To support formal education, television can be attached with school curriculum and time-tables. It can enhance quality in education and reduce dependence on verbal teaching and teachers. It can stimulate learning and give opportunity for mass education.

In non-formal education, television can directly or indirectly teach many things. Television benefits the masses by making them conscious of the environment, their rights, duties and privileges. It is a source of teaching etiquettes, language skills, hobbies, social relations and religious beliefs.

On the other hand, the role of television in entertainment is indubitable. As in this contemporary, busy world, majority of people lead a stressful life, and they require a sort of passive entertainment to feel relaxed. There are countless channels on TV providing entertainment in the form of soaps, video songs, movies, and game shows. Thus, every person irrespective of his age group can find something interesting to see on TV. Moreover, today the smart TV is capable of recording our favorite programs, which we can enjoy in our free time. It also offers thousands of games to play.

I believe that TV is simultaneously doing both – entertainment and education. Even the daily soaps that we see provide some social education. So the role of TV is overlapping as far as education and entertainment are concerned.

To sum up, television is equally meant for education and entertainment both. To use it solely for education or for entertainment would be wrong.

Plan followed

Intro: Equal role

Para 1: Role in education

Para 2: Role in education

Para 3: Role in entertainment

Conclusion:

92.Some people believe that watching TV is good and makes life more enjoyable. Others, however, feel that it is a waste of time. Do you agree or disagree? Give your own opinion.

Some individuals opine that TV adds joy and fun to our lives, whereas others believe that it is a total waste of time. In my opinion, both perspectives have some element of truth in them. TV is our source of happiness, but only if we know where to draw the line. Otherwise, it can eat away all our leisure time and we would miss out on many other things, which could bring us greater joy than this idiot box.

On the one hand, the usefulness of TV in entertaining us cannot be denied. There is a huge variety of TV shows available. It is a nice way to relax after a busy day. In this day and age of global competition, everyone is leading busy and hectic lives. Due to such busy routines, people are not able to take out time for leisure, like in the past. They do not have time to meet their friends and relatives very often. They can remain in the comforts of their home and watch shows of their choice.

Secondly, TV keeps us up-to-date with what is going on all around, and it can also be very educational. It is now possible to see new places, learn about their culture and food, without visiting those places. Not only that, through this armchair tourism, we can see animals, which we may not get a chance to see in reality. Watching TV can be coupled with some other task such as walking on the treadmill. In all these ways, TV has enriched our lives.

On the other hand, TV has destroyed social interaction. In a recent survey it was seen that an average person watches approximately 3 hours of TV per day, which accounts for more than half the leisure time in a 24-hour day. More productive things could be done in that time, such as playing with other children, reading books, doing homework and so on.

Another reason, which goes against TV is that some of the shows that teenagers watch are very negative and destructive to their mind. On top of that, many youngsters have started developing unhealthy habits in front of the TV. Snacking while watching TV is very common and these things make people obese and lazy. It has been proven that the more time a person spends sitting in life, the sooner he is going to die. Sitting, as they say, is the new smoking. Being active is one of the most important necessities of a person's body. Leisure time we have is limited, so the onus is on us not to waste it on wasteful TV viewing.

To sum up, watching TV is good entertainment, But if we don't limit our TV viewing time, it can prove to be a sheer wastage of time.

Plan followed

Intro:

Para 1: How TV is entertaining

Para 3: How it is a waste of time

Para 2: How it is a waste of time

Conclusion:

93.Among Internet, radio, TV and newspaper, which has the greatest effect on the social activity of people? Give reasons.

In the last 50 years the media influence has grown exponentially with the advancement of technology. Each of these four media - internet, TV, newspapers and radio - impacts the social life of people in different ways. All these media shape people's opinions, provides entertainment and information, is a link between the government and the people and helps in providing justice at times. All these media have their own importance and uniqueness. However, TV has the greatest influence on society as it is the most pervasive of all media.

Newspapers have better breadth, which means that a large number of items, issues and viewpoints can be covered. They also have better depth, which implies news can be presented in detail. Newspapers can also be read and re-read at one's convenience, as opposed to being scheduled to run only during fixed time periods as is the case with TV and radio. The disadvantage of newspaper is that the ability to comprehend news in print depends on educational and literacy level, which is a clear-cut advantage in case of radio and TV.

Radio, can be accessed in a variety of situations. People listen to radio while they dress and eat in the morning, commute to and from work, perform work or study, have meals and so on. Radio news reporters can provide live, local coverage in a timely manner. However, television has an edge over radio as it combines both sight and sound, which are the two major human senses for communication, and is therefore more appealing. With the appearance of all-news cable television networks, it is now possible to bring news coverage of important global events instantaneously.

The Internet is the newest source of news and is fast becoming popular among the computer literate sections of society. However, its usage depends on availability and affordability. Theoretically, we can say that the Internet incorporates characteristics from ALL of the traditional media, such as sight, sound and online versions of newspapers and magazines. The youth are the most influenced by the Internet. The social network sites on the Internet have made it possible for the youth to have the widest circle of friends.

To conclude, all these media are not equivalent and interchangeable with each other, as they have unique characteristics. It is very difficult to pin point which one is the best. Television, however, is the most pervasive news media.

Plan followed

Intro: Tell how media affects people. TV has the maximum impact

Para 1: advantages of newspapers

Para 2: Advantages of TV and radio with some comparison

Para 3: Advantages and limitations of the Internet especially on youth

Conclusion: very difficult to pin point which is the best. All have unique characteristics.

94. Radio will no longer be able to hold its presence, as television and Internet media will replace it very soon. Do you agree or disagree?

In the past, radio was considered the most convenient and important source of information. Even today, despite the emergence of other media such as the TV and the internet, the radio has held its place as an important mass medium. I strongly disagree with the notion that the radio will lose its importance in the future. In fact its popularity will grow even further. A number of arguments surround my opinion.

One of the main reasons why radio will retain its value is because of the fact that driving has become very popular across the world as a way of life. Radio is a regular piece of equipment installed in a car, and to car users, listening to the radio while driving is an effective means of taking full advantage of their time and keeping abreast of the latest information, such as news, weather forecast, share markets, and so forth. As car use is likely to increase in future, the popularity of radio will also grow.

Secondly, for those people who have no time to watch TV, radio provides immediate and easy access to information. Another advantage of its continued popularity is that it is highly affordable. Radio broadcasting is free to the public, unlike TVfor which one has to pay for the channels of choice. Furthermore, the radio is portable. On occasions where people cannot watch TV, read newspapers or surf the net, they can listen to the radio.

The newer technologies are also responsible for the popularity of radio. For example, people can get radio via satellite, the internet and cable nowadays. There are many other electronic devices, such as MP3 and MP4 players, which allow people to listen to the radio more easily and to use it for various entertainments, such as sharing their music collections. The only disadvantage of the radio is that it is unable to convey messages with sight and motion, as television or internet do. However, the radio is still able to serve the needs of audiences as it always did.

To conclude, the radio has many advantages that give it an edge over TV and the internet. Therefore, it will always remain popular.

Plan followed

Intro: Disagree

Para 1: Advantages while driving

Para 2: highly affordable. – even radio broadcast is free //Portable

On the occasions where people cannot watch TV, read newspapers or surf the net, they can listen to the radio.

Para 3: The newer technologies are also responsible for the popularity of radio.

Conclusion:

95. Nowadays people depend on newspapers, radios, television and the Internet for news and information. Which in your opinion is the best way for getting news and why?

People receive news from different sources. This essay shall compare four popular media from which people receive news - newspapers, radio, television and the Internet and then come to a conclusion as to the best one out of these four.

Newspapers have better breadth, which means that a large number of items, issues and viewpoints can be covered. They also have better depth, which implies news can be presented in detail. Newspapers can also be read and re-read at one's convenience, as opposed to being scheduled to run only during fixed time periods as is the case with TV and radio. The disadvantage of the newspaper is that the ability to comprehend news in print depends on educational and literacy levels, which is a clear-cut advantage in case of radio and TV.

Radio, can be accessed in a variety of situations. People listen to radio while they dress and eat in the morning, commute to and from work, perform work or study, have meals and so on. Radio news reporters can provide live, local coverage in a timely manner. However, the television has an edge over radio as it combines both sight and sound, which are the two major human senses for communication, and is therefore more appealing. With the appearance of all-news cable television networks, it is now possible to bring news coverage of important global events instantaneously.

The internet is the newest source of news and is fast becoming popular among the computer literate sections of society. However, its usage depends on availability and affordability. Theoretically, we can say that the Internet incorporates characteristics from ALL of the traditional media, such as sight, sound and online versions of newspapers and magazines.

To conclude, all these media are not equivalent and interchangeable with each other, as they have unique characteristics. It is very difficult to pin point which one is the best. The television, however, is the most pervasive news media.

Plan followed
Intro: Opinion to be reached after comparing the four media.
Para 1: advantages of newspapers
Disadvantage
Para 2: Advantages of TV and radio with some comparison
Para 3: Advantages and limitations of the Internet
Conclusion: very difficult to pin point which is the best. All have unique characteristics.

96.More and more media attention is being paid to famous people who are successful in sports and movies. Why do you think this is happening? Is this a good thing?

It would not be unfair to say that today's world is saturated with celebrity related news and gossip. We have access to the very latest news in the world of celebrities via different mediums. This essay shall delve into the causes of this phenomenon. It is definitely not a good thing.

The main reason for this is that people idolize celebs and want to know more about them. Celebs are role models for many. People want to be like them and that is why they want to know everything about them. The media is only responding to people's desires. To survive in today's world, the media, whether it is e-media or print media, has to focus on these big shots. Another reason for this is that the celebs themselves need the media coverage to survive in today's era of cut-throat competition. That is why the extent and quality of celebrity news in the media is multiplying manifold.

However, too much focus on the lives of celebrities is certainly harmful for the people as well as the celebs themselves. Too much focus on celebrities is diverting people's attention away from more important issues such as politics and the environment. For example, the public knows more about Salman Khan and his broken relationships than about many political issues. Another important point is that sometimes these celebs are negative role models for people. For instance, if a celebrity drinks or smokes then young people may copy him thinking that it is glamorous to drink and smoke.

Too much celebrity gossip can be detrimental for the celebs themselves. Everyone knows that Princess Diana died because she was being followed by the paparazzi. Celebrities' lives do not have any privacy and they cannot enjoy the simple things of life like a common man does. This increases the stress in their lives and consequently, their careers also suffer.

To conclude, the media does focus too much into the lives of famous people because of several reasons. However, it should understand its responsibility and use its power for the right cause. It should know where to draw the line and should also know how much is too much.

Plan followed

Intro: This essay shall delve into the causes of this phenomenon. It is definitely not a good thing.

Para 1: Reasons

Para 2: Why it is not good for people

Para 3: Why it is not good for celebs

Conclusion:

97.Should media networks such as newspapers publish people's private information?

Media plays a very important role in our lives. Through the different media, be it print or broadcast, we get to know about the local, national and international news and along with that it helps spread awareness and brings to our notice the various issues and helps form our opinion. In this day of competition, in order to increase the sales or the TRP, many media people publicize the private life of celebrities and other famous people. In my opinion, this is not justified.

It is true that the reason why such private information is publicly disclosed is because there isa demand for such details by the masses and people relish such news. However, that doesn't give anyone the right to publish such information, especially without the consent of the person concerned. Every individual has a right to privacy and journalists and other media persons should not invade the privacy of anyone, be it a common man or a famous person.

Moreover, most of the celebrities act as role models for many youngsters. If negative or uncensored information is published about famous people, many people may follow them and indulge in the same kind of behavior as their role models, even if it is something wrong, like drinking or smoking excessively or using abusive language. To add to it, if some private aspect of that person's life is published or broadcast, it may affect the career of a celebrity adversely. Ultimately it is a loss for the public as well, as an artist is lost in the process.

My final argument against publicizing private lives of celebs is that when the paparazzi make their private lives public, it sometimes affects their performance, which is the loss of the common people. These celebs entertain us, and if they don't perform well, they cannot entertain us well.

Opponents may say that any public figure has to accept this as a part of their lives, as they chose this way of life, when they chose to become a celebrity. However, I strongly believe that this still does not give anyone the right to invade someone's privacy and make it public.

To sum up, it can be said that we all have a right to privacy and so do the famous people. It is not right for the media networks to publicize anyone's personal and private information.

Plan followed

Intro: They should not
Para 1: first reason
Para 2: second reason
Para 3: third reason
Para 4: My view
Conclusion

98.Some people say television contributes more than other modern inventions to the quality of life of ordinary people. Do you agree or disagree?

The television has become arguably the greatest invention of the past century. There is no doubt that it has significantly changed the life of the ordinary man. However, I disagree that it adds more to the life of the common man. I believe that the mobile technological gadgets of today have surpassed the TV, as they also provide TV on the go along with all other benefits of the phone and the computer.

Undoubtedly, the TV is still very important to us. We watch TV in the morning to receive the daily news. We eat watching it. We watch it before going to bed. Thus the television eats up most of the time we get to stay at home. What is more, the advertisements succeed in giving rise to strong materialistic wants in us, which must be one of the reasons why we are becoming increasingly consumerist.

On the other hand, modern gadgets have accelerated the pace of communication, and now we are able to communicate with anyone in any corner of the world. Long distance communication has also become much cheaper than before. Newer jobs have been created because of these technologies. Many people work in the programming field, as systems analysts and web designers.

Furthermore, businesses can expand globally with very little investment. They can develop a network of customers and get instant feedback on their products or services. Payments can be sent and received by wireless terminals, like PayTM. Another big advantage is to the students. Students can create documents and immediately upload them to a teacher's electronic folder. Teachers can then view the documents immediately, and keep them permanently stored. It works in reverse, too. Teachers can upload assignments, links, or feedback for students via these shared resources or folders.

Moreover, these gadgets have proved an asset in healthcare also. The tablet and smartphone are becoming nearly as ubiquitous in healthcare as the stethoscope. One survey in 2013 discovered that 86% of physicians used smartphones. In one handheld device, doctors can access patient information, research medical literature, and securely communicate with patients and colleagues.

To sum up, it can be said that television has been the leader in changing the life of man till the beginning of the 21st century, but mobile communication technology has now surpassed all other inventions in affecting the life of the common human being.

Plan followed

Intro: Disagree
Para 1: What all we see on TV – When-when we see the TV – Ads on TV
Para 2: How modern gadgets are better
Para 3: More advantages of modern gadgets
Para 4: More advantages of mobile gadgets.
Conclusion: reiterate your points

99.Some people are interested in international news, others prefer watching national news. Discuss both views and give your opinion.

All cultures whether literate or not have a thirst for news. News plays a vital role in human affairs and also keeps us in touch with our environment. Some people just like to watch national news whereas others want to know all about the international arena. Before rendering my opinion, I think it is important to look at the argument on both sides.

Those in favour of national news contend that it is enough to know what is happening around them in their own country. They believe that what is happening a thousand or more miles away has no bearing on their lives and it is futile to go into the depth of that news. Their curiosity is satiated with political, social, sports and entertainment news of their own country. For example, most people in India follow the national political developments as it affects important aspects of their life such as their finance, health and education. They like to discuss national issues and express their concern over them.

Those interested in global news say that global news gives us a big picture view of what is happening around the country and the world. Today, the world is becoming more and more interconnected and a well-rounded understanding of politics, the environment, social structures and the global economy is needed in order to make important decisions of their lives. Some like to invest in the stock market which is affected by any happening anywhere in the world. For example, when a tsunami struck Japan in 2011, stock markets around the world saw a sudden dip.

Another reason of taking interest in international news is that today people travel the world for various purposes. Tourism has taken mammoth dimensions. For example, today people go for business tourism, religious tourism, educational tourism, medical tourism, sports tourism, political tourism and remote tourism. Keeping in touch with international news affects our decisions regarding our destination of travel and many more factors. Therefore international news is of paramount importance today.

To conclude, international news is very important in today's times. It does not, however, mean that national news is not important. I firmly believe that news of our own country is very important, but today we belong to a small global village and not a huge planet Earth. Therefore all news is local news.

Plan followed

Intro: it is important to look at the argument on both sides
Para 1: views of those in favour of watching national news
Para 2: views of those in favour of watching international news
Para 3: more views of those in favour of watching national news
Conclusion: your opinion - news of our own country is very important, but today we belong to a small global village and not a huge planet Earth. Therefore all news is local news.

100. Recently, more and more people use the Internet to get information and buy goods. What do you think about the advantages and disadvantages of this phenomenon?

The Internet is probably one of the greatest inventions of the century. This essay intends to discuss the pros and cons of the Internet.

Information is probably the biggest advantage that Internet offers. Internet is a virtual treasure trove of information. There is a huge amount of information available on the Internet for just about every subject known to man, ranging from government laws and services, market information, new ideas and technical support. Another big advantage of the Internet is speedy communication. Now, you can communicate in a fraction of second with a person who is sitting on the other side of the world. With the help of such services, it has become very easy to establish a kind of global friendship where you can share your thoughts and explore other cultures.

Entertainment is another popular reason why many people prefer to surf the Internet. Downloading games and songs or just surfing the websites are some of the uses people have discovered. Finally, with numerous online services you can now do net-banking, book tickets for a movie, pay utility bills, taxes etc., sitting at home.

On the other hand, if you use the Internet for online banking, social networking or other services, you may risk a theft to your personal information such as name, address, credit card number etc., which may land you in serious trouble. Secondly, Internet users are often plagued by virus attacks on their systems. Virus programs may end up crashing your software and sometimes even hardware. Furthermore, Internet allows you to access and download millions of pornographic photos, videos and other X-rated stuff. This can be detrimental for children and teenagers.

Finally, people now only meet on social networks and face to face communication has taken a back seat. More and more people are drifting apart from their friends and family. Even children prefer to play online games rather than going out and mingling with other kids.

To conclude, with all its faults the internet has the potential to make your life simple and convenient, as well as wreak havoc in your life. With clever use, you can manage to harness its unlimited potential.

Plan followed:
Intro
Para 1, 2 and 3: Advantages
Para 4, 5 and 6: Disadvantages
Conclusion

101. Films can have effect on children's education and teach them many things. Do you think it is always a positive influence? Discuss.

It is irrefutable that movies can be very educative for children. However, the effect of movies is not always beneficial. In the following paragraphs, I intend to discuss the positive and negative effects of movies on children.

On the positive side, movies are enjoyable for children of all ages. They stimulate children's emotions, imaginations and conversations. Movies also introduce children to cultures and historical events. Movies used in the classroom enhance learning. Therefore, if the movies are good they can have a very positive influence on a child's growth.

On the downside, children are negatively affected by movies with sex, violence drug abuse and offensive language. Older children and adolescents may copy the risky things they see in movies. What is more, movies glamorize things like smoking and drinking and children are quick to pick up these traits.

Furthermore, watching too many movies can impede the development of healthy habits like playing outdoor games, reading and spending quality time with family. Children who are avid film viewers are more likely to suffer from obesity related problems throughout their lives.

I believe that as everything has its pros and cons, movies too can have both - good and bad influences. It is very important for parents to check the movie ratings before allowing their children to watch any movies. The best thing for parents could be to watch movies with their children. Watching movies together could be a very rewarding experience.

To summarise, movies can have a positive or a negative influence on children but if parents take steps in choosing their children's movies, then the effect can be largely positive.

Plan followed
Intro: It has both positive and negative effects
Para 1: Positive effects
Para 2: Negative effects
Para 3: Negative effects
Para 4: Own opinion
Conclusion: Reiterate opinion

102. Today the Internet has replaced traditional books as a source of information. Discuss the advantages and disadvantages of this development.

The Internet as the mainstream of media plays a very important role in transferring information. Some people assert that Internet would take the place of books in the future. However, in my opinion, each medium has its own advantages and disadvantages. Books will always hold a place in our lives.

Admittedly, Internet has made our lives very convenient. Firstly, it can transform information instantly. It can tell us what happened in the world right away with very impressive pictures. Secondly, it plays an important role in education. People can study history, culture, language and cooking skills from the internet. Even books are now available in electronic format (e-books) and that is the reason some people find it a threat to the traditional, physical, book.

However, we should not neglect the importance of books which are very convenient to carry and easy to get. Books are available everywhere, such as in the library, in the book store, in your pocket or beside the pillow. After a day's work we can relax in our bed or sofa by reading some book or magazine. Books are also very good travel companions.

Moreover, it is very difficult to sit for long hours glued to the monitor screen. Eye strain and back pain are also some disadvantages of the internet. With so many power cuts, as in my country, we cannot rely on the internet. Last but not least, the day is still very far when all people will be able to afford the internet connection and read e-books.

To conclude, despite the threat of the internet, the book has maintained its place. So I feel we'll never go without books because they have served us so well for so long.

Plan followed

Intro: a balanced approach as it is a discuss essay.
Para 1: Advantages of internet over books
Para 2: Advantages of printed book
Para 3: Disadvantages of internet
Conclusion: Despite the threat of the internet, the book has maintained its place.

103. As communication technology develops, people are interacting with each other in different ways. Does this trend have more advantages or disadvantages?

Technology has revolutionized the concept of communication. It has brought in the market many gadgets to facilitate communication. This has led to a considerable change in the type of relationships that people have and largely these changes have been positive although there is a downside to this phenomenon as well.

The most significant impact of technology on communication is that the speed of communication has increased manifold and the cost has been cut drastically. In the pre-information technology days, a document often required re-typing on the typewriter before the final version. Sending a letter across to someone else required a visit to the post office and a postage stamp. Faster methods such as telegrams had severe limitations in text, and remained costly. Computers and the internet have eased the process of creating and editing documents and applying features such as spell check and grammar check automatically. Email allows sending the document to any part of the globe within seconds, making telegrams, and even ordinary letters mostly obsolete.

The accessibility of communication has also improved because of its low cost. Relationships have become better because people are connected to each other all the time and there is little chance of misunderstanding due to communication gaps. Finally, technologies such as the internet help spread the net of communication by tracking down old friends, shedding light on new business opportunities, and the like.

On the downside, the possibility of high quality communication from anywhere in the world to anywhere else at low costs has led to a marked decline in face-to-face communications and to an increased reliance on electronic mediums. Communication has become concise and short, and the adage "brevity is the soul of wit" finds widespread implementation, though unintentionally. The small keyboards in mobile phone and other hand held devices that make typing difficult has resulted in a radical shortening of words and increasing use of symbol and shortcuts, with little or no adherence to traditional grammatical rules.

Summing up, as every garden has weeds, similarly the effect of technology on communication has a downside. Overall the positive effects far outweigh the negative ones.

Plan followed

Intro: these changes have been positive although there are some negative changes also

Para 1: Advantages

Para 2: Advantages

Para 3: Negative side

Conclusion: Overall the positive effects far outweigh the negative

104. Some people say now there is less communication between family members than in the past. To what extent do you agree or disagree?

I do not completely agree that nowadays there is lesser communication among family members than in the past. What has actually happened is that most of the communication has changed from direct face-to-face communication to blind communication via the computer screen or the cell-phone.

To begin with, even today, the family is the center of many people's lives. As many people study or work in the same city and live in the same flat or house, family members have numerous opportunities to talk to each other. The whole family also gets together to have dinner at night at the same time, and exchange information about their day's happenings. Last but not least, on weekends, the whole family goes for outings or shopping together and on these occasions gets opportunities to communicate with each other.

On the other hand, in this era of cut-throat competition, people spend more time on their study and work. Meanwhile, compared to the past, people have to face fiercer competition and suffer greater pressure nowadays. Therefore, they have to devote more time and energy to their careers. For example, many jobs require people to work in other cities and many children have to leave their parents at an early age to study or work elsewhere. That is why to some extent communication has decreased among family members.

Today families communicate with each other as much as or even more than the past via the cell phone and internet. Earlier, when a member of the family went to another city or country for study or for a business trip, the landline phone or the traditional letter was the only means of communication. Today, families have minute-to-minute information about each other and many applications such as Skype have made video chat so easy and good that distances seem no barrier at all and communication has become even more frequent.

To sum up, it can be said that, even today families communicate with each other in many ways. To some extent the fast paced life has decreased interaction among family members but technology has brought in newer means to ease communication.

Plan followed
Intro: I do not completely agree – communication has changed – some decrease is there
Para 1: How families communicate even today
Para 2: How communication has decreased
Para 3: How communication has changed
Conclusion:

105. Nowadays people like to use new electronic equipment. Do you think this is a positive or negative development?

Technology has practically taken over our lives. Electronic devices have become an integral part of our lives. Such devices range from cellphones and notebooks to washing machines, microwaves and dishwashers at home. We use electronic gadgets not only for work in offices and industries, but also in our homes. Every day there is a new invention that makes our work easier and convenient. This development has both merits and demerits. In my opinion its pros are more than its cons.

At work, the use of computers has made the work of the employees faster and their productivity and efficiency has improved immensely. For most of the jobs, having computer skills has become a pre-requisite. Electronic devices can be used not only at work, but also for education and for domestic purposes. For instance, we don't have to go anywhere to buy groceries and vegetables. These can be ordered in a few clicks of the mouse and are home delivered. The time saved with the use of such equipment can be utilized to pursue our hobbies and other interests. Even for hobbies, people take online classes or watch videos and learn new things, like recipes, guitar lessons, language lessons and so on.

To add to it, most of the schools have classrooms equipped with electronic equipment, like smart boards, projectors, TV screens, etc. The use of technology in education has improved the quality of learning among students. Furthermore, communication has been revolutionized with the use of such devices. We can connect with anyone, in any corner of the world, within a matter of seconds. Through video calls, people cannot only stay in touch with friends and relatives, but it has also helped many people expand their business globally.

On the downside, we have become too dependent on electronic equipments and gadgets. Without these devices, people start feeling helpless and it seems that our work and world has come to a standstill. Also, the over-dependence on technology has led to many health-related problems, due to less physical activity and less utilization of our brains, making us less creative. We are so reliant on technology that a system failure for a few seconds at the stock exchange, can lead to huge losses, affecting an entire county's economy.

To conclude, I would reiterate that the increasing use of electronic devices has brought tremendous, positive changes in our lives. However, it is in our hands to mitigate its negative effects, by not becoming over-dependent on electronic devices. It has been rightly said, "Technology should improve your life, not become your life."

Plan followed

Intro:

Para 1: Electronic devices at work and home – Benefits   Para 2: Benefits in school

Para 3: Drawbacks   Para 4: More drawbacks

Conclusion:

106. Computers have made our world a better place to live in. Do you agree or disagree?

Computers are ubiquitous nowadays and almost every home, office, or school has a computer of some kind these days. There can be no denying that this is because of the plethora of benefits we get from using computers. Therefore, I agree with the given statement that computers have transformed the world for better.

To begin with, our personal and professional lives have improved because of computers. We can now do more things and do them more easily than we could before. Checkout lines at stores move faster because a computer scans the prices. The bank manages our account more easily because of computers. The weatherman reports the weather more accurately with the help of computers. A computer is involved in almost everything we do, or that is done for us. Most people these days do their jobs with the help of a computer. Architects use computer programs to help them design buildings. Teachers use computers to write their lessons and get information for their classes. Pilots use computers to help them fly planes. With the help of computers, people can do complicated jobs more easily.

Furthermore, through the Internet, computers have made communication much more convenient. E-mail has made it possible to communicate with people instantly at any time of day. The Internet has made it possible to find out the latest news right away - even if it is news that happens someplace far away. The Internet has made it possible to get almost any kind of information from any place quickly, right in your own home or office. To add to it we can now do net-banking, online shopping and even do air and rail reservations online.

Undoubtedly, there is a dark side to this man-made machine called the computer. Many jobs have been lost due to the fact that computer can do a lot of tasks more efficiently than humans. This has led to high unemployment in many countries. What is more, kids, if left unsupervised, would spend all of their time playing games on the computer rather than using it for educational purpose. Moreover children might use the internet to access pornographic material. Furthermore some people when working from home with computers are far more likely to feel cut off from the rest of the world. Also frequent and prolonged computer exposure may pose health risks especially for children. The most frequently cited are visual strain, harmful effects of radiation and posture problems. Last but not least, in case of a network failure, the whole office work may come to a standstill. Despite all these drawbacks, the computer has made life without it inconceivable.

To sum up, computers and the internet have come to stay. Obviously, the whole world has changed for the better.

Plan used

Intro: agree

Para 1: Advantages   Para 2: Advantages through the internet

Para 3: disadvantages   Conclusion: pros more than cons

107. More and more adults are spending time playing computer games. Why are adults doing so? Is it good or bad?

Video games and computer games are heavily marketed towards teens and young adults, but recent studies show that the average video game addict is 35 years old. This essay intends to analyse the reasons why adults choose to play video games. I believe that playing video games is good in adulthood, but only until it does not become an addiction.

There are many reasons of adults playing video games. The first is that these games act as stress busters. In the hectic life of today, adults have a lot of responsibilities. They have to balance demanding jobs, look into the needs of spouses and children, and also deal with problems of ailing parents or friends in crisis. So, they need time to relax, unwind, and take their minds off the realities of life.

However, when adults develop an addiction to video gaming, they suffer a lot of problems. Firstly, there is an increased risk for depression, anger and mood swings. Secondly, these gamers withdraw from friends, family, or spouses to the point that family, social or work life is disrupted. In addition, the gaming addict may neglect household responsibilities and chores, and may lie to family members about the time he spends on these games.

In addition, adults addicted to gaming may have physical symptoms like difficulty sleeping, migraines, back and neck aches and dry eyes. Video game addicts mayalso become so preoccupied with earning the high score or reaching the next level that they forget to eat, shower, shave, or take care of basic hygiene. The addicts also lack physical exercise and so also suffer from an elevated BMI (Body Mass Index).

To sum up, video game addiction is not just limited to teens, but has also engulfed the adults. These games are addicting and isolating and so it would be better for adults to refrain playing such games.

Plan followed

Intro: Cause effect essay

Para 1: Reasons

Para 2: Harmful effects

Para 3: More harmful effects

Conclusion:

108. Many jobs used to be done at home by hand, but nowadays an increasing number of them are done using machines instead. Discuss the advantages and disadvantages of this development.

Modern technology has equipped us with machines. There are positive and negative effects of these machines on the individual and the society, which I shall highlight in this essay. Overall the cons outweigh the pros.

On the positive side, machines are faster, more convenient and energy saving. Households and industries are much facilitated with machines. Personal use of machines gives people more free time to spend with family and pursue hobbies. Likewise, industrial use of machines reduces manpower for work and increases output. In the words of Oscar Wilde – "The fact is that civilization requires slaves. The Greeks were quite right there. Unless there are slaves to do the ugly, horrible, uninteresting work, culture and contemplation become almost impossible. Human slavery is wrong, insecure, and demoralizing. On mechanical slavery, on the slavery of the machine, the future of the world depends."

On the negative side, machines reduce the need of manual work, which can lead to unemployment especially in the developing countries. What is more, insufficient knowledge of machine handling and operating is detrimental to uneducated workers and they end up getting injuries or disabilities while working with machines. Technical failures can also disturb the whole working system and lead to losses.

Other negative effects of machines are on the health of individuals especially the housewives who rely heavily on machines for the household chores. Machines are a failure where creative work is required. For example, the unique and original work done by many artisans can never be reproduced by any machines. It has been rightly said that a machine can do the work of a thousand ordinary men but no machine can do the work of one extraordinary man.

Overall, the negative effects of machines outweigh the positive effects on the individual and society. In order to meet the employment needs of the population, a balance has to be maintained between manual work and mechanization.

Plan followed
Intro: Discuss essay intro
Para 1: Advantages of machines
Para 2: Disadvantages of machines
Para 3: Other negative effects
Conclusion: Machines are good but should be used judiciously in developing countries because may lead to unemployment

109. Some people think the mobile phones are most useful for their professional lives, others think mobiles phones are most useful in their personal life. Discuss both of them and give your opinion.

The mobile phone is ubiquitous these days. I believe that mobile phones are very beneficial in both - personal as well as professional lives.

In personal life, the main advantage of a mobile phone is that it keeps people connected to their kith and kin at all times. Today we live in nuclear families but are connected to our extended family network all because of the cell phone. Secondly, it saves a lot of time. In the spare time that a person gets while travelling or waiting for someone he can carry out a number of tasks such as paying bills, ordering grocery, booking tickets and so on. Nowadays we all know that both parents are working. If they do all this work while commuting to and from work, they can give more time to their children once they are home. The world would be a lot slower had the mobile not been there. What is more, children who have to leave their elderly parents at home because of work, feel comfortable because they know they can be called any time their parents need them.

On the other hand, in professional life also, the cell phone has proved to be an asset. Professionals can use functions like call conferencing and video call conferencing instead of traditional face to face meetings. This saves a great amount of valuable time and cost for the companies. In addition, last-minute information that could make or break a project can also be delivered if a business cell phone is kept on hand. For instance, in the case of an emergency, having a business cell phone allows workers to call their fellow co-workers at all hours. Moreover, phones with advanced features, such as global positioning systems (GPS), also help you navigate with ease, making sure that you are able to reach your destination even in unfamiliar locations.

It is difficult to decide which sphere of life has been influenced more with a mobile phone. In many cases it is difficult to draw the line between personal and professional use. For example, a busy gynaecologist having to attend a patient in labour can attend to her children also side by side in the time before delivery. This way neither the personal life suffers nor the professional life. Ten years ago the cell phone was a luxury; today it is a necessity to balance personal and professional life.

To conclude, the cell phone has revolutionized communication and brought equal benefits to both personal and professional lives.

Plan followed

Intro: Discuss essay intro

Para 1: Advantages in personal life

Para 2: Advantages in professional life

Para 3: Overlapping role of cell phone

Conclusion: equal benefit

110. Some people are making new friends by using socializing network websites and internet chat rooms. Some people say that this is a good thing. Others say that people should make new friends by face-to-face chat. Discuss these views and give your own opinion.

Some individuals are of the opinion that it is good to make friends online on various social networking sites and internet chat rooms. However, others are in favour of making friends by direct face to face chat. This essay intends to look at both perspectives. I personally side with the latter view.

On the one hand, social network sites like 'Facebook' provide a great opportunity for people to socialize with one another and find common ground, before even meeting. Online social groups have become fundamental building blocks of modern human societies. They have a beneficial effect on our way of life. They increase our social interaction and give us more ways to make social connections. Earlier our social interactions were constrained by national boundaries, but now the Internet has turned communication into a global phenomenon. Today, our network of friends stretches across the globe.

On the other hand, making friends through direct contact is definitely better as social media sites can cause more harm than good. People can make fake IDs and cheat anyone. Every now and then we hear stories how girls and boys were cheated through such sites and after months of friendship, the original identity of the person turned out to be very different. Cyber criminals can hack the IDs of people and chat on their behalf which may cause huge misunderstandings.

Furthermore, face to face friendship is better because it is a friendship which has a deeper bond than online friendship. Man is after all a social animal and friends are meant to be there when you need them the most. Online friends cannot be with you when you are sick and you need a friend's touch. Face to face friends are with you in thick and thin and this can never be possible with online friends.

To sum up, even though the growing majority of the world's population abides by the social meme: "I love my computer, because my friends live in it", I still reiterate my opinion that face to face friendships are stronger and longer-lasting.

Plan followed:
Intro: Discuss essay intro
Para 1: Advantages of online friends
Para 2: Advantages of face to face friends
Para 3: More advantages of face to face friends
Conclusion:

111. Many adults think that childhood and schooldays are the best years of a person's life. What's the reason for this? Do you agree or disagree?

Everyone has nostalgic memories of one's childhood days and would like to return to them if given a chance. Therefore, it goes without saying that childhood and early school days are the golden periods of one's life. However, the later school years, the teenage years, do have some stresses.

To begin with, there are many positive aspects of being a child. One of the biggest benefits is in the area of sleep. Generally, parents encourage children to 'go to bed early' for one reason or another. Sleep seems to be something that most adults wish they had more of. Another benefit of being a child is in the area of responsibility. The only person a child is responsible for is himself. Life is therefore less complicated and slower-paced. In addition, children are normally not engaged in full-time work. This means the stress of finding and keeping a job is not a part of their life.

Moreover, people tend to treat children with love and care and generally tend to ignore their mistakes, which if done by an adult are taken seriously. A child is inexperienced, and lacks understanding about life; he or she must go through a period of learning basic 'life skills' such as manners and appropriate language. All this is also a fun part of growing up.

On the other hand, the teenage years have some tensions. Teenagers face the identity crisis, which means that they are neither considered children, nor adults. If they play like small children, they are rebuked and if they sit with adults, they are asked to go away. They also face some hormonal changes of puberty, which are very stressful for some. Then they have the stress of choosing their career because the subjects relating to one's career have to be finalized in secondary school. Nonetheless, these stresses are minor if compared to the responsibilities and tensions of adulthood.

To conclude, childhood for most people is certainly a stress-free time. I believe that childhood and primary school days are among the best times in a person's life. Teenage years do have their downside but still they are better than older years.

Plan followed

Intro: Agree

Para 1: reasons

Para 2: Other reasons

Para 3: stresses or teenage years

Conclusion: childhood and early schooldays the best.

112. Some people think parents should control the behaviour of children from a very young age but others think we should give them more freedom. Discuss both views and give your own opinion.

Young children are beginners. They have lots to learn and one of the biggest lessons they must learn is to behave or act in an acceptable manner. So parents have the onus of instilling the best values in their children. Some people say that parents must pull the reins on their children from a really young age but others opine that children should be given freedom. This essay shall look into both views.

Firstly, restrictions create responsible and respectful children who, in turn, mature into respectful adults. They know the value of respect for others. They know the importance of relationships. They know their cultural values as well. They know their boundaries. Moreover, children are like sponges, who very easily absorb what is taught to them. If you teach them good values, they will imbibe them. If parents don't realize their role and don't bother much, children will learn from other sources like TV and the people around them. They learn whatever they see and observe and if no one tells them at an early age what is wrong and what is right, they may learn vulgarity and violence. Later on parents may find it impossible to make them unlearn those things.

Furthermore, if parents don't control their child's behavior from a very young age, they may fall into bad company. They may start taking drugs under peer pressure. Once children become drug addicts, it is very difficult to bring them to normalcy once again.

On the other hand, those who believe that children should be given freedom are of the view that if children are controlled too much, they may become rebels. It would also snub their individuality and creativity. They may withdraw into a shell and sometimes go into depression. Therefore, they opine that children should be handled with soft gloves.

To conclude, parents are responsible for bringing children into this world and it is their responsibility for instilling good behavior in them. So, the earlier they do so the better. If they keep waiting, things may go out of hand.

Plan followed

Intro: Discuss essay intro
Para 1: restrictions create responsible and respectful children
Para 2: if parents don't control their child's behavior from a very young age, they may fall into bad company
Para 3: if children are controlled too much, they may become rebels
Conclusion: Controlling them is better

113. Today, majority of children are raised by their grandparents due to the fact that their parents are busy working. To what extent do you think it affects the whole family?

It is irrefutable that both parents are working nowadays and as a result children have to be raised by either maids or grandparents. Definitely, grandparents are better than any other option and this situation affects the family in both positive and negative ways, which I shall highlight in this essay.

On the positive side, looking after the grandchildren keeps the grandparents energetic and vibrant. Grandparents bathe, feed and even read books to the child. This leads to a sort of symbiotic relation in which both grandparents and grandchildren are benefited. In other words we can say that it is a win-win situation for both. Grandparents don't suffer from loneliness and depression, which is very common at that age, and children are also well looked after.

Moreover, such a situation encouragesa joint family system. Therefore, all the benefits of a joint family are there. There is security in the family as we all know that there is security in numbers. Another big advantage is that grandparents teach moral values to children. If grandparents do not look after children then parents use TVs as baby-sitters and children can become couch potatoes.

On the negative side, it is generally seen that grandparents are over-doting and, out of love, may pamper and spoil the grandchildren. Another disadvantage is that if there is not enough harmony between the parents and grandparents then it can lead to frustration and spoil the whole atmosphere of the house. In such cases children are the worst sufferers.

To conclude, it is very beneficial if grandparents look after their grandchildren. Both parents are free to pursue their careers, grandchildren learn moral values, are looked after well and grandparents enjoy themselves and don't suffer from loneliness and depression.

Plan followed in the essay

Intro: address the essay question appropriately.

Para 1: Advantages to grandparents and children

Para 2: More advantages

Para 3: Disadvantages

Conclusion: it is very beneficial if grandparents look after their grandchildren.

114. Teenagers have problems at home and school. What difficulties are they facing now? What should parents and schools do to help them?

Teenage years are the most delicate years of a person's life. These are beautiful years but have their share of difficulties. This essay shall delve into some problems teenagers face at home and school and also suggest some ways forward.

The main problem teenagers face at home is the identity crisis, which means that they are neither considered children, nor adults. If they play like small children, they are rebuked and if they sit with adults, they are asked to go away. They also face some hormonal changes of puberty, which are very stressful for some. To add to it parents have become workaholics and do not give the required time, which teenagers need in these crucial years.

Furthermore, parents want to take decisions for their teenagers like selecting their subjects of study. They do not give any importance to the aptitude of the child and force the subjects of their choice on them. They also want their child to excel in everything, which can lead to a lot of stress. They expect their teens to follow the traditional culture whereas teens want to follow the more liberal, western culture, which they are exposed to. To tackle these problems, parents need to spend quality time with their children in these impressionable years. The child's aptitude should not be ignored and choice of subject should be left on the teenager.

In schools also teenagers are not without challenges. Pressure of studies is just one problem. Classroom bullying by some students and favouritism shown by the teachers can be very stressful. To add to it some of them are being sexually harassed and abused daily at school by other teenagersand teachers. Some of them are too hurt to tell anybody while others feel embarrassed to share their experiences. Peer pressure is also an issue of concern in these years. Teens can easily be swayed to take drugs under peer pressure. At school taking part in extra-curricular activities keeps teens happy. These activities act as stress-busters. Teachers should have an unbiased attitude and treat all students equally.

To conclude, there is no doubt that teenagers face a lot of problems at home and school but simple measures taken by parents and teachers can help make these years pleasant and memorable. The onus is on the parents and teachers to make these teenage years stress-free.

Plan followed

Intro: This essay shall delve into some problems teenagers face at home and school and also suggest some ways forward

Para 1: Problems at home

Para 2: More problems at home and solutions

Para 3: Problems at school and solutions

Conclusion:

115.   More and more young children have mobile phones. Some people say it is a good thing for them, while others say it is a bad thing. What is your opinion?

Mobile phones have certainly become ubiquitous, especially in the hands of children. As with any other gadget of technology, cell phones also have pros and cons. If used wisely and within limits, the advantages are more than the disadvantages.

To begin with, if children have mobile phones, they feel safer because they are never out of contact with their parents or guardians. Cell phones provide a way to quickly contact someone if they are in trouble or are lost. Children having cell phones helps parents feel more at ease.

Secondly, having a mobile phone helps children to learn in a lot of different ways. First they learn about technology; about how to use the mobile phone. Second, most phones today have apps through which they can access online courses and lessons which can be provided in fun ways and can in some cases instantly tell you if you have the right answer. It may even sometimes be possible to do homework on a phone and send it to the teacher. Even without the internet phones can be used to provide short assignments, or to provide reminders to study.

On the other hand, today's cell phones are not just phones; they are smart phones. They give too much power in the hands of the children. If misused, they can play havoc with the children's lives. Most parents cannot keep an eye on what their children are using the cell phone for. Secondly, children get distracted when crossing the road while texting on the phone and this can lead to accidents.

I believe that merits of cell phones outstrip the demerits if parents make a conscious effort to choose the right phone for their child. They can block unwanted calls, set time limits for phone usage, prevent access to web sites, set school-accepted usage limits, and locate their child with the built-in GPS feature.

To sum up, for the safety of the child and to keep parents' mind at ease, children should have a cell phone but the onus is on the parents to make the right choice of phone.

Plan followed

Intro: advantages are more than the disadvantages

Para 1: Advantages

Para 2: More advantages

Para 3: Disadvantages

Para 4: Own opinion

Conclusion:

116. It is better to teach sports to young people at school as an alternative to playing computer games at home. Why is it important? Give your opinion and examples from your own experience.

I agree that it is advantageous for young people to engage in sports activities in school instead of playing computer games at home. I have several arguments to support my perspective, which I shall elaborate in the upcoming paragraphs.

To begin with, outdoor activities are good for the physical health of the child. Obviously, if a child is playing outside he/she will be a lot more active than the child that stays indoors. As it is childhood obesity is a serious problem and has to be tackled on a war footing. Children who take part in outdoor sports are less likely to suffer from this problem.

Secondly, outdoor activities are good for mental health. It has been proven by researches that by outdoor activities, the brain develops at a much faster rate than by playing indoors. Moreover, researchers have found a new disorder called 'Nature Deficit Disorder' seen in children who don't play outdoors. It has been seen that children who play outdoors are less stressed out with life. Not only do they become better learners, and do well in school, but they are also much happier. All these benefits accrue by just playing outside.

On the other hand, playing video games is also essential. These games introduce children to technology. They enhance critical thinking and improve visual and motor skills. They can be played indoors, when the weather outsidemay not be good. However, there should be a limit on these games because they are addictive and children forget everything else such as homework, when they start playing. These games are also isolating, as they are usually played alone.

To sum up, it can be reiterated that it is more beneficial for children to play outdoor sports in school than to play video games at home.

Plan followed
Intro: Agree
Para1: sports increase physical health
Para 2: Sports increase mental health
Para 3: Advantages of video games ending with disadvantages
Conclusion:

117. Some parents believe that watching TV and playing computer games should be limited and substituted by reading books. Do you agree or disagree? Give your opinion.

TV and computer games have become an obsession with children and therefore some parents believe that the time children spend on TV and electronic games should be cut down and allotted to reading books. I definitely agree with this perspective. A number of arguments surround my opinion.

There are many advantages of watching TV and playing PC games, provided it is done in moderation. To begin with, video game playing introduces children to computer technology. Secondly, some games provide practice in problem solving and logic e.g. Age of Empires. Video games have proved to improve visual skills. They also improve motor and spatial skills. Children who play video games have better reflexes. Watching TV also is very educative for children.

On the other hand, reading books is also important because it provides an active learning for learners while TV is a passive one. Reading can greatly enhance people's imagination. For example, individuals make different images in their mind when they read some articles or sentences and then use their imagination to put the story together whereas the TV audience just passively accepts information from the TV screen.

What is more, reading can also contribute a lot to language skills. Reading begins the journey through one's language development stages. Reading opens doors to all kinds of new worlds for people. Reading and writing are important ways we use language to communicate.

To summarise, on the whole these games and TV are very good, but only if a balance is maintained between these activities and reading books. For the holistic development of children all these are required. The onus is on the parents to allocate equal time for these to their children.

Plan followed

Intro: Agree

Para 1: Advantages of TV and computer games

Para 2: Importance of books

Para 3: More advantages of reading

Conclusion: Reiterate opinion

118. Young people these days tend to be less polite and respectful than in the past. What are the causes?Suggest some solutions.

It is unfortunate that in the midst of vast progress in every field of life, we also see increasing anti-social behaviour, with people becoming less respectful of each other. This essay intends to analyze some causes of this phenomenon and suggest some ways to ameliorate the situation.

Today, we live in an era of technology in which the whole Earth has shrunk and become a global village. Everybody is connected to everybody through telephone lines and the Internet, but the warmth of relationships has taken a back seat. Most people have more than enough wealth, comfort and freedom, but their hearts desire even more. To satisfy their hearts greed people have become workaholics, and as a result have no time for family and friends. People have become selfish, isolated and indifferent. Each person is busy in his own quest for more. To add to it, the youngsters who are at ease with the new technology think that the elderly are good for nothing and that is why they don't respect them.

The changing family structure is another big cause of this phenomenon. Earlier, people lived in joint families and the grandparents were there to supervise the children. Now there are nuclear families in which both parents go out to work, and children are left unattended in the hands of pervasive media like the TV and the Internet. No one monitors what they watch and they see programs full of violence and crime, which makes them anti-social. The pressure of consumerist society and peers also breeds anti-social behaviour. To add to it, the values of traditional culture are being lost and people are following the global culture, which is also considered anti-social by the orthodox elderly.

There are many solutions to this problem. To begin with, people have to learn to strike a balance between work and family life. Government should also fix the maximum hours a worker can work per week so that exploitation is not there in the job market. People should revert back to the old joint family system. This would benefit everyone. The children would learn moral values and the elderly would be well looked after. Negative effects of excessive consumerism should be taught to the people. Media can play a big role in highlighting the good points of the traditional and the western culture so that the people can adopt good social values. Neighbourhood associations should be set up to connect people to each other.

Summing up, anti-social behaviour and mutual lack of respect in today's times can be dealt with by taking simple measures, and individuals and governments should collectively take these steps.

Plan followed

Intro: I intend to explore the possible causes of this situation and suggest some ways forward.

Para 1: Causes

Para 2: More causes

Para 3: solutions

Conclusion:

119. In some countries around the world men and women are having children late in life. What are the reasons for this development? What are the effects on society and family life?

In modern society, young people have a tendency of postponing their parenthood until late 30's or even early 40's. This essay shall deal with the reasons for this phenomenon and the effects this has on the families and societies.

Many factors could be responsible for this trend. The most important reason is that in today's era of cut-throat competition, young people have to focus on their jobs and therefore have little time for their families. What is more, women of today have become more career oriented and do not wish to be held back by family responsibilities. Obviously, under such circumstances, committing to a serious relationship or starting a family, which means tremendous responsibility and dedication, is not a preferable choice. The cost increase of raising a child is another barrier to late parenthood, and this is especially obvious in major cities around the world.

This change of lifestyle can have some negative effects on society as a whole. Firstly, low birthrates can result in an ageing population and a lack of labor force in the future. A graying society is a dependent society and is a burden on the shoulders of the government. Medical care services can be in high demand and medical cost can rise significantly.

The families too cannot escape the brunt of such a situation. The most disturbing effect is that chances of congenital anomalies rise significantly if a woman bears the first child after the age of 40. The families with mentally or physically challenged children can never be happy families. Another effect can be that the age gap between parents and children is too much and so chances of generation gap are strong.

Summing up, there are many reasons, which are responsible for people marrying late and having babies late in life and this definitely is detrimental for the societies and families. Therefore, young people should learn to give importance to both, a career and a family life.

Plan followed:

Intro: This essay shall deal with the reasons for this phenomenon and the effects this has on the families and societies.

Para 1: Reasons

Para 2: negative effects on society

Para 3: negative effects on families

Conclusion:

120. Parents, usually mothers, give up work, choose to stay at home and look after families. Some people think the government should give them salary. Do you agree or disagree. Give the reasons from your own knowledge and experience.

Ensuring the health and wellbeing of children has never been more critical to a nation's political and economic future than in the 21st century. That is why some people hold the opinion that a parent (usually mother), who quits her job to look after the child should be remunerated by the government. I agree that government should support stay-at-home mothers for the first few years until the child starts going to school.

The most important argument for the state funding of stay-at home mothers is the aging demographic trend. Many women are delaying motherhood or are choosing not to have children as it may impact them professionally and financially. However, this declining birth rate means that in future there will be a very small population of workers and consumers to drive the economy of the nation forward. The government must ensure that this relative shortage of children, the future workforce, does not occur. Giving salary to the stay-at-home mother would encourage many young couples to have children.

Secondly, the child's upbringing is best done by the parent. Otherwise the child has to be left behind in a crèche or in the care of a nanny, which is not the most desirable. Only the parents can give their child a loving, stimulating and stress free environment. Neurological research shows that early years play a key role in children's brain development. The emotional, social and physical development of young children has a direct effect on their overall development and the adult they will become. So, if the government pays the parents who give up their career to care for them, it should be considered as an investment for the future success of the society.

However, this support by the government should only be till the child starts going to school. After a child starts going to school, the mother should go back to work. Women have the education and talent to work. If they don't go back to work, the nation loses the services of half of its workforce.

To sum up, I reiterate my opinion that investment in the health and wellbeing of children is the best and most valuable long-term investment that any government can make, and giving salary to stay-at-home mothers is one good way to do so.

Plan followed

Intro: Agree

Para 1: Reasons

Para 2: Another reason

Para 3: this support should only be until the child starts going to school

Conclusion: Women should be supported by the government to look after the baby and themselves. This can contribute a lot to social welfare.

121. Caring for children is important for any society. It is suggested that all mothers and fathers should be required to take childcare training courses. To what extent do you agree or disagree?

In recent years, childcare has gained as much importance as any other subject of academic studies. Current research has shown that the early years (ages 0-5) are the most sensitive for brain development. Over 90% of brain growth occurs during this period. The people who care for the child are also those who shape the child's mind. I firmly believe that all parents should get childcare training, even if they have to hire professionals for this purpose.

Childcare courses are important for many reasons. Firstly, traditional childcare skills, which are passed on from one generation to another, through oral and informal instruction, are not sufficient in today's era of nuclear families. So parents should undergo childcare training. It is also a misconceived idea that childcare is a simple process of feeding children, changing diapers and making them sleep regularly. Contemporary childcare is not limited to this. Childcare is a complex science that goes beyond nutrition. It involves the physical and emotional wellbeing of children. Therefore, with the changing times and changing family structures, childcare training courses should be the norm for all would be parents.

Secondly, childcare training teaches parents how to take a holistic approach to caring for their children. Many people might wrongly think that childcare is all about love. Parents have to learn when to be firm, and when to give some room to children. For example, children eat a lot of candy, without the knowledge that candy can cause obesity and tooth damage. Parents should not respond to children's needs for candy frequently.

Furthermore, quality childcare has many other far-reaching benefits. Studies show that children who get good care, enter school with better maths, language and social skills. Parents, who have themselves done such courses, can monitor the childcare being given by a professional nanny, better. Thanks to surveillance cameras, parents can keep an eye on what is happening at home from their cell phones, even during work hours.

To summarise, successful childcare does not lie only in love but also in other skills. Children's healthy development is measured not only by physical wellbeing but also by growth in other dimensions. With these borne in mind, parents should now be compelled to join childcare training.

Plan followed

Intro: Parents' participation in care training is advisable.

Para 1: Childcare is much more than changing diapers and feeding children

Para 2: Childcare training teaches parents for a holistic approach of childcare.

Para 3: Far reaching benefits of quality childcare

Conclusion:

122. There are some violent cartoon characters on TV such as Mickey Mouse, which bring negative influence to children. Do you agree or disagree? What types of TV programs are suitable for children?

A child's mind is like a sponge. It absorbs everything they see and hear. If they are constantly exposed to cartoons with violence and fighting it will affect them morally and may lead to teenage violence in the future. Therefore, I agree that violence in cartoons has a detrimental effect on children. A number of arguments support my opinion.

To begin with, a major effect that has been proven by psychological research is that children who watch cartoons full of violence may become less sensitive to the pain and suffering of others. They do not fear violence nor are they bothered by violence in general. If one character gets killed, the other cartoon characters don't care, and they may even laugh. TV makes violence and even death seem funny and unreal. Children do not learn to respect life because violence shown on television desensitizes them.

Secondly, children try to copy what they see and as a result become aggressive by nature. They cannot tell the difference between real and unreal. The characters in the cartoons are make-believe. Young children are unable to realize that when a character attacks someone it is not real and should not be imitated. Children have imaginative play, which is very important for the development of their character. Unfortunately, research proves that watching violent cartoons decreases the imaginative play for the children, and increases the imitative play in which the child imitates the violent and aggressive actions observed in cartoons.

There are many types of TV programs which may be better for children. Educational cartoons are a good way to instill positive values in a child. However, it is the parent's duty to make their children watch cartoons that entertain and educate them, without being violent. Parents must watch the cartoons with their children, and evaluate these cartoons together. Talking with the children about the cartoons they watched is very significant, because parents then will be able to know if these cartoons affect their children positively or not. The government should also take steps to increase the amount of educational programming available to children.

To conclude, children will try to mimic anything they see or hear and cartoon violence is no exception. So, it is the onus of the parents to see to it that they do not see violent cartoon programs and see educational cartoons instead.

Plan followed

Intro: Agree

Para 1: First negative effect of violence on TV – desensitizes children

Para 2: Second negative effect of violence on TV – children imitate the characters and become aggressive

Para 3: Examples of good programs for children. Parents and Government's onus.

Conclusion: Restate opinion

123. Some people argue that a growing number of young people spend too much time in watching TV. Why does this phenomenon happen? And what kinds of activities should they be encouraged to do?

Television has become ubiquitous nowadays. Most families have more than one television in their houses. This essay shall outline some of the reasons why the youth of today spend too much time watching TV, and also suggest some other activities, which they should be motivated to engage in.

First of all, television is usually one of the first media which young people meet with. Parents use this medium as baby sitters for their convenience. This habit continues as the child grows. What's more, TV seems to be the most convenient medium. There's no need to move anywhere, just to push the button and then they can see a completely different world. Then, there is the peer pressure; those who are not up to date with the latest programmes on TV, are considered as inferior by their peers.

In addition, the TV of today has so much to offer. There are uncountable channels running 24/7 to suit every taste. The satellite TV has brought in all foreign channels right into our bedrooms. The youth of the global village of today keep themselves at par with each other through these channels. Last but not least, the reality TV shows of today such as Dance India Dance and Indian Idol have given an opportunity to today's youth to show their talent to the whole world and get name and fame overnight. So, because of all these reasons, the youngsters of today watch too much TV.

Because of TV, children are being alienated from the outside world. They should travel, read books and play outdoor games. Parents and teachers should take the onus of diverting children's mind away from TV and towards other healthier activities. Sports stadiums, gyms and playgrounds should be there in cities, so that the youth are motivated to use them. Parents should act as role-models, by themselves staying away from TV as much as possible. TV should not be there in each and every room of the house. There should be one TV per family. All these steps can prove very useful to motivate the youngsters for other activities.

In summary, there are a plethora of reasons why young people watch too much TV. There should be some control on this and they should be encouraged to do other outdoor activities also.

Plan followed
Intro:
Para 1: Reasons of watching too much TV
Para 2: More reasons
Para 3: other activities – travel - read books - play outdoor games
Conclusion:

124. Some people think that watching TV programmes can help children's development while others disagree. What is your opinion?

Watching TV programs can help children's development in both positive and negative ways. If there is a limit to the number of hours a child sits in front of TV and a control over the type of channels a child is exposed to, then TV can be very good. However, if children watch too much TV and if they are allowed to watch almost any type of program then TV can be detrimental for them.

Television definitely has its good side. It can be entertaining and educational, and can open up new worlds for children, giving them a chance to travel the globe, learn about different cultures, and gain exposure to ideas they may never encounter in their own community. Shows with a pro-social message can have a positive effect on children's behavior; programs with positive role models can influence them to make positive lifestyle changes. The opponents may say that there are plenty of different medium of information such as books, magazines, teachers etc. But, in our modern world children must learn faster and use all contemporary technologies in order to succeed in competition.

On the other hand, watching too much TV can be very harmful. The major hazard is a matter of what children watch. There are many contents that are unsuitable for young people, like violence or porn. These can badly disturb the process of mental development and make children less sensitive. Secondly, television may affect students' schoolwork. Many students spend most time watching TV in the night although they have a lot of homework to do. Some young people even watch TV until midnight. Therefore, it not only affects their work, but also influences their spirits and physical strength. In the morning, students may feel sleepy in class.

Finally, the most serious problem is that television viewing may affect young people's health. It not only affects their eyesight but also leads them to be obese. Children who watch TV are more likely to be inactive and tend to snack while watching TV. On top of that, many TV ads encourage unhealthy eating habits. After-school TV ads target children with ads for unhealthy foods and beverages, like fast food and sugary drinks.

In conclusion, it can be said that it is really important to watch TV properly. Only when children's TV programs are chosen wisely and watched moderately, can they benefit them in positive ways. Therefore, parents should take the responsibility and supervise their children's TV watching activities.

Plan followed

Intro: If watched in moderation, TV is beneficial – otherwise detrimental

Para 1: Positive effects

Para 2: Negative effects

Para 3: Other negative effect

Conclusion – reiterate opinion

125. Most children want to watch the same TV programs and play the same computer games like their friends do. Should parents allow them to do like this?

Psychologists, dealing with the study of child development, believe that peer relationships provide a unique context for cognitive, social and emotional development of children. This is the reason why most children engage in parallel play and tend to do the same types of activities as their peers do. A child who copies other children may pick up good habits but may also pick up bad ones. So, sensitive parenting is required and children should not be allowed to watch the same types of TV shows and play the same types of games as their friends watch and play. A number of arguments support my opinion.

Firstly, all TV shows are not safe for children to watch. Even some cartoon characters are so violent that children learn nothing fruitful from those programs. Such programs may make them insensitive to the pain of others. It is surprising that even watching news could have negative outcomes for a child. For example, sometimes news broadcasts portray suicides glamorously and children may take it as a viable option for stress. As a result of this cases of 'copycat suicide' occur. Therefore parents should not allow their children to see such shows even if their friends are watching the same.

Similarly, all computer games are not good for children. Mind games like solitaire are good but some action games and fighting games can harm children. For example, in a small fight between my niece and nephew last year, my nephew hit my niece so badly that she suffered internal bleeding and had to be hospitalized for few days. When I asked my nephew from where he had learnt to hit like that, he replied he had learnt it from a computer game. In short, children mimic everything innocently without knowing the consequences, so a constant check is required.

Moreover, if parents allow children to watch or play anything just because their friends do so, then children start thinking that they can get away with this excuse every time and by the time parents realize that children are going astray, it may be too late. So, it is necessary to keep an eye on what their children are playing or watching on TV.

To conclude, I reiterate my opinion that children should not be allowed to watch the same TV programmes that their friends watch, or play the same games which their friends play just because their friends are doing so. Parents should carefully monitor what their children play or see.

Plan followed:

Intro: Children should not be allowed to watch and play same type of TV programs and same type of computer games as their friends watch and play.
Para1: All TV shows are not safe for children to watch.
Para 2: All computer games are not good for children.
Para 3: if parents allow children to watch or play anything just because their friends do so, then by the time parents realize that children are going astray, it may be too late
Conclusion: Reiterate opinion

126. In many countries around the world young people decide to leave their parents' home once they finish school. They start living on their own or sharing a home with friends. Do you agree or disagree with this approach? Give your opinion.

The trend of living alone or with friends rather than families has gained popularity among the youth all over the world. It has some advantages as well as disadvantages. I agree with the current trend of young people leaving their parents' homes and living alone. A number of arguments surround my opinion.

Living alone or sharing an apartment with a friend teaches the young adults many things. They become independent, more confident, develop decision-making skills and learn to deal with situations and problems on their own. It is true that these things can be taught at home, while living with their parents, however, there is always a sense of dependency and security that the children feel when with their parents, which may come in the way of their handling things on their own. For instance, children who live with parents till a late age are too dependent on someone else to give them suggestions, or make decisions for them. They may never step out of their comfort zone and consequently, cannot handle challenges very well.

Furthermore, living away from home encourages the young people to explore more and learn more. They gain more experience by meeting new people from different backgrounds and culture. It also helps them become more social, whereas, if they stay with their parents they may not feel the need to socialize or there may be restrictions at home. Such generation gap may spoil the parent-child relationship. It has been rightly said that 'Distance strengthens relationships.'

To add to it, when parents know that their children are going to stay on their own just after school, they also start imparting moral values to their children in early childhood, and so by the time the children step out of their homes, they are mature enough to understand the difference between right and wrong. They also learn how to manage expenses related to rent, bills, food, etc. They would never learn to handle these things when staying with their parents.

The opponents of this view say that such freedom to the youth usually takes them on the wrong path like drug addiction, petty crimes, etc. However, I still believe that with freedom, a sense of responsibility is developed and by the time children reach adulthood, they have been taught about moral values and ethics and they are mature enough to understand the difference between what is right and what is not.

To conclude, I reiterate my opinion that young adults should live independently, as experience is the best teacher, especially for learning life skills. Family will always be there to support them even if they don't live with them. In this world of competition it is very important that the youngsters learn to fend for themselves.

Plan followed

Intro: Agree

Para 1: benefits of living on their own

Para 4: Opponents view

Para 2& 3: More benefits

Conclusion: Reiterate opinion

127. Some people claim that family members are more important than friends; do you agree or disagree with this statement?

Human development is a complex interplay of many factors. Some individuals are of the opinion that parents are more significant for children whereas others opine that friends have a more important role. It is necessary to look at both arguments before forming an opinion.

Parents have direct interactions with the children. They provide a sense of identification to the child. These have their greatest effect on intellectual development and character traits. They also play a very important role in the socializing process of the child. Right from the bedtime stories to the behavioural habits parents play a very important role in making a child a responsible citizen. They know their child's temperament better than anyone else. They can provide critical input better than anyone else. That is why it is believed by some that parents have the strongest role in a child's development.

Friends, on the other hand, are important in order to help children grow emotionally and socially. Children find out who they are by comparing themselves to others. They learn about attitude, character and personality. Building good relationships boosts a child's self-esteem and they find comfort in those friendships when things get tough such as losing a pet or facing family problems. Therefore, friendships are essential to assure children develop a healthy psyche. When kids are surrounded by friends or have one close friend, they have better self-esteem, feel a sense of well-being and experience fewer social problems.

In my opinion, we cannot generalize as to what has more significance. In the early years family generally has more impact but in adolescence friends may impact more. It appears that the power of the peer group becomes more important when the family relationships are not close or supportive. For example, if the parents work extra jobs and are largely unavailable, their children may turn to their peer group for emotional support.

To conclude, children are affected by many different factors such as parents, friends and environment. All these are inextricably linked in the development of children. There is individual variation and therefore it is difficult to generalize which factor plays the most significant role.

Plan followed

Intro: It is necessary to look at both arguments before forming an opinion
Para 1: Role of parents
Para 2: Role of friends
Para 3: your opinion
Conclusion: Cannot generalize. Both are important and individual variations are there

128. Playing team sports can teach students more than just games themselves. What do young people learn from playing team games? How are they useful in their later life?

Both teamwork and individual work require different skills and teach different things. However, team activities are opined by some to be more beneficial than solo activities. While, I do believe that individual activities are important, team activities certainly hold more relevance in today's era of increasing dependence.

There are many significant skills learnt by working in a group such as communication skills, cooperation and conflict management skills. All these are only learnt through teamwork. In solo activities, people do not need to communicate, and so people do not learn these skills. However, when people step into daily life, they realise that communication skills are the most needed skills. They also have to co-operate with their family members, colleagues, friends and neighbours in daily life. When they do team activities, they learn cooperation also. Conflict management skills are also learnt when they do team activities. People have differences of opinion and people learn to manage tough situations very diplomatically.

Furthermore, team activities also broadens a person's horizons as they get to interact with people from diverse backgrounds. Individuals learn to how to make their voice heard, and also learn how to accept the suggestions of others. Finally, people learn sportsman-spirit, which is a very good trait. They learn to accept victory with modesty and defeat with grace. This is an important life skill.

On the other hand, people learn many skills of life through solo activities also. People learn a sense of competition and perseverance through individual activities. All life skills are important. However, people cannot forget that man is a social animal, and cannot live alone. Especially today due to segregation of work people are more dependent on each other than ever before. Success in life today depends upon how people deal with others and how they adapt to working in different situations, which is learnt only by working with others.

To conclude, I would reiterate that team activities and individual activities – both teach important skills of life, but the skills learnt by working with others have a lot more importance.

Plan followed

Intro: agree

Para 1: Communication skills, are only learnt through team sports.

Para 2: co-operation and conflict management skills

Para 3: Leadership skills, decision-making and critical thinking skills while doing team sports

Conclusion: reiterate opinion

129. In some countries more people choose to live alone or by themselves in recent years. Why is this the case? Is it a positive or negative development for the society?

As any country develops, people are faced with new challenges and set new goals for themselves. Many individuals have to leave their families and as a result this trend of living alone or in nuclear family units has increased. This essay intends to explore the reasons of this phenomenon in depth. I believe it is largely a negative development, although there are a few advantages, too.

The first possible reason of this changing family structure is globalization. The huge planet Earth is now a small global village. This situation has opened lots of opportunities for people to travel to and work in other countries. Moving to foreign countries or even in far-off places in one's own country is not possible with the whole family. So this has led to the breaking of joint families into nuclear units. When children of such nuclear families grow older, they live individually to explore new avenues for themselves.

The second important reason is the growing generation gap. The elderly want to stick to their tradition and culture whereas the youngsters want to adopt the global culture. This leads to conflicts and so there is lack of harmony among the family members. The senior members of the family do not want to let go, but the youth want to be free birds and so living individually is the only option once they are able to earn for themselves.

This situation is both positive as well as negative, but the demerits outweigh the merits. Man is, after all, a social animal. Living alone may seem good for some time, but this isolation can lead to depression. There are many ups and downs in life, when a person needs the loving and tender care of his nears and dears. In addition, children of nuclear families are often left unattended when both parents are working. They can become self-centered or can even go astray. The elderly also need the love and support of their children at this age. They are forced to live lives of isolation and depression. This has also led to the mushrooming growth of old-age homes. On the positive side, this leads to faster progress, as people are not held back by family ties. Nuclear families are easy to maintain. Conflicts are also less and so love among the extended family members is maintained. Family get-togethers are celebrated with great enthusiasm.

To sum up, living alone has become common because of many reasons, which have been discussed above. In my opinion, the cons of this situation, overpower the pros.

Plan followed
Intro:
Para 1: First reason
Para 2: Second reason
Para 3: positives and negatives of this situation.
Conclusion:

130. Nowadays young people prefer to move to big cities; older people, however, are the opposite and prefer to stay in the countryside. What are the positives and negatives of this trend?

Rural ageing, or in other words more elderly in the rural areas, has become very common almost everywhere in the world as the young move to the cities in search of better opportunities. This essay intends to analyze the pros and cons of this demographic shift. I believe that the demerits of such a situation are more.

The advantages to the young to move to cities are obvious. Cities are full of opportunities for the young. Job vacancies can be filled. Economic growth can be sustained. The pension gaps can be filled by the contributions of new young workers and they also pay taxes.

Similarly, the elderly who don't migrate to cities are at an advantage. Ageing in the rural setup is healthier than ageing in the urban areas. For instance in a recent survey, 70% of the elderly in rural areas reported their health as good as compared to only 52% in the cities. Then, there are strong social networks in rural areas, where life is comparatively slower. Also there is a strong sense of attachment to the place. The elderly feel more comfortable in familiar environment.

On the other hand, this urban migration of the young is challenging for the youth. The young migrants may be exploited as increasing competition may make them willing to work for low pay. Increase in urban population may put pressure on resources. Unemployment may arise if there is unrestricted number of workers.

Furthermore, the rural areas may face economic disadvantage, as there are fewer young workers. Agricultural production would suffer and there would be reduced family support for the elderly. In such a situation, additional pressure would fall on the governments.

To sum up, young people moving to cities and elderly staying behind in villages would have both positive and negative effects. Concrete steps have to be taken by the governments to ameliorate the negative effects.

Plan followed

Intro: Discuss essay intro

Para 1: advantages to the young

Para 2: Advantages to the elderly

Para 3: Disadvantages to the young

Para 4: Disadvantages to the elderly

Conclusion:

131. Some people say that it is impossible to live comfortably in big cities. What problems are faced by the people living in big cities? What steps can be taken to solve those problems?

Cities are growing. Unfortunately this development has made it difficult for people to lead a comfortable life in cities. This essay intends to analyze the problems faced because of this situation and suggest some solutions.

To begin with, the most common problem in many cities is environmental pollution and unhygienic surroundings. This is because cities act as magnets for people of the rural areas as a result of which cities have to house more people than they can possibly afford. Therefore it is hard to maintain cleanliness. Unhygienic surroundings are the breeding ground for germs and cause many health problems. On top of that, the spending capacity of people has gone up and so more and more people are buying their personal vehicles. This vehicular pollution affects the quality of air and leads to many respiratory ailments. All of these affect the quality of life in cities.

Furthermore, the cost of living is also pretty high in metros. In large cities, land prices are exorbitant. Consequently, people are forced to buy ridiculously small homes for huge prices. Those who cannot afford to do so spend the whole of their lives in rented apartments. Worse still, the law and order situation in many big cities is not particularly good making them unsafe for visitors as well as those dwelling in those localities.

The solutions are not simple, but many of these problems can be solved with a little bit of planning. High population density is the main reason that reduces the quality of life in cities. Although this is not exactly avoidable, governments can reduce the migration to cities by making jobs available in smaller towns as well. For example, industrial units can be set up in small towns and villages. If these units employ the people living nearby they will not have to move into large cities. What's more, the fact that cities are home to a large number of people makes it possible for civic bodies to collect more money from taxes etc. If these taxes are utilized properly civic authorities can build better roads and flyovers that will ease the traffic congestion. And by improving the quality of public health care, the government can ensure that all people get medical attention when they need it.

To sum up, poor planning and the centralization of jobs is the main reason that reduces the quality of life in large cities. However, these problems are solvable to a great extent. The governments just need to make a determined effort to decentralize the jobs.

Plan followed:

Intro:

Para 1: causes Para 2: More causes

Para 3: Solutions Conclusion:

132. Parents often buy their children many toys. What are the advantages and disadvantages of children having a large number of toys? Use examples from your personal knowledge and experience.

Toys are not just playthings. They are the building blocks of our child's future. They teach our children about the world and about themselves. That is precisely why parents always want to provide their children with toys. The issue of concern here is regarding the number of toys children are given. While some parents fill their children's rooms to the ceiling with toys, others limit the number of toys that children have to play with.

On the one hand, there are a few advantages of children having a plethora of toys. They have more variety to play with and they can pick out their personal favourites from those toys according to their taste. Moreover, parents can be satisfied that their children have enough to play with when they are themselves busy.

On the other hand, too many toys prevent kids from fully developing their gift of imagination. Children learn to be more creative with fewer toys. To cite an example, an experiment was conducted in Germany in which all toys of a kindergarten classroom were removed for three months. It was observed that children soon began to use their basic surroundings to invent games and use imagination in their playing.

Furthermore, children with fewer toys establish better social skills. They learn how to share with other children. Also, they develop a greater love for reading, writing, and art. Fewer toys also make children to become resourceful by solving problems with only the materials at hand. And resourcefulness is a gift with unlimited potential.

Children with fewer toys become less selfish. Those who get everything, believe they can have everything they want. This attitude is definitely detrimental to a child's psychology. They do not even value the toys they have. Another advantage of not having a basement full of toys is that children are more likely to play outside and have the much needed physical exercise which results in healthier and happier bodies. Finally, fewer toys result in a less-cluttered, cleaner and healthier home.

To conclude, toys are very much needed for the development of children, but there should be a limit on the number of toys a child should have. Excess of everything is bad.

Plan followed

Intro: a balanced approach as it is a discuss essay.

Para 1: Advantages of having too many toys

Para 2: Advantages of fewer toys

Para 3: Other advantages of fewer toys

Para 4: more advantages of fewer toys

Conclusion: fewer toys are better

133. Young people have different ideas and attitudes with their parents and grandparents. What are the differences? What problems may be caused?

The differences in the thinking of parents and children have been there since age-old times. These differences are referred to as the 'Generation Gap'. This essay shall delve into these differences and the problems caused by these differences.

To begin with, it is generally seen that older people have more traditional views on the world. For example, younger people tend to have a more relaxed view on marriage and divorce, whereas our parents and certainly our grandparents considered marriage to be a sacred and important institution. What is more, parents have many years of life experience behind them, and want to impart this knowledge to their children, but the children do not always want to hear. They want to be free, independent, to live their own lives, and make their own choices.

Furthermore, the older generation believes in going to bed early and getting up early, whereas the young belong to the 24/7 society, where the waking and sleeping patterns are different. What is more, the elderly want them to wear traditional clothes, whereas the youth want to wear the global wear that is jeans and T-shirts because they feel comfortable in it. Another difference is that the parents want their children to follow the careers of their choice. However, youngsters want to walk on the un-trodden path and pave new ways for themselves.

These differences can lead to a strained relationship between young people and their parents. Children can rebel against their parents because of this generation gap. Today's 'Generation Gap' is a lot different from the 'Generation Gap' of yesteryears. Earlier children were dependent on their parents and grandparents for all knowledge and information. They accepted meekly what was told to them. Today's children belong to the age of the IT revolution and are part of a global village. In many ways they are much more well-informed than their parents and grandparents. Today, the onus is on the parents and grandparents to walk fast and catch up with their children to bridge this gap.

To sum up, I would like to say that generation gap is nothing new and only the parents can take a step forward in this direction and bridge this gap.

Plan followed

Intro: This essay shall look into the causes and problems caused by the generation gap.

Para 1: Differences

Para 2: More differences

Para 3: Effects

Conclusion: Onus on parents to bridge the gap

134. Some people believe that children should be brought up in cities. Others believe that the countryside offers a better environment for children. Discuss both views and give your opinion.

Some people believe that growing up in a big city provides children with many advantages, whereas others, including some educators and social scientists, agree that the countryside is better for the health and physical development of children. This essay shall discuss both views. I, however, side with the former view.

Admittedly, there are some advantages of raising children in the countryside. Firstly, the countryside is virtually pollution free as a result of which children can breathe fresh and healthy air. Secondly, parents do not have to worry about where their children are playing because there is a lot of open space and there is no risk of being hit by any vehicles. Finally, children brought up in the countryside are more in touch with their culture and tradition than those in cities. In villages people have still retained the community spirit whereas in cities people don't know their next-door neighbours.

On the other hand, living in a big city almost guarantees children a chance of receiving a better education than in the countryside. Cities are equipped with more schools and facilities such as large libraries, museums, zoos and other educational establishments that can assist children in their overall education. Parents can choose where to send their children to school based upon their own set of requirements and special needs or abilities of the children. In contrast, the children living in the countryside normally have few, if any, choices concerning where they attend school and the educational facilities mentioned above are also next to nil.

In addition to a better variety of educational opportunities, children can learn through more cultural experiences when growing up in a big city. Since cities are busy places with events always going on, on the weekends children can have the opportunity to attend concerts or view exhibits in museums and be exposed to many different kinds of people with different backgrounds. On the other hand, children in the countryside are very limited as to their exposure to cultural events and the types of people they see. Seldom do they ever even enter a museum or come into contact with people different from themselves. This can limit their knowledge and views of people outside their communities.

To conclude, while the countryside surely provides benefits such as cleaner air, less noise and a calmer lifestyle, the benefits of living in a big city far outweigh those of living in the countryside. This is due to the fact that children can gain a better education and more cultural experiences when they grow up in a big city.

Plan followed

Intro: This essay shall discuss both views before forming an opinion.

Para 1: advantages of raising children in the countryside

Para 2: Advantages of raising children in cities

Para 3: more advantages   Conclude: Raising in cities is better

135. Nowadays in some countries children are given fewer responsibilities compared to the past. Some people believe it is a positive development while others argue otherwise. Discuss both views. What is your opinion? Give some relevant examples from your own experience.

There have been many changes in the way children are brought up now, as compared to the past times. One such change is that the children of today have lesser duties and obligations than in the earlier times. Some individuals consider this change as positive and others opine that it is detrimental for the children and society. I will delve into both these perspectives in this essay. I, however, side with the latter view.

In the past, children had more tasks as compared to the present era. In those times there were a lot of adverse situations that the children had to encounter, like freedom struggles, wars, revolutions, etc. Such situations led the children to become more mature and thus, more responsible at an earlier age. Another reason is that the family structure was such that each family had many children. Consequently, the elder siblings were given the responsibility of taking care of the younger ones in the family. As a result, the family bonds were stronger and children valued everything more.

In the contemporary era, children are not given too many responsibilities. The competition has become global and children focus only on the academics. They are not given any extra burden or duties by the parents. They enjoy outdoor sports, extra-curricular activities and have time for their hobbies too. This leads to the holistic development of children. Such children are more focused and career oriented. However, the downside to this development is that the children become responsible much later in life and face many difficulties when they come across hardships. Also, according to some studies, there are more chances of such childrenbecoming insensitive or selfish when they grow up. They may not even take care of their own parents when needed.

Admittedly, it is important that children of the contemporary world need to focus more on their academics and future. However, for the holistic development and to inculcate in children attributes like self-discipline, being caring, responsible and for stronger family ties, it is important that parents involve the children in the household chores. These chores can be made interesting for the children.

To conclude, it is true that children of today do not have so many responsibilities, but I believe that it will be damaging for the society if the children are not involved in the household chores. Parents need to instill confidence in children by assigning them some tasks, which they carry out responsibly.

Plan followed

Intro:

Para 1: Earlier situation   Para 2: Present situation

Para 3: Own view   Conclusion:

136. In many countries, children are getting fatter and less fit day by day. Why is it so and suggest solutions.

It is irrefutable that childhood obesity is a burgeoning problem these days in many parts of the world. In this essay I intend to discuss the causes of this problem and suggest some ways forward.

The most important reason for this unfortunate situation is unhealthy diet. Children are attracted to fast food, which is rich in sugar and fat. They are ignorant of what constitutes a healthy diet. Parents nowadays are busy in their work and are not present to guide their children. To add to it, children are bombarded with advertisements from fast food companies.

Another important factor is that children are much less active than they used to be. In the past young people took part in activities that burned a lot of energy. However, today they spend a lot of their time indoors, sitting in front of computers or playing video games. This sedentary life style is playing havoc with the health of young people.

There are a number of steps that need to be taken to solve this problem. The first is to educate children about nutrition. Health education should be incorporated in school curricula. Schools should organize compulsory lessons to explain the main elements of a healthy diet and teach pupils how to prepare healthy meals. Parents should also cook healthy delicious meals at home so that children are deterred from eating fast food. Furthermore, governments should have some restrictions on the type of adverts shown in children's programmes. Finally, children should be encouraged to take part in sports. Schools have a great role to play in this.

To conclude, childhood obesity is a serious problem and it should be tackled on a war footing, otherwise the young people of today will have a very unhealthy middle and old age.

Plan followed:
Intro: In this essay I intend into the causes of this problem and suggest some ways forward
Para 1: First reason
Para 2: Another reason
Para 3: solutions
Conclusion

137.   People say that a child's success is dependent on the way parents bring them up. To what extent do you agree or disagree?

Success in a person's life does not come overnight. One cannot buy success from a store. It is something that requires the continuous investment of time and effort by the parents. Therefore, I agree with the given statement that nurturing by parents contributes a great deal to a child's success.

There is no doubt in the upbringing of a child, the most important part is played by parents. Parenting consists of balanced development of children's physical, emotional and intellectual qualities. Parents provide shelter, food and clothes and also promote the healthy growth of their children. Parents provide a safe loving environment and have a mental bonding with their children. All these things do play a part in the child's success in his later life.

Undoubtedly, there are other factors such as good schooling, good teachers, peers and the media. These too have a role in success of a child; but ultimately it is the parents who select the schools for their children. Good schools have good infrastructure and good faculty. They also have regular parent-teacher meetings. These interactions between parents and the pedagogues are helpful in understanding the aptitude of the child and guiding him towards the right career path.

Furthermore, the friend's circle of the child also matters in his success. Here too, there is the role of the parents. Good parenting involves keeping an eye on the child's peers. If parents are themselves friendly with the child then their children will introduce them to their friends also. This is very important in the most impressionable adolescent years of a child's life. Finally, there is the role of media. Here too parents can intervene and monitor what their children are watching.

To sum up, parenting is not an easy task. Becoming a parent is the easiest part, whereas, being a conscious and positive parent is a momentous task. Parenting is the most important role one faces in a lifetime. Parents who provide an encouraging environment for their children are rewarded when, as adults, their children become successful in life.

Plan followed
Intro: Agree
Para 1: Parents' role
Para 2: Role of schools – but suggest that ultimately it is the parents role
Para 3: Role of peers and media – but ultimately it is the parents role
Conclusion: reiterate opinion

138. In some countries, the age of 18 means adults, while in others, it is older. What is your opinion and talk about the responsibility of an adult?

The legal age of adulthood ranges internationally from ages 15-21, with 18 being the most common. In this essay, I shall discuss what the ideal age of adulthood should be, and also discuss the responsibilities that adulthood entails.

It is indeed difficult to draw a line between adulthood and childhood. Nonetheless, it is important to set an age for recognising a person as an adult. This is mainly to protect a minor against his inexperience. In my opinion, the legal age of adulthood should be 18. I believe that by the age of 18, a child is mature enough to know what is right or wrong. He/she should be given some freedom, and should be held responsible for his actions.

As far as the responsibilities of an adult are concerned, adulthood has to be looked at from a social context. So, it is a combination of age and social milestones. Adults are expected to be responsible and accountable for their actions. For example, if they get a driving licence, it is expected that they drive responsibly, abide by all the traffic laws and be held accountable if they do not do so.

Furthermore, an adult is expected to get a job, earn an income and use it to pay for his needs and wants. Adults are answerable for their life obligations, whether that is in marriage, at work or in the community being a worthwhile citizen. Getting married and having children are individual responsibilities that are expected of adults as being part of the society they live in.

To sum up, adulthood is a very subjective term. A person may be biologically an adult, but may be considered a child if he is below that legal age when he can be called an adult. Conversely, he may be much older, but behave childishly. However, to generalize, the age of 18 is ideal to be called an adult and there are many responsibilities that are expected of adults.

Plan followed:

Intro: This essay shall deal with the responsibilities of an adult

Para1: Which age should be the legal age of adulthood.

Para 2: responsibilities of an adult

Para 3: more responsibilities

Conclusion:

139. Some people agree that children should do what their parents tell them to do. Other people think children should learn how to think for themselves. Discuss both views and give your opinion.

Bringing up children the right way has been a long debated issue. Some individuals are of the opinion that parents should decide everything for their children, while others opine that children should be made independent and should take their own decisions. This essay intends to analyze both the perspectives. I am of the opinion that children should be allowed to think freely and take decisions, but with the guidance of the parents.

The main reason why some people say that parents should tell their children what to do is because children are immature and do not know right from wrong. Children do not have the awareness, experience, knowledge and wisdom that their parents do. So, children should do as their parents say. Moreover, it cannot be denied that parents only want the best for their children and will never misguide their children. Following what their parents say also makes the children more disciplined and respectful of others.

On the other hand, there are many benefits of encouraging the children to learn to think for themselves. First, they become more responsible and independent soon. These attributes are essential in today's era of competition. This can be done by making the children decide their own activities, choose the sports they like, pursue their interests and not restricting them with rules. Furthermore, such freedom leads to creativity and originality in children and they grow up to be successful in their career.

In my opinion, children should not be restricted and should be encouraged to be creative and free thinkers. However, parents need to play the role of guides and coaches. They need to ensure that while the children are making their own decisions, they are shown a path and a direction. For instance, when parents ask children to do household chores, it should be in such a way that the children feel that they are in-charge of the activity. This motivates them to complete the tasks independently and without any restrictions.

To conclude, it can be said that it is important to give liberty to children to make choices and decisions, but the parents need to show them the right direction by guiding them and supervising their activities.

Plan followed

Intro: Discuss essay
Para 1: In Support of Parents
Para2: For Children
Para 3: For Children
Conclusion

140. Nowadays, fewer people tend to look after their old relatives and send them to some old age homes. What is the situation in your country? In your opinion, who should be responsible to look after the elderly?

Demographic trends suggest that we are heading towards a graying society and it is the bitter truth of today that children are sending their elderly parents to live separately in old age homes. Fortunately, in my country India, the old-age homes are still in their infancy. Ideally, the children should look after their elderly. However, I have strong arguments to suggest that the elderly should live separately in old-age homes.

The ideal situation would be that the elderly should be looked after by their children. Parents spend their whole life toiling hard to provide the best to their children and now it is the children's turn to pay back. It is their moral responsibility to look after their parents. However, it has been seen that most elderly are leading miserable lives with their children. They are leading isolated lives amidst their family members and that is why I firmly believe that they should live separately.

My first argument is that living separately will give them a feeling of independence. Moreover, by doing so, they will command more respect in the eyes of their children. It is irrefutable that relationships become strong and meaningful when people are not under the same roof. Hence, if aged people are away from their children physically, both will be closer to each other emotionally.

What is more, the mushrooming growth of old age homes is ample evidence that they are a boon for the society. They give the opportunity to the elderly to be in the company of people of similar age and experience. They also remain healthy with timely day-to-day activities. In such homes, the elderly also get a chance to do some social service activities, which in turn help the society.

Furthermore, the culture of the old age homes tends to refine some attitudes of the aged such as short temper and negative thinking. Old age homes are also a boon for those elderly who face social isolation in their own homes where their so-called loved ones neglect them badly and have no time for them.

To conclude, the elderly should live with people of their own age group, in old age homes, where they enjoy the retired period of their life nicely, comfortably and productively.

Plan followed

Intro: Agree. Old people should live separately

Para 1: Ideal situation

Para 2: this will give them a feeling of independence.

Para 3: Advantages of old age homes

Para 4: More advantages

Conclusion: Reiterate opinion

141. In many countries, people are not taking care of their elderly relatives but seeking help of professionals to look after them. Do you think this is a positive or a negative development?

In the contemporary world, more and more people are hiring specialists to take care of the elderly members of the family at home or in old age homes. I believe this as a positive development and a number of arguments support my perspective, which I will discuss in the forthcoming paragraphs.

The merits of hiring professionals to take care of the senior members of the family are numerous. In this fast paced world, everyone is leading hectic lives. People do not have enough time to spend with their family and take care of the elderly. So, it is better to have the experts take care of the elderly members of the family, as they are the best people to provide them not only with the medical care and attention they need, but also keep them company while the family members are busy at work or with their studies. This avoids the complications that arise in old age due to loneliness.

Furthermore, there are several senior care options available today in the form of old age homes, in-home caregivers or in assisted living communities. People can choose and decide on the best possible option that can be given to the elderly members of the family. Of course, this should be done with the consent of the elderly and also depending on the amount of care required for them. There are certain old age related conditions, which are best treated under specialists' care. So, in such cases, this care can be given in-home or in a nursing home, under proper supervision of the experts.

Undeniably, it is the responsibility of the children to take care of their parents in their old age. That being said, the family members may not have the time to be able to provide them with the care that is needed by old aged members. Moreover, life expectancy has increased all over the world and there are two generations in many families that fall in the elderly group, needing the same kind of care and attention. So, this burden falls on the younger generation and it is impractical for them alone to bear this responsibility. So, the specialists need to be hired in such cases.

To recapitulate, it can be safely said that the younger family members should provide the best care to the elderly family members and in this modern era, hiring professional caregivers is the most befitting and practical approach.

Plan followed:
Intro:
Para 1: benefits of hiring professional
Para 2: reasons why care cannot be provided at home
Para 3: diificult for younger generation to bear the responsibility
Conclusion:

142. Nowadays, people are living an increasingly longer life and in many countries there are more old people than young people. What are the advantages and disadvantages of this trend?

It is the inescapable truth that we are heading towards a graying society, which means that the population of the elderly is soaring. Scientists predict that there would be fewer youth than olds in the near future. Although the population ageing should be seen as a success story, it brings social and economic challenges for the nations. So, it can be said that this situation is both, positive as well as negative.

First, there will not be a large enough workforce to keep the economy running. Lesser number of youngsters would mean lesser people working, which will decrease the revenue received by the government from taxes. To increase the labor pool, the government will need to spend a lot to invite foreign skilled workers to fill the job vacancies. This is exactly what is happening in developed countries like Canada and Australia, which have opened doors for skilled workers to immigrate and settle there permanently.

Second, health care costs are four to five times higher with the elderly because of their deteriorating health. Wear-and-tear on their bodies accumulated over the years makes their immune system more susceptible to disease. It will be necessary to allocate a considerable budget from the government to improve the quality of their life. No wonder, nanny care courses are in full demand in developing countries because professional nannies are required to look after the elderly and are being paid handsomely.

On the other hand, we cannot demonize the older population, because one day we, too, will pass through that stage. We cannot deny we've made progress. We've given ourselves the great gift of longer life and better health. So anything we face in terms of the challenges of dealing with this, does not outweigh those benefits. The challenge for the future is to ensure that people everywhere can grow old with security and dignity, and that they can continue to participate in social life as citizens with full rights. One way out would be to increase the age of retirement, and to give part-time work to the willing elderly. This could help in a big way to the predicted worker shortage. Also, part time, older workers don't need the benefits, don't get called home for sick kids, are more mature, and approach their jobs with more patience and better perspective. Working part time also allows retirees to stay active while maintaining their lifestyles, feel productive and interact with others, which is a win-win situation for all.

In summary, aging is inescapable. A predominantly old-aged society will certainly have a negative impact on a country's advancement, and so it has to be planned well. The countries will have to spend on ensuring the quality of life for the senior citizens, and providing job opportunities to them for as long as they are able to remain productively engaged.

Plan followed:
Intro:
Para 1: negative effect on economy
Para 2: Healthcare costs
Para 3: Positives of a graying society and how to meet the challenges
Conclusion:

143. There are more and more old people in many parts of the world. What are the causes of this and what are the solutions.

Demographic trends suggest that today we belong to a graying society. This essay shall delve into the reasons of this phenomenon and also suggest some ways to deal with this situation.

The main reason for the increased life expectancy of people is the development in health care. Years ago, people died young because of simple things such as an infection or a virus. Now we have antibiotics and other medicines to help cure infections. Many incurable cancers and diseases such as tuberculosis are now completely curable. Due to technological advancements, many diseases such as breast and uterine cancer can be diagnosed so early that the evil can be nipped in the bud. What is more, advances in surgical techniques have made miracles happen. Transplant surgeries have increased the life of many.

Another reason of people living longer is that there is better access to health care. Earlier if a person suffered a heart attack or a stroke, a lot of harm was done before he could reach the nearest super-specialty hospital. Now faster modes of transport and the mushrooming growth of such hospitals provide timely treatment. To add to it, people can now get consultation from any doctor in any part of the world because digital x-rays, MRIs and CT scans are there which can be sent at the click of a mouse.

A final reason for this is that there is more personal awareness. The quality of nutrition has also improved. People eat more healthfully than they used to. It is now common knowledge that eating low fat food can prevent heart disease, and we know that eating fruits and vegetables can prevent cancers. Now people have begun to realize the importance of exercise. Walking, yoga and gym culture has become very popular not only among the youth but also with the octogenarians and centenarians of our society.

These demographic changes are the reality of today. There is no going back. A lot of planning is needed at the individual level and at the government level to meet the challenges of old age. Governments have to provide special privileges to the elderly so that they don't face any problems and at the individual level people should plan their retired life nicely so that they may lead a happy life. For whatever reason people are living longer, what is important is that living longer is one thing, while living healthier and leading productive lives is another.

To sum up, people are living longer because of many reasons and many steps can be taken to face the challenges of this demographic trend.

Plan followed

Intro:

Para 1: first reason - Para 2: another reason – Para 3: another reason –

Para 4: steps to tackle it   Conclusion:

144. It is a fact that people nowadays are under a lot of pressure and their lives are becoming increasingly stressful. What could be the possible reasons for this? What are some solutions to address this issue?

It is irrefutable that everyone in this fast paced world of today is suffering from some form of stress or the other. This essay intends to look into some major causes of stress in people's lives and suggest some ways to overcome it.

To begin with, there is a lot of stress in the workplace. Managers are expected to deal not only with their own pressure, but also with the pressure of the people they manage. There are some people who are being squeezed from above and below. And when people themselves feel pressurized, they often put additional pressure on their colleagues, which is their outlet of stress.

Not only at the workplace, there are stresses even at home. The demands of the children are rocketing in this era of consumerism. Inflation is going higher and higher. Children and teenagers have their own share of stress of this highly competitive era.

The solutions are not easy. There can never be one way of effectively dealing with pressure, since no two people are affected by stresses in the same way. One man's stress may be another person's excitement. And, of course, depending upon what else is going on in a person's life, what feels manageable one day, may feel overwhelming the next.

Fortunately, there are things one can do that help manage the pressure. To begin with, one should do a stress audit. By identifying what stresses which overwhelm you, you can look at prevention as well as cure. Secondly, one should set realistic goals. Trying to make big changes usually results in failure and disappointment. By lowering your standards, you can create far more 'wins' for yourself, and 'wins' make us all feel great. Then, misunderstandings are another big cause of stress. Therefore, anything that improves communication or clears the air will reduce pressure.

To sum up, there are many causes of stress in people's lives today. But steps can be taken to manage it.

Plan followed

Intro:

Para 1: Causes

Para 2: Causes

Para 3: Solutions

Para 4: Solutions

Conclusion:

145.   Old people think that life was better in the past than what it is now. Do you agree or disagree? Give your reasons and examples from your own life.

Although it is true that a great many people now have a higher standard of living than in the past, it does not seem that it makes people any happier. In many ways and in many places, life is much easier and more comfortable than it used to be, but I agree that life was better in the past. A number of arguments surround my opinion.

One feature of modern life that has changed in many places is that people have less contact with each other, and there is less of a feeling of belonging to a community. People leave their hometowns more than they used to and so family ties are not as strong as they used to be. In cities, people often do not know their neighbours. As a result of all this, people can feel isolated. People help each other less and there is much more emphasis on the individual. Earlier, people had slower lives and they knew each other and led happier lives with a feeling of belonging for each other

Modern life has also brought with it problems that people do not think existed in the past. For example, many people are concerned about rises in crime, and they also feel that life is much faster and more stressful than it used to be.

Another reason for people's unhappiness is that they have higher expectations than they used to have. They have more but they want even more. This leads to feelings of disappointment and even anger when people do not have everything they think they should have. People take for granted all sorts of comforts and material possessions that people in the past would have considered luxuries. They don't appreciate what they have. They simply want more. In the past, society was not consumerist. People bought only what they needed and were happy and contented.

It is also true, in my opinion, that when people have all the basic needs for survival, they are likely to become more introverted and think about life more. This can lead to feelings of depression and dissatisfaction with their lives. If you are struggling to survive, you do not have the time or the opportunity to think so much about the meaning of life.

Of course, it is impossible to return to the past and nobody would want to exchange the comforts of modern life for the way that people used to live. However, in many ways, progress has not made people happier. Therefore, I reiterate my opinion that life was better in the past.

Plan followed

Intro: Agree

Para 1: isolated lives today

Para 2: More crime and more stress today

Para 3: Consumerist society. No contentment

Para 4: People think about their needs more as basic necessities is not a problem today.

Conclusion

146. Some people prefer to live in hot climate, while others like to live in cold climate. Discuss both of the views and give your own opinions.

There are various factors which a person considers while deciding a place to live in and climate is just one of them. This essay shall discuss why some people prefer a cold climate and others choose to live in a warmer one.

There are several benefits of living in a country with a hot climate. The main advantage is that people can afford being outside in the sun and doing outdoor activities. For example, residents of the hot countries spend their time sunbathing, swimming in the sea and eating in the open air. Another benefit of warm weather is that it is cheaper and easier to buy clothes and wearing less clothing gives you a feeling of freedom. Also many elderly people choose to move to hotter climates for health reasons and to avoid the harsh winter conditions.

On the other hand, cold climate also has its advantages. The main advantage is economic benefits. Many people like snow activities such as skiing, sledding and building snowmen and therefore they come to these places as tourists for such activities, enabling the residents an opportunity to gain economically from these tourists. What is more, people don't have to worry about sweating and suffering from heat strokes.

Personally, I believe that extremes of both hot and cold climate are not good. Both types of climates have their share of pleasures and challenges. In India, we generally have the tropical climate in which there are four seasons – summer, winter, autumn and spring. Summers are generally very hot and winters very cool. Autumn and spring generally have pleasant weather which is neither too hot nor too cold. So we get to enjoy all types of weather.

To conclude, it can be said that there are pros and cons of both types of climates and choosing to live in any climate is a matter of personal choice.

Plan followed

Intro: Discuss essay intro

Para 1: Advantages of hot climate
- people can afford being outside in the sun and doing outdoor activities
- it is cheaper and easier to buy clothes and wearing less clothing gives you a feeling of freedom
- many elderly people choose to move to hotter climates for health reasons and to avoid the harsh winter conditions

Para 2: Advantages of cold climate
- main advantage is economic benefits
- people like snow activities such as skiing, sledding and building snowmen
- people earn from tourism

Para 3: own view – refer to climate of your country   Conclusion: it is a matter of personal choice

147. To what extent do you think governments should be held responsible when problems of homelessness and unemployment arise?

When a country has a large number of homeless and unemployed people, it is a clear indication that something is wrong with the way it is governed. However, I do not agree that the governments can be held completely responsible for loss of jobs and homes. A number of arguments surround my opinion.

It is a well known fact that the economy of any country depends on internal and external factors. A government can be held responsible for the internal conflicts that might be causing joblessness and homelessness. However, no government in the world can effectively control external affairs. For example, a lot of people lost jobs due to the economic crisis in 2008. In fact, the US recession caused job loss in countries like India and China. It affected India's booming outsourcing industry. And because it was an external factor, the governments in India couldn't be held responsible for this situation.

Nonetheless, there are many things that governments can do to reduce the severity of these problems and protect their citizens. Governments collect taxes from the wealthy people. It is definitely the onus of the government to use this money effectively to improve the living standards of the poorer sections of the society. If a government fails to do it, it is certainly inefficient. In India, for example, the government has launched several schemes to provide housing and employment to people. Although the country still faces these problems, the situation has considerably improved in recent years. This is a clear indication that political willpower and proper governance can improve the economic status of a country and its people.

To sum up, it is difficult to arrive at the conclusion that governments can be held completely responsible for problems like job loss and unemployment. Of course, the governments have a role to play in easing these problems, but factors outside the control of a government too can upset a nation's financial status.

Plan followed

Intro: I do not agree that the governments can be held completely responsible for loss of jobs and homes
Para 1: External factors can cause homelessness and unemployment
Para 2: how good governance can help ease the situation
Conclusion:

148. Some people believe that hobbies need to be difficult to be enjoyable. To what extent do you agree or disagree?

Hobbies of people change over period of time. Some hobbies are relatively easy, while others involve more of a challenge. Personally, I believe that hobby is an activity which can give us pleasure and hence both types of hobbies can be fun for different people and therefore I disagree with the statement that hobbies need to be difficult in order to be enjoyable. A number of arguments surround my opinion.

Firstly, one follows a hobby for relaxation and enjoyment, so it is practiced with ones heart; it is not at all necessary for the hobby to be difficult to derive fun from it. Many people enjoy easy hobbies. One example of an activity that is easy for most people is watching movies or listening to music which is one of the most popular hobbies of mostly all families in my town. Another instance is playing some easy games like angry birds or snakes which does not involve as much difficulty as some other games, even though they become more popular hobbies of many people in short time. These kinds of hobbies require no hardship; they are simple and yet people enjoy them a lot. .

Moreover, some activities which can be very tough for one can be easier for others who follow it as a hobby. For example, knitting is my passion and I find it very easy. I can even make very complicated patterns and knit all types of sweaters with ease. But when my sister tries to knit, she finds it really hard and cannot do it well even if she tries very hard. So, I believe it is not the degree of difficulty which makes a hobby more interesting or enjoyable but the interest we take in it.

On the other hand, there are some hobbies which involve some challenges can give us sense of satisfaction or sense of achievement, and sometimes this sense of achievement makes us enjoy those hobbies more. However, I still believe that a hobby is an activity which provides us fun and this could be anything from playing with one's favourite pet to filling colours on canvas. One can get fun from anything and, it is not essential in every case to face a challenge to enjoy it.

To summarise, choosing hobbies and enjoying them varies from person to person. It is not necessary for any activity to involve some difficulty to become enjoyable. In fact a simple hobby can give us a lot of pleasure with relaxation.

Plan followed:
Intro: Disagree
Para 1: Firstly, one follows hobby to get fun and so he does it with heart, it is not necessary to have difficult hobbies to get fun from it. Give examples.
Para 2: What is tough for one may be easy for others.
Para 3: there are some hobbies which involve some challenges
Conclusion:

149. Some people believe that old public buildings in cities should be restored while others say that they should be demolished and new buildings should be built instead. Discuss both sides and give your opinion.

It has been a matter of intense debate for quite some time now as to what should be done with old buildings. Some opine that it is futile to spend money on their restoration and upkeep, while others want to see them restored to their old glory. I believe that those old buildings which are neither beautiful nor useful, should be demolished whereas those buildings which add character to a place, give it a unique identity or have a historic significance should be repaired and restored at all costs.

There are many arguments in favour of demolishing old buildings. It is not very uncommon to hear news on TV that a building in a particular city crumbled killing a few people. Such buildings should be demolished even if they have an emotional value for the owners. The maintenance costs of such buildings, which are in a very bad shape, are much more than the cost of demolishing and building new ones instead.

What is more, the newer buildings could be made in such a way that they can accommodate more people in the same amount of space. These buildings could also be made to be energy efficient by using newer technologies, which could save a lot of energy later on. For example, double glass panels could be used for insulation and the terraces could be made as to accommodate solar panels. All these measures are the need of the hour considering the rapidly occurring climate changes and the burgeoning population.

On the other hand, there are some old buildings, which give a unique identity to a place and with a little maintenance can be used effectively even today. For example, the Sainik School of Kapurthala was the home the maharaja of Kapurthala, Jagatjit Singh. It is a magnificent piece of architecture and is now serving a very good purpose. There are many other such buildings which house important government offices or have been converted to hotels for tourists. The Umedh Bhawan Palace in Jodhpur, Rajasthan has been converted into a hotel and is a good source of revenue for the government. We would be losing a lot of our historical and cultural background if we demolish such buildings.

To summarise, the decision to preserve or demolish old buildings should be made after considering many factors. If the old building can be used effectively or be made into a tourist attraction or is giving a unique identity to a place, it should definitely be preserved. If a building is occupying a lot of space and is unfit to live in, then it should be demolished.

Plan followed:

Intro: Discuss essay

Para 1: arguments in favour of demolishing old buildings

Para 2: Advantages of newer buildings

Para 3: Advantages of restoration   Conclusion:

150. Too many old historical buildings are in danger and destroyed in many countries. What are the main reasons? How to protect them?

Modernization of cities is the need of the hour as a result of which many historic buildings are being destroyed. This essay shall highlight the reasons for this phenomenon and also suggest ways to protect these buildings.

The main reason for the demolition of these old historic buildings is to meet the needs of the growing population. Sky-scrapers are part of modern cities and they are needed today as land is becoming scarce. Some old historic buildings are serving no purpose today. They are neither safe to live in nor are attracting tourists. On top of that they occupy a lot of space. Everything has a life and if these are not demolished or renovated, these may crumble anytime and cause threat to life.

Furthermore, road systems are being expanded to meet the needs of the growing number of vehicles. Many old buildings come in the way of these road systems. That is why these buildings need to be destroyed. The benefits of these changes are becoming obvious as traffic jams are becoming things of the past in these places.

Some steps can be taken to preserve these buildings. There are some old buildings which give a unique identity to a place and with a little maintenance can be used effectively even today. For example, the Sainik School of Kapurthala was the home the maharaja of Kapurthala, Jagatjit Singh. It is a magnificent piece of architecture and is now serving a very good purpose. There are many other such buildings which house important government offices or have been converted to hotels for tourists. The Umedh Bhawan Palace in Jodhpur, Rajasthan has been converted into a hotel and is a good source of revenue for the government. Therefore, if we renovate these buildings and make them utilitarian, then we can preserve them.

To conclude, demolishing old buildings for modernization is definitely advantageous. However, if the historic building is a tourist attraction or is giving a unique identity to a place, it should definitely be preserved.

Plan followed
Intro: This essay shall highlight the reasons for this phenomenon and also suggest ways to protect these buildings
Para 1: Reasons
Para 2: More reason
Para 3: Steps to preserve
Conclusion:

151. Many old cities around the world are going through a major process of modernization. What are the advantages and disadvantages of modernization?

Modernization is the process by which cities are being transformed under the impact of scientific and technological revolution. Modernization is usually associated with urban and industrial development. Cities are growing as economic and cultural centers, and new technologies have transformed almost every aspect of life. As everything has its pros and cons, similarly modernization also has its good and bad points which I shall discuss in this essay.

On the one hand modernization of cities is very beneficial to meet the needs of the growing population. Sky-scrapers are part of modern cities and they are needed today as land is becoming scarce. Modern architecture uses pre-fabricated material instead of wood for the doors and windows, which is also the need of the day. Modern buildings are also being made to be energy-efficient. For example, walls are being insulated so that lesser air-conditioning is needed. This is also a big plus point as we are all facing energy crises today.

Furthermore, road systems are being expanded to meet the needs of the growing number of vehicles. The benefits of these changes are becoming obvious as traffic jams are becoming things of the past in these places. Finally, as globalization is opening doors for the developing countries to expand their trade, modernization is becoming mandatory to attract foreign investments in these cities. It goes without doubt that these changes are bringing tangible benefits to these cities. For instance, various multinational companies have opened in these cities and these are providing employment to many.

On the other hand, in the process of modernizing, most of the city administrators just copied the architecture of other cities from the developed world and this resulted in cloning of cities. Very naturally, to rebuild any city with modernization while maintaining its historical and cultural uniqueness is a difficult task that demands know-how in many areas. Copying is relatively simple and fast. Most of the cities now look similar and this has led to a loss of architectural diversity.

Summing up, modernizing cities is the need of the time and it has obviously much more advantages than disadvantages. However, care should be taken, as far as possible, to preserve some of the historic and cultural uniqueness of these cities.

Plan followed

Intro:

Para 1: Advantages

Para 2: more advantages

Para 3: Disadvantages

Conclusion

152. Discuss the advantages and disadvantages of living in a house and living in an apartment and give your opinion as to which is better.

Many people nowadays face a difficult decision when they buy their own home. The question is whether they should buy a house or an apartment. This essay shall discuss the advantages and disadvantages of both options before forming an opinion.

Perhaps the major advantage of living in a house is the issue of privacy. Typically, there is more opportunity for peace and quiet, if you live in a house. This is particularly the case if it is a detached house. Other significant advantages are that houses are generally more spacious and on the whole have gardens. This is especially important if there is a family so that the children can have a safe environment to play in.

There are, of course, negative aspects to living in houses. The greatest of these is that they tend to be more expensive to purchase and to maintain. Indeed, a large majority of people choose to live in apartments because they cannot afford the mortgage to buy a house. Another possible problem is that there are fewer houses in cities than the countryside. So the facilities of urban life may be far away.

On the other hand, in an apartment there is always somebody near to help you in an emergency or watch your flat when you are away. As well as this, flats have very low maintenance costs. For example, with only a balcony, there are no bushes to trim, no lawn to mow and no leaves to rake. Finally, flats are usually located closer to city centre and so public transport is easy to get.

The downside of apartment life is that the neighbours may be noisy and bothersome. This can be extremely unpleasant, particularly if your sleep is constantly interrupted. Also, living in a neighbourhood crowded with blocks of flats means that parking is limited and finding a space for your car could take a considerable amount of your time.

To conclude, it can be seen that there are probably an equal number of pros and cons to making either choice. Ultimately, whether you decide to live in a house or a flat depends on your family and financial circumstances.

Plan followed

Intro: Discuss essay intro
Para 1: advantages of living in a house
Para 2: disadvantages of living in a house
Para 3: advantages of apartments
Para 4: disadvantages of apartments
Conclusion: Matter of individual taste

153. Many people think living in high-rise apartment blocks makes people feel lonely and unhappy, while others argue it has advantages. Discuss both views and give your own opinion.

The number of high rise buildings has grown many-fold in the past few years. This essay shall discuss the advantages and disadvantages of high-rise apartments.

There are many advantages of living in high-rise apartment buildings, the main one being that everything that you need is just a stone's throw away. This is because high-rise apartments or condominiums tend to be either very close to or right in the middle of downtown. Some apartment buildings may be located near beautiful, natural surroundings such as parks, gardens, and white-sand beaches. A person can relax and escape from the stresses and hassles of city living by going up the top floor and marvel at the cityscape with the wonderful perspective of everything around you.

Furthermore, there are shared amenities in the building such as swimming pools, recreation centers and gyms which one can enjoy. You can actually socialize with the other families, get to know them, and create a better sense of community also. When neighbors get to know one another, they tend to look out for one another, and this generates a greater sense of safety and security, and this only adds to the advantages of high-rise living.

Along with certain living advantages, there are also plenty of disadvantages of such sky-scrapers. When it comes to high rises, the balcony is a possible safety hazard because of a growing number of fatalities associated with suicide and accidental falls. What is more, high-rise fires are the worst nightmare for people living in tall apartment buildings because of the cramped conditions when doing an evacuation out of one's apartment space. Another issue about high-rise apartment buildings is the fact that everything is compact and you don't have a lawn and a spacious yard where you can play with your kids. Finally, there are many people living in such buildings and so residents do not question the presence of strangers. Therefore, security can be a big problem.

To sum up, there are both advantages and disadvantages of high rise apartments. However, feeling lonely is not one of them. Whether to live or not to live in a high-rise apartment is a matter of personal choice.

Plan followed

Intro: Discuss essay intro

Para 1: Advantages of high-rise apartments

Para 2: More advantages

Para 3: Disadvantages

Conclusion:

154. Countries' population is increasing so people believe we should build new homes in existing cities instead of building new towns in the countryside. What do you think about that and give example or your own experience.

The burgeoning population has led to the debate whether the remote and rural areas should be developed by making new towns there or if more housing be made in the cities already existing. I am of the view that new towns should be made in the countryside. A number of arguments support my opinion, which I will discuss in the upcoming paragraphs.

There are a plethora of benefits of making new towns in the countryside areas. Firstly, the housing in these new areas will be affordable for many, as the land/property rates will be much lower as compared to the cities. Furthermore, the present cities are already congested and there is a lot of burden on the resources, like electricity, water supply, transport system, etc. So, when people move to new towns outside the cities, it will reduce the burden on the resources and allow people to lead a better quality life.

Another advantage of making new towns in the rural areas is that the new towns can be planned to be more energy efficient, and the issues that the present cities now face can be taken care of right from the inception stage. For instance, the plan should include more green spaces/belts; solar energy and other such renewable sources should be used; public transport systems like Metros and subways can be planned ahead, and many more such things can be looked at when planning a new town. Moreover, this will lead to development of areas, which might have been left neglected and will provide opportunities for the people living there to have a better life and enjoy the modern resources and facilities of a town.

Admittedly, there are some disadvantages of making new towns, rather than adding to more residential areas in the present cities. For instance, if people move out to live in the new towns, then there will be a decline in the local economy of the city. Many businesses may shut down. Also, people will move away from their workplaces and this move will affect many households. For example, the commute time may increase for many people and the children may have to change schools when the family moves to a new town.

To conclude, I would reiterate my opinion that to deal with the problem of the increasing population, adding more houses to existing cities will only increase the burden on such cities. Making well-planned new towns in the countryside is more advantageous.

Plan followed
Intro:
Para 1: Advantages of making new towns
Para 2: More advantages
Para 3: Disadvantages with refutation
Conclusion:

155. In some countries, most people prefer to rent their homes rather than buying them. What are the advantages and disadvantages of renting a home?

Every one aspires to live in a dream house. The choice between buying a home and renting one is among the biggest financial decision that many adults make. The huge cost of buying a house and complications involved in renting make it a hard choice to decide which is a better deal. This essay intends to analyse the pros and cons of renting a house.

The proponents of renting a house cite a host of benefits. Firstly, it has financial benefits. One can invest such a large sum elsewhere, such as in one's business and earn manifold. Secondly, one doesn't have to pay any taxes on the property or troubled by regular maintenance charges. Also, one can always change one's place of residence by renting a home close to one's work place and save time. Another advantage is that if for some reason a person doesn't like a place because of the neighbourhood or weather, he is not obliged to stay there a lifetime. Finally, a person's work may require shifting places and so it would be futile to invest a fortune in a place where one cannot live.

On the other hand, the disadvantages of renting a house are also numerous. Firstly, being able to call a place as one's own cannot be achieved in a rental home. Secondly, buying a home can be more profitable in long run, as the person is making an asset for life. While renting a person is indirectly paying someone else's mortgage. What is more, while renting, a person has to sign a lease and vacate accordingly.

I believe that whether to own a house or to live in a rented house is a matter of personal choice and should be decided according to one's own circumstances. Sometimes it is smarter to rent, and sometimes buying can work in one's favor. One should carefully weigh the merits and demerits of both approaches before reaching a conclusion.

To conclude, renting a house has its benefits and drawbacks, and so the decision should be made considering ones needs and aspirations.

Plan followed
Intro:
Para 1: Advantages of renting
Para 2: Disadvantages of renting
Para 3: Own view
Conclusion:

156.   Many people think that zoos, which keep wild animals in a man-made environment should no longer exist in the 21st century. To what extent do you agree or disagree with this statement?

I agree that there is no place for zoos in the 21st century. I feel that zoos are an unsuitable environment for animals, and therefore should be abolished. A number of arguments support my opinion.

Firstly, zoo animals are kept in very confined areas compared with their vast natural habitat. Due to this, zoo animals develop unnatural habits like pacing back and forth or swaying from side to side. For example, polar bears are given about 10 metres of walking space, whereas in their arctic home they roam for hundreds of kilometers. Similarly, lions and tigers are confined in cages where they lack exercise and stimulation. What is more, it is very common for visitors to tease and provoke caged animals. This also leads to unnatural behavior in animals.

Secondly, the breeding programmes taken up by zoos are not very successful. For instance, the 'Panda Breeding Programme' has been very costly and unsuccessful. Also, zoo life does not prepare animals for the challenges of life in the wild. They are provided good food in the zoos, but if left in the jungle, they may die of starvation because they cannot hunt for themselves.

Finally, the zoo is an unnatural environment that exposes animals to many dangers. Diseases often spread between species that would never live together naturally. For example, many Asian elephants have died in African zoos after catching herpes from African elephants.

To sum up, I would like to reiterate my opinion that zoos are unnatural habitats for the wild animals and there is no justification in caging these marvelous creatures of God. It is not true to say that zoos are educational or that they help to save endangered species. In reality they only teach us how wild animals behave when they are cramped in small spaces. Breeding programmes provide zoos with good publicity, but in fact most of them are failures. Finally, zoo animals are more at risk of dying from disease or injury than their wild counterparts. It is time we abolish these cruel institutions.

Plan followed

Intro: Agree – means that you are against zoos

Para 1: Reasons why zoos are not good

Para 2: more reasons

Para 3: more reasons

Conclusion:

157. Some people argue that the purpose of zoos is only to entertain people. What do you think? What are the other purposes of zoos?

It is irrefutable that zoos provide recreation to people. However, zoos have a lot of other advantages besides entertainment. This essay shall highlight these functions of zoos.

To begin with, the main advantage is the education that people receive when visiting a zoo. Someone has rightly said that zoo animals are ambassadors for their cousins in the wild. Zoos provide a rare and unique opportunity to peer into the wild without actually traveling to forests. Zoos contain a range of animals such as giraffes, elephants, lions and even large and venomous snakes. People receive firsthand knowledge of how animals behave and act. Most zoos also provide interactive shows with some of the animals during specific times throughout the week. Surrounding the exhibits, zoos usually have information describing the animal, its history and natural location.

Furthermore, learning about animals also brings empathy to many people. Zoos help to promote awareness by educating people on how to protect animals that face extinction. By doing so, researchers can receive funds to repopulate these animals. What is more, zoos often take an active approach in helping animal populations. For dwindling species, many zoos breed species in an attempt to increase their numbers. After raising sufficient numbers of the populations, the animals can then be released into the wild in order to encourage population growth. Many animals have been tremendously helped this way, including the white tiger and panda bear.

Moreover, zoos help to attract tourists and thus boost the economy. People buy tickets to visit zoos and a number of people get employment in zoos. Workers are needed to look after the animals and provide them timely exercise and food. Finally, entertainment is also there when people visit zoos. Everyone enjoys looking at these marvelous creations of the almighty.

To summarise, zoos provide education, awareness and boost the economy in addition to providing entertainment.

Plan followed

Intro: zoos have a lot of other advantages besides entertainment

Para1: main advantage is the education

Para 2: more advantages

Para 3: more advantages

Conclusion:

158. Some people think that Government should invest money in wildlife projects and protect them. Other people think it is better if the government invests money in other projects. Discuss both views and opine.

In recent times, there has been a great hue and cry over the money and efforts being spent on conservation of wild animals and birds. Some say that the government should fund such wildlife projects, whereas others say that priority should be given to human projects. This essay intends to analyse both perspectives. I side with the former view.

The most important reason for saving wild animals and birds is that they are part of our ecosystem. Every species of wildlife plays a role to maintain the balance of life on Earth. Thus, the loss of any species can affect us directly or indirectly. For example, there are many bat species that are becoming extinct. Such bats help keep the insect population in control. If these bats die then the insects will increase a lot and destroy our crops. So, we will have nothing to eat. In addition, many animals, like rodents, help in the dispersal of plant seeds and in the pollination of plants. By protecting endangered animals we ensure not only their survival but also the biodiversity that is necessary for the ecological health of the planet.

Secondly, wild animals provide many valuable substances such as medicine and fur. The horn of the rhinoceros has medicinal value, and the fur of the mink is very valuable. Moreover, the recreational viewing of animals at zoos is also a source of revenue. Thus, the financial value of wild species is important to the economies of many nations. Furthermore, wild animals have aesthetic appeal. They are beautiful creatures of nature and are a part of our bio-diversity.

On the other hand, some people say that humans are suffering from poverty, hunger, homelessness, unemployment and ill health. These areas should be the priority for human spending. They opine that human needs must come first. They have a point, but I still believe that conservation of wildlife is as important for humans as any other thing.

To sum up, the resources spent on these animals and plants are well justified. Wildlife is Mother Nature's greatest treasure. To protect it, we must take every measure.

Plan followed

Intro: Discuss

Para 1: Part of ecological chain – interconnected

Para 2: Provide us many things

Para 3: Other view and refutation

Conclusion:

159. Nowadays we see more advertisements on the streets and on our TV screens. What are advantages and disadvantages of these?

Advertising is a powerful and persuasive medium and advertisements have become a part of our lives. Advertisements have both positive and negative effects, which shall be discussed in the following paragraphs.

On the positive side, ads tell us about the new products that are launched in the market. They also tell us about the working of these products. After seeing the ads, consumers can go to the market and select things of their choice. What is more, the advertising industry provides jobs to many.

Furthermore, advertisements touch social issues. For example, when Amitabh Bachchan tells people to bring their children for pulse polio immunization, people listen. Then there are ads against female foeticide which are very informative. Advertisements also teach us a lot about the country from where the ads come. This is because through satellite TV we can see ads from all over the world. When we see a Japanese advert of a lady in a kimono, we come to know about the clothes of Japan.

However, adverts also have a downside. There are many advertisements which make many false claims about their products. For example, I recently bought a floor cleaner which claimed to remove rust stains from floor effortlessly but when I used it in my kitchen, the rust stains did not go at all. It also goes without saying that when businesses hire celebs to endorse their products then definitely they have to pay them exorbitant amounts of money and all this increases the cost of the product.

Furthermore, advertisements can cause people to be dissatisfied with what they already have and make them want more. Being exposed again and again to products which one cannot afford leads to dissatisfaction. Moreover, not all parents are in a position to afford the goods which the children see advertised and want to possess. This often leads to feelings of inadequacy among them. In addition to this, advertisements lead to materialism and people lay too much emphasis on material goods. People are prepared to work long hours or even turn to crime to get these goods.

To conclude, adverts have pros and cons. Without adverts we would lose a valuable source of revenue, which is used for the benefit of majority. Our lives would be dull without these ads.

Plan followed
Intro:
Para 1: Advantages of ads
Para 2: Advantages
Para 3: Disadvantages
Para 4: Disadvantages
Conclusion

160. Consumers are faced with increasing numbers of advertisements from competing companies. To what extent do you think are consumers influenced by advertisements? What measures can be taken to protect them?

Advertising is the heart of trade. To survive in the competitive market of today, every product has to be advertised. There is a huge impact of these ads on the people, which is both positive, as well as negative. This essay shall analyse these effects on the common man, and suggest ways to protect people from the negative effects of adverts.

There are many ways in which these ads are helpful. First, ads tell us about the new products that are launched in the market. They also tell us about the working of these products. After seeing the ads, consumers can go to the market and select things of their choice. What is more, the advertising industry provides jobs to many. Many models and other people make a living through this industry. Ads also touch on social issues. For example, there are ads which make people aware that they can stand up against domestic violence and female foeticide. We also have ads which warn people about the harmful effects of smoking. Another big positive influence of the ads of today is the entertainment they provide. They are made so hilarious that you feel like watching them again and again.

On the other hand, advertisements promote consumerism. Ads can cause people to be dissatisfied with what they already have and make them want more. Not all parents are in a position to afford the goods which their children see advertised and want to possess. This often leads to feelings of inadequacy among them. In addition to this, this materialism leads to workaholism. People are prepared to work long hours, or even turn to crime to get these goods. Finally, ads can be very irksome at times. This is especially true of Internet ads. The increasing number of advertisements and the never-ending list of ad-networks are making the Internet users' experience worse than ever. The ads which have audio are very troubling, while some ads are flash based. Telephone ads are also very irritating. When you are driving or in an important meeting, the bell rings and disturbs everyone.

The solutions are not simple as advertising is a very persuasive medium. It would be unwise to ban ads, as this would cause more problems than it would solve. However, advertisements which make false claims should be banned. Advertisements for liquor and those ads which show stunts, should also be banned. Then there should be consumer awareness programmes. Consumers should be warned against too much consumerism. Our celebs have a big role in selecting what products they should endorse. People, who follow these celebs would buy anything they say even without needing it.

To conclude, today we are influenced a lot by adverts, both in positive and negative ways. Without adverts we would lose a valuable source of revenue, which is used for the benefit of the majority. However, many steps can be taken to mitigate the negative influence of ads.

Plan followed

Intro –   Para 1 – positive effects   Para 2 – advertisements have negative points
Para 3 – solutions are not simple   Conclusion:

161. There is an increasing amount of advertising directed at children, which encourages them to buy goods such as toys and snacks. Many parents are worried that these advertisements put too much pressure on children, while some advertisers claim that they provide useful information to children. Discuss both views and give your opinion.

Advertisements are all around us, especially advertising targeting children, who are considered vulnerable targets by companies. As a result, many parents are worried that their children are being wrongly influenced by ads. However, some advertisers claim that they provide beneficial information to children. In the following paragraphs I intend to discuss both perspectives.

It is not difficult to see why parents' worry is justified. Children, under a certain age, lack abilities to make wise judgments as to what they really want. They are attracted by colourful pictures on advertisements, and swayed by misleading information. So, they pester their parents to buy those things, and this can upset the budget of many families. Even the advertisements of fast foods are bad for children. Children cannot understand that the slim-trim models advertising Mac Donalds burgers hardly ever eat such foods themselves. They are attracted to fast foods and these are very detrimental for their health.

What is more, some ads show some stunts, and although it is written that children should not copy these stunts, children hardly ever read that part and in their ignorance try to perform those stunts and get hurt. For example, in my neighbourhood, one child tried to jump from one rooftop to the other after seeing the ad of Thumbs Up and ended up with a plaster on his leg. Therefore, parents are rightly worried.

On the other hand, advertisements also provide beneficial information to the children. For example, the advert of Colgate toothpaste, which tells that we should brush our teeth twice daily, is good for children. Then there are ads about health drinks such as Complan and Bournvita, which are good for children. Furthermore, advertisements also touch important issues, such as ads against wastage of water, ads for tree plantation, ads against wastage of electricity and ads for keeping the surroundings clean. Children are motivated by these ads and try to follow the good things they learn.

To conclude, it is true that some adverts have a detrimental effect on children and should be subject to some regulations, but at the same time it can also be not be denied that adverts enlighten children in many ways by providing a lot of useful information.

Plan followed

Intro – Discuss essay intro

Para 1 – Parents view

Para 2 – Parents view

Para 3 – advertisers view   Conclusion: ads have both – good as well as bad effects

162. In the past people used to wear their traditional clothes depending on their culture. Nowadays the trend is changing and people wear different clothes. Is it a positive or negative development? How does it affect certain societies and people's behavior?

The global era of today is all about choices. People are aware of fashions all over the world, and are adopting whatever suits their fancy. This phenomenon is largely positive, although there is a downside to it as well. This essay intends to analyze the pros and cons of this change and also discuss its impact on certain societies and people's conduct.

On the one hand, the trend to wear clothes not related one's culture is bound to erode the cultural identity of nations. Many nations are known by their national dress. For instance, 'sari' is the national dress of India and 'kimono' is the national dress of Japan. These dresses are also linked to certain customs and traditions. If these attires are lost, the customs and traditions will also be lost.

On the other hand, there are countless advantages of this trend. People adopt things which they find comfortable and which suit their pocket. If jeans and T-shirts are comfortable, people will wear them. Such clothes are easier on the pocket too. For instance, two pairs of jeans and a few T-shirts are enough for the whole year. The traditional clothes like suits and saris are noticeable when worn repeatedly. So, a huge collection is needed. Finally, wearing clothes according to the latest fashion makes people feel more confident as they are portraying that they are up-to-date.

There are noticeable influences of globally similar clothing on people and societies. When people of global communities look similar, they find it easier to accept each other. It leads to better harmony among people. People feel united and work together for uplifting the global communities. People feel part of a global village and it makes them feel more confident.

In my opinion, wearing clothes, which are comfortable and make you feel confident and happy, is better and needed in today's fast paced life. I don't believe that not wearing traditional clothes takes you away from your traditions and culture. Traditions and culture are deep rooted and can never fade away with the clothes we wear. On our festivals and cultural events, our traditional clothes are still very conspicuous.

To sum up, people are following fashion in clothing according to the times, and it is certainly a positive trend.

Plan followed

Intro: Para 1: Disadvantages

Para 2: Advantages   Para 3: Effect on individuals and societies

Para 4: Own opinion   Conclusion:

163. Nowadays, the traditions and customs of the food we eat and the way we eat it are changing; what is the way they have changed, and what do you think of the change.

In this era of technology and globalization, all spheres of life have changed dramatically and food is also no exception. This essay intends to discuss the ways in which the traditions and customs relating to food are changing. I believe this change is largely negative.

There are a lot of changes in the foods we eat and also in the ways we prepare these foods today. Firstly in this torrid pace of life, people are working till their death. They have no time to prepare and enjoy traditional home cooked food. Ultimately, they switch to an easy option of restaurants. McDonalds have become a ubiquitous term in every home. Secondly, there is the influence of occidental culture over the oriental one. People are forgetting their roots. For example, in earlier times all family members used to sit together and eat, and over the dining table they shared their happenings of the day. Fast foods, however, are eaten alone mostly because they don't appeal to the palate of the older members. As a result, family bonds and relationships are getting adversely impacted. Moreover, the art of home cooking is suffering a lot.

Admittedly, this trend has harmful effects on individuals. Undoubtedly, people are affected by health hazards like obesity and other diseases. Obesity is the root cause of many other diseases. Fast foods are rich in fats and salts which are not good for health. An obese person is more likely to suffer from diseases like hypertension and diabetes.

There are tangible consequences on society too. Broadly speaking, as people get inclined towards fast food and restaurants, local culture dies out. It is because traditional food is inextricably linked with culture. Undoubtedly, the identity of the society and nation will fade away. It will be monopolized by western norms. Also, if people are not healthy, the productivity of the nation will come to a standstill. Last but not least, fast foods promote use-and-throw culture which adds to the problem of garbage dumps, contamination, pollution and eventually many diseases.

To summarise, international fast foods have carved their niche and traditional food has taken the backseat. Certainly, this has adverse effects on individuals, families and societies.

Plan followed:
Intro:
Para 1: Ways of change
Para 2: Effects on individuals
Para 3: Effects on societies
Conclusion:

164. Nowadays, some people are changing their way of look through hair color, clothes, cosmetics and even plastic surgeries. What are the reasons? Is this a good thing?

For centuries, men and women have beautified their eyes, lips and body. Now modern science and cosmetology have merged to create various techniques for enhancing one's looks. Many individuals, nowadays, are giving themselves a complete makeover by using these new techniques. This essay shall discuss the reasons for this development. I believe it is good only upto some limit. A number of arguments augment my opinion.

The most important reason is that in today's society, changing one's appearance through hair color, eye contacts, and cosmetic surgery, seems to be the answer to looking good. It is a general perception that when you look good, you feel better; when you feel better, you behave better; when you behave better, the people around you tend to respond to you positively. Earlier, when all these facilities were not there, people had to accept themselves as they were and a person who was not born with good features always lived with some inferiority complex and remained an introvert throughout life.

Secondly, in today's competitive era, looks are very important, so much so that some professions are totally dependent on looks. Many film stars have got face lifts and other cosmetic surgeries done on their faces to look younger and thus further their longevity in their careers. Even in some other jobs such as receptionists in offices and air hostesses, looks are given weightage over other aspects. Moreover, some people have their faces disfigured due to accidents or any other trauma. For example, one of my friends lost her ear in an accident. For months she kept that side of the face covered by her hair and could not wear any jewelry and therefore suffered a lot of mental trauma. Finally, she consulted a plastic surgeon and got an ear implant. Now she has regained her confidence.

I believe that this is a positive trend, but only within limits. If it is done after an accident then it is good, but if people spend exorbitant amounts just to look like their favourite celebrity then it is not justified. One must remember that ultimately what matters is the inner 'you'. It is more important to be beautiful from within. What is more, cosmetic surgery is not without its side-effects. Even the products used on hair and face may damage the hair and skin permanently. Finally, terrorists may get cosmetic surgeries to look different and prevent being identified and this may prove very detrimental to society.

To conclude, changing one's looks through hair colour, beauty products and surgery is good only if done within a limit and for some reason like after an accident. The outer appearance may have a temporary appeal but what ultimately matters is the person within.

Plan followed

Intro:

Para 1: First reason

Para 3: It is good if done within a limit

Para 2: Other reasons

Conclusion: reiterate what said earlier

165. Wearing fashionable clothes is becoming important today. Is the attitude to wearing fashionable clothes leading to a positive development or negative development?

Fashion has never been out of fashion. It is a way of life. It has been evolving ever since Eve decided to start wearing a fig leaf. However, it is also true that it has become very essential in today's time to look fashionable. This is both a positive as well as a negative development.

To begin with, fashion plays a foremost role in giving the crucial first impression. In the period of cut-throat competition, a lot of weightage is given to personality that is our dress and demeanour. It has become a barometer to measure our social standing and success. What is more, it adds variety to our life when we try out new apparels. It also satisfies the creative urge in us, for only man is gifted with an aesthetic sense that makes him want the things around him including his attire to look beautiful.

Perhaps the biggest advantage of this trend is that it has given rise to an entirely new industry which is worth over a thousand crore rupees. No wonder, large educational institutes are imparting specialised fashion technology courses such as the NIFT and NIFD. It has given rise to a plethora of new industries ranging from apparel to accessories. It has become a lucrative career option for the youth today. Many fashion houses of India are exporting clothes to foreign countries and earning valuable foreign exchange.

On the other hand, it has become an exclusive preserve of the rich and the influential for they have the means and the resources to indulge in this luxury. This creates a sharp divide between the haves and the have-nots which in turn creates a psychological imbalance in the youth. They try to ape their affluent friends, but in the absence of means resort to unlawful and unethical means. A lot of petty crimes are committed by today's youngsters just to buy a pair of fashionable shoes or acquire something fashionable that may catch their fancy.

The need is therefore to strike a balance between being fashionable and wearing what is right for us. We must not blindly follow fashion but we should wear what suits us and in what we feel comfortable. The clothes, which look good on others may not suit us and wearing those clothes may make us a subject of ridicule.

Summing up, we must be in fashion to add flavour to our lives, but we must beware of the 'herd' instinct, which impels us to emulate others without considering its suitability for us.

Plan followed

Intro: This is both a positive as well as a negative development.

Para 1: - advantages

Para 2: advantage

Para 3: disadvantages

Conclusion: Following fashion is good but within a limit and according to what suits us.

166. Modern lifestyle has made it harder for people to live a healthy and active lifestyle. What are the causes of this situation? Suggest what can be done by the government and large organisations to improve it?

Modern man is an unhealthy man. Today, people have to spend wealth to buy health, all thanks to the modern lifestyle. This essay intends to analyse the reasons why people's lifestyle is unhealthy and suggest ways to alleviate the problem.

One of the major causes of this unhealthy and inactive lifestyle is the highly competitive work culture. With people working up to 14 hours a day, , cut-throat competition, hire and fire culture, target-based compensation, insecurities and excessive availability of manpower, every employee finds himself tied only to the office chair. Consequently, his health gets compromised. It is apt to mention here that the growing materialism in this capitalist world is adding to the travails of the modern man. High living standards, higher cost of living, dreams for luxuries and more money are only adding to the problem.

Furthermore, gadgets and machines that were intended to help mankind have also chained him and made him sedentary. Even children are glued to gadgets. Adults have professional requirements for the gadgets, but children no longer play in the open. These unhealthy habits develop inadvertently and continue into adulthood.

However, some steps can be taken to mitigate the problem. Large organisations must start considering humans as an asset and not a liability. They must be treated humanely and not like machines. Rest hours, weekly offs, fixed daily work schedules, incentives to efficient workers, training to keep fit, awareness campaigns and special awards for the fittest employees should be incorporated to improve the unhealthy and inactive lifestyles of employees.

As far as governments are concerned, they must stop focusing on Gross National Product Index and start focusing on Gross National Happiness levels, which include sustainable development, health and happiness levels of citizens, education and environment conditions. Moreover, easily accessible parks and gyms should be open to public for free. Children shouldn't be confined to books only, but play outdoor games. Unhealthy youth should be fined if they don't get fit and junk foods should be taxed more to discourage their sale.

To recapitulate, it can be said that health is a choice. It doesn't come easily. We have to work for it and forgo the laziness. The above-mentioned suggestions, if implemented can save the situation of today's unhealthy man from further deterioration.

Plan followed

Intro:

Para 1: Reasons

Para 2: More reasons

Para 3: Solutions at organisations level

Para 4: Solutions at government level

Conclusion:

167. Many people are not as fit or as active as they used to be, and it is having long term effects on them. Why is this happening and what are some ways to solve this? OR
Nowadays many people have unhealthy diets and do not exercise regularly. Why is this happening? How can we encourage these people to live a healthy lifestyle?

Obesity and its related problems are a growing cause of concern. The main reason is a sedentary lifestyle and fast food culture. This essay shall delve into the reasons why people choose to eat an unhealthy diet and not do exercise. Some measures to motivate people to adopt a healthy lifestyle shall also be discussed.

The fast paced life of today is the most common cause of this habit. People have become workaholics in their rat race after material possessions and as a result don't have the time to cook healthy food and even do any exercise. Whole foods require time to prepare;however, processed or ready-to-eat foods are being consumed nowadays, which are definitely less healthy.

Another reason is the taste factor. Given the choices of steamed broccoli versus macaroni and cheese, or baby carrots versus potato chips, or an apple versus a candy bar, most people would choose the latter simply because it tastes better. The mushrooming growth of fast food outlets have also made them very affordable and very easily available. Finally, perhaps the most significant reason is lack of awareness that obesity caused by such a lifestyle is not just one disease; it has many other deadly diseases like diabetes and hypertension associated with it.

People can be encouraged to adopt a healthier lifestyle in many ways. The government can make people aware about the ill effects of obesity through the media. Sports stadiums and well equipped gyms should be made available in the propinquity of residential areas so that people don't have to go far to access them. Benefits of healthy eating habits and daily exercise should be told to people through the media. Last but not least, the family meal should be encouraged. People tend to eat better when they are sitting down at a table. There is better control of the serving size. There is more focus on interaction and discussion and not only on the food.

Summing up, people eat unhealthy and don't exercise enough but if they are made aware about the ill effects of such a lifestyle and motivated to make some lifestyle modifications then surely it will make a big difference.

Plan followed

Intro:

Para 1: Reasons   Para 2: more causes

Para 3: How people can be encouraged for healthy life style

Conclusion:

168. In many countries people of all ages do sports and exercises a lot. Does this trend have more advantages or disadvantages? Give reasons for your answer and include examples from your own knowledge and experience.

Healthy living has become a buzzword in the recent years. Exercising is the sine qua non of the routine for people of all age groups. This has led to the question if excess of exercising among different age groups has more benefits than drawbacks. In my opinion, exercising should be done with proper guidance, keeping in mind the age and any medical condition the person has, as excessive exercise can lead to more harm than good.

To begin with, exercising a lot can have adverse effects on the body. There are many serious injuries that the body can sustain if too much exercise is done. After any exercise, there should be proper rest time given to the body. If the body doesn't get that rest, it can lead to injuries like muscle, tendons, bones and ligament damage. Admittedly, exercise has myriad benefits and we need some physical activity to stay fit and healthy. However, that needs to be done depending on our age, metabolism, any medical condition or injury we are suffering from and some other such factors.

To add to the above mentioned point, excess exercise can lead to a loss of appetite and thus unwanted weight loss. Research has shown that exercise addicts may develop eating disorders like anorexia, bulimia and orthorexia. Such disorders lead to further side effects like loss of bone density, excessive weight loss and cardiac conditions. It is good to be careful about what we eat and we should avoid unhealthy foods, but that should not become an obsession. It may also lead to a weakened immune system and changes in hormone levels, resulting in adverse effects on the body.

On the psychological front also, obsessive exercising has severe effects. People are not satisfied with the results and look for the next physical target to achieve. It also leads to sleep disorder, which is one of the root causes of problems like depression, stress, excessive fatigue, irritability and lack of concentration. While exercise is essential, we should follow a training schedule provided by a professional trainer and a diet recommended by a nutritionist or a dietician. We shouldn't overdo any exercise as our body is like a machine and we may damage it by excessive use.

To sum up, it can be reiterated that excessive exercising in any age group is not advantageous. It should be done within limits and under proper guidance to reap the maximum benefit for our body and mind.

Plan followed

Intro:

Para 1: negative effect   Para 2: negative effect

Para 3: negative effect

Conclusion

169. Fast food is becoming a part of people's daily life everywhere, and this has had negative effects on our lifestyles and diet. Do you agree with this statement?

In this era of technology and globalization, all spheres of life have changed dramatically and food is also no exception. I agree that international fast foods and restaurants have become part of life and this has had a detrimental effect on our lifestyles and diet. A number of arguments support my opinion.

There are a lot of detrimental effects of fast foods. Firstly, because of the easy availability and affordability of fast foods, people do not spare time to prepare and eat traditional home cooked food. Secondly, there is the influence of occidental culture over the oriental one. People are forgetting their roots. For example, in earlier times all family members used to sit together and eat, and over the dining table they shared their happenings of the day. These fast foods are eaten alone
mostly because they don't appeal to the palate of the older family members. As a result, family bonds and relationships are getting fragile. Moreover, the art of home cooking is suffering a lot.

Furthermore, this has a harmful effect on people's health. Undoubtedly, people are affected by health hazards like obesity and other diseases. Obesity is the root cause of many other diseases. Fast foods are rich in fats and salts which are not good for health. An obese person is more likely to suffer from diseases like hypertension and diabetes; obesity also aggravates cases of arthritis.

There are tangible consequences on society too. As people get inclined towards fast food and restaurants, local culture dies out. It is because traditional food is inextricably linked with culture. Undoubtedly, the identity of the society and nation will disappear. It will be monopolized by western societies. Also, if people are not healthy, the productivity of the nation will come to a standstill. Last but not least, fast foods promote use-and-throw culture which adds to the problem of garbage dumps, contamination, pollution and eventually many diseases.

To conclude, international fast foods have carved their niche and traditional food has taken the backseat. Certainly, this has had an adverse effect on our lifestyles.

Plan followed
Intro: Agree
Para 1: Effects
Para 2: effect on people's health – obesity
Para 3: effects on society
Conclusion:

170. International sporting events could contribute greatly to peace and stability in the world. Do you agree or disagree? Support your opinion with relevant examples.

I agree with the given statement that International sports events could contribute to peace and stability in the world. This essay intends to provide arguments to support the role of sports in international peace.

Sports provide people of all age groups and cultures with entertainment and something to get excited about and they are topics for conversation. They provide a common bond for complete strangers and a common team to cheer for. The Olympics are one of the best examples of how sporting events can bring people of different nations together. In ancient times, the Greeks and Romans would interrupt battles to participate in games. Sport has, for example, facilitated dialogue among conflicting countries, such as the United States and China, Pakistan and India, or the Koreas. Although sports cannot prevent conflicts, it can certainly unite people across the political divide .

Another important contribution of sports is that it can bring about social change. Sports can trigger mutual respect and understanding among athletes and among supporters. Through role models, sports can reach out to youth. Adding an educational message to sports or sporting events can raise awareness on societal issues, such as HIV/AIDS. Sports can reach a much larger audience than any other event.

Opponents of the view claim that sports can also bring out some of the more troubling sides of human beings, such as intolerance, corruption, mindsets that seek to win at any cost. They cite many examples of violence and conflicts, which such games have brought about. Football hooliganism or football violence is well known to all. That is why some people hold the opinion that such games divide people.

However, I still believe that in general, sports promote peace and development in the world. No wonder, many representatives from the world of sport, such as from International Sports Federations and the National Olympic Committees have joined hands to strengthen international efforts to further promote and use sport as an effective tool for development and peace.

To conclude, international sporting events generally bring people together and promote peace and harmony in the world. There are a few instances when over-patriotism prevailed and people got divided but such incidents can be counted on the fingertips.

Plan followed:
Intro: Agree
Para 1: Reason   Para 2: Another reason
Para 3: Opponents view
Para 4: Refutation of opponents view
Conclusion:

171. Some sports are extremely dangerous but many people still like them very much. Why do people take part in dangerous sports? Give some suggestions on how to deal with these dangers.

In recent years we have seen a considerable rise in dangerous or extreme sports. This essay shall discuss some of the main reasons why people engage in such sports and suggest ways in which some risks involved in such sports can be reduced.

The main reason why people go for dangerous sports is that they get a thrill out of them. They like taking risks. They like to challenge their abilities and potentials. They feel a sense of satisfaction when they come face to face with fears while bungee jumping, rock climbing and so on. In addition, going through a dangerous experience gives them courage and confidence to face the hurdles of their daily life.

Another reason for pursuing such sports is that there is a lot of fame and money involved in them. They get attention by doing stunts on motorcycles and jumping from tall buildings. They make headlines in newspapers and TV News Channels. They feel great when their name comes in the Guinness Book of World Records. Once they get famous they get a lot of money also. For instance, many businesses hire them to endorse their products. They also get jobs on the basis of such skills.

Many steps can be taken to reduce the risks are that involved. Firstly, these sports should be done under strict supervision. All safety precautions should be taken. Such sports should be performed after sufficient training and under supervision of professionals. Sport companies which cater to such sports should require a license for providing such training. Some people suggest banning such sports. However, I do not believe that banning is a good solution. We all know that forbidden fruits taste sweeter and people will indulge in such sports surreptitiously which would increase the risks involved.

To conclude, people engage in such sports for fun, for money and for fame. However, such sports should be performed after sufficient training from licensed companies and under professional supervision.

Plan followed

Intro: Address the question appropriately.
Para 1: Why people take part in dangerous sports
Para 2: Another reason
Para 3: Solutions
Conclusion:

172. Some people think government should ban dangerous sports, such as skydiving and rock climbing. Do you agree or disagree?

In recent years we have seen a considerable rise in dangerous or extreme sports. Although I do not support an outright ban on such sports, I do feel that the government should regulate such sports, so that they are played under supervision, which will minimize the risks.

Those who maintain that the government should ban dangerous sports activities argue on the grounds that a government has a responsibility to protect its population. In other words, there should be a law to prevent citizens from taking risks endangering themselves, whether deliberately or unintentionally. These sports can be highly dangerous and sometimes life-threatening. More than that, it is not just the participants who are at risk, but spectators too can be seriously injured. If, for example, a Formula 1 car crashes, while the driver may escape unharmed, there is a possibility that a bouncing tire or debris may fly into the crowd. Given this level of danger, it is understandable why people call for the authorities to take action.

However, banning such sports is not the answer. Instead, the government should ensure that the companies or centres, which provide the facilities for such sports should meet the required, legal safety standards. Another argument against banning is that then people would play these sports in hiding, and then they would be even more risky. After all we all know that forbidden fruits taste sweeter.

A further point is that in statistical terms there is a low probability of injury in many so-called dangerous sports, and people are at greater risk carrying out everyday activities such as crossing the road or cooking a meal. With the rapid development of advanced technology and medical insurance in our society, the security systems of these extreme sports have maturedadequately to protect people who participate in these challenging activities.

What is more, those sportsmen who excel in such sports bring name and fame to their country. They break records set by others, and when they do so, the name of their country shines in the whole world. I also believe that people should be allowed to go for whatever risk they choose. So, if someone wishes to free-fall from a plane at 30,000 feet, then he should be free to do so and it should be accepted that it is not the place of the government to dictate how they lead their lives. Not infringing on citizens' freedom should be regarded as a standard government policy.

To sum up, it can be said that such sports should be performed after sufficient training and under supervision of experts. Companies in this business should require a license for providing such training. To lay a blanket prohibition on such sports is not the answer.

Plan followed

Intro: Disagree

Para 1: Arguments for banning   Para 2: Arguments against banning

Para 3: Arguments against banning   Para 4: Arguments against banning

Conclusion: should not be banned but regulated

173. Holding International games such as the Olympic Games is an exciting event. Some people think it has positive effects while others argue it is a waste of money. Discuss both sides and give your own opinion.

People are divided on the issue of hosting Olympic Games. Some individuals opine that it is advantageous to host such events, whereas others believe that this could be detrimental for the host country. This essay shall look into both arguments. I, however, side with the former view.

There are many advantages that can ensue from hosting such events. To begin with, such events would mean an influx of a large number of international tourists, which in turn would mean a lot of tourist dollars. For example, during the Olympics many athletes, spectators, officials, sponsors and broadcasters come to the host country and spend money on hotels and restaurants. What is more, the country also earns by selling tickets and souvenirs. Additionally, many people get employment because of the jobs related to hosting such events. For instance, there are many new jobs in construction projects of stadia and hotels and also in advertising related to such events. All this improves the overall economy of the people and the country.

Furthermore, the host country gets recognition in the whole world because of media exposure. It is also an opportunity for the host country and its people to know about the culture of other countries. This broadens the outlook of people and helps to make them true citizens of the global village of today. Last but not least, the infrastructure of the host country develops at an accelerated pace. For example, when New Delhi hosted the Commonwealth Games, many flyovers and stadia were built which changed the overall look of Delhi and now, all these new facilities are being enjoyed by the local people of Delhi.

On the other hand, it is also easy to see why some people are opposed to hosting such events. The main reason is that the development of that part of the country is at the expense of other parts. This is because the government of the host country usually prioritizes the allocation of its resources to the development of infrastructure related to the event. Another reason why people are against such events is because of the Olympic drain associated with such events. In other words, the tourism in the neighbouring area suffers, as all visitors are attracted towards the host city. Finally, crime is another factor why people don't like such events. When many people get together at the same place, there are chances of petty crimes and the host city needs to deploy more police officers.

Looking at both arguments, it is clear that there are both – advantages as well as disadvantages of hosting such events, but on the whole the pros far outweigh the cons.

Plan followed

Intro: Discuss essay   Para 1: - advantages   Para 2: advantage

Para 3: disadvantages   Conclusion: pros outweigh cons

174.   Do you agree or disagree that improvements in technology reduce the role of Olympic Games.

Olympic Games are the world's most important international athletic competition. They bring together thousands of the finest athletes to compete against one another in a variety of individual and team sports. Although technology is having an impact on the Olympics in a profound way, I disagree that it is reducing the role of Olympic Games. I believe that technology allows us to more fully appreciate everything about the competition and the athletes who commit their lives to fulfill their dreams.

To begin with, winning an Olympic event is the highest honour an athlete can achieve even in the modern times. Unknown athletes get the chance to attain national, and in particular cases, international fame. Secondly, Olympic Games are the best medium of culture exchange even today. People of different countries, religions, cultures etc. get together at Olympics and the participants get a chance to know about other cultures. The Games also constitute a major opportunity for the host city and country to showcase themselves to the world.

Although the technological realities of the modern times have brought many changes in the Olympic Games of today, they have not eroded the importance of the Olympic Games. Technology plays a part in every aspect of these games, from the first torch relay hand-off to the closing ceremonies. Athletes and trainers use technology in preparing for the games to optimize their training. Sports equipment manufacturers use design technology to build improved apparatus, gear and more that will enable their clients to deliver a high level of performance. Broadcasters use technology to better inform viewers of all aspects of the events. As a consequence, more and more people are exposed to these games.

People who opine that technology has reduced the role of Olympic Games, say so because the ugly claws of commercialism have crept into this field also. As a result, the Olympics have shifted away from pure amateurism to professionalism. A win-at-all-cost attitude has emerged and many use unethical means to win. They also say that only the rich can afford technology to boost their performance and this creates a gap between the rich and poor. However, I still believe that without inherent ability no amount of technology can make anybody a winner or loser.

To sum up, technology has brought colossal changes in The Olympic Games of today but in no way have they decreased the role of Olympic Games.

Plan followed:

Intro: Disagree

Para 1: Role of Olympics

Para 2: How technology has increased effect of Olympics

Para 3: Why people say that technology has decreased the role of Olympics

Conclusion: Reiterate opinion

175. Nowadays football supporters behave violently. What is the cause? How we can solve it?

Football hooliganism is not a new phenomenon. It dates back to 14th century England, when this sport was banned by the king of that time. In the modern form of football, such violence has also been reported many times. This essay intends to analyse the causes of this phenomenon, and suggest ways to mitigate the problem.

The main reason of violence by football supporters is that football is a competitive, physical sport, which is played by and attracts an audience, which is youthful and aggressive. The supporters of the teams form gangs, and these gangs want to assert themselves over their rivals. They have strong emotional ties with their teams. The Heysel stadium disaster is an example of such hooliganism, in which Liverpool supporters and Juventus supporters had a fight, because of which a wall collapsed and there were 39 casualties.

Secondly, the influence of alcohol is there on football violence. There were clear evidences that most of those involved in football hooliganism were drunk. Finally, the media is also considered a culprit in contributing to football violence. Studies have suggested that the language of war and combat employed by the media in covering football, incited the young supporters to indulge in violence. For instance, the Daily Mirror's headlines "Achtung! Surrender" before the match between England and Germany in 1996, was very provocative for the young supporters.

Many solutions have been proposed and tried, which has resulted in a significant decrease in football hooliganism. Such measures should be implemented more stringently to completely eradicate the menace of such violence. First of all, sophisticated policing measures should be employed. Spotting and barring the identified hooligans to attend further matches would be very helpful. Alcohol consumption during the matches should be banned. Finally, the media should be wise enough to play its role in such a way that it does not give air to hooliganism.

To sum up, football violence is a problem, but many effective steps can be taken to address the issue and prevent further mishaps.

Plan followed
Intro:
Para 1: reason
Para 2: More reasons
Para 3: Solutions
Conclusion

176. Many people think that the behavior of professional sportsmen/sportswomenon or off the field is not important as long as they are good players. To what extent do you agree or disagree with it?

I disagree that the conduct of professional sportspersons on and off the field is not significant. I believe our sportsmen are role models for the masses and therefore their behaviour, both on and off the field, should be very good. A number of arguments support my opinion.

To begin with, people especially the youth, worship their favourite sportspersons as their idols. They follow these sportsmen as their role models. The good behaviour of sportsmen both on and off of their playing field can have a positive effect on the spectators. Qualities such as teamwork, motivation, and dedication can all be easily spotted on the field. Sportsmen can also help promote eating healthy and staying in good physical condition. There are also many qualities off the playing field that can be viewed as positive influences for children. Some professional sportsmen are very active in charities and foundations for the sick and less fortunate children and others visit students in schools. For example, our famous cricketers, Sachin Tendulkar and M.S.Dhoni have started charities in their names to help raise money for children suffering from cancer or other diseases.

On the other hand, if their behaviour on and off the field is not good, they can set negative examples. Some sportsmen can get carried away during a game and become very rude and disrespectful towards coaches, other players, and even fans. There are also problems off of the field such as drugs and gambling that tends to get a lot of sportsmen into trouble. Just as the good examples can be mimicked by children, the bad examples can and unfortunately will be mimicked too.

Furthermore, these sportspersons are ambassadors of their respective countries and people of any particular country are judged by the behaviour of their sportspersons. When they win matches, they raise their nation in the eyes of the world. When they cheat to win, they lower the name of their nation. Finally, their bad behaviour affects their game. For instance, when Harbhajan Singh, a famous cricketer slapped another player Shrisanth on the field, he was fined heavily and also barred from playing for some time.

To conclude, sportsmen can set an example wherever they are, whether on the playing field in front of thousands of people or off the playing field doing their own thing. They can be both a positive and encouraging role model or they can be viewed as someone who is not a good example for children today. So, their behaviour on and off the field is very significant.

Plan followed

Intro: Disagree. Their behaviour both on and off the field is very important

Para 1: They are role models.

Para 2: Their bad behaviour has negative impact

Para 3: They are ambassadors of their respective nations.

Conclusion: reiterate opinion

177. Some people think competitive sport is important for a child's education. Others think it has negative effects on children. Discuss both views and give your opinion.

In recent years, due to stiff competition in almost every area some people opine that competitive sports have a beneficial impact on children's education. However, there are some who disagree with the above notion. Before presenting my view, I intend to explore both sides of the argument.

There are many advantages of competitive sports. The first and foremost advantage is that such sports prepare children for a society that thrives on competition. Competition is a normal part of human nature and a part of everyday life. Secondly, competitive sports provide challenges and help children deal with such challenges. Finally, these games teach discipline and help build character and confidence.

On the other hand opponents of competitive sports argue that these sports lead to stress which is detrimental to the mental health of children. If these games are played with a win-at-all-cost attitude then sometimes unethical means are adopted to win and this is definitely not what children should learn in schools. Competitive sports also have a toxic effect on the relationship among children. Each child may regard others as a rival to his own success and it may lead children to envy winners and laugh at losers.

In my opinion, competitive sports are good but over competitiveness should be discouraged. The win-at-all-cost mentality should not be there. In childhood, competition should be introduced gradually and children should build skills, participate fully and focus on playing rather than winning.

To conclude, competitive sports have more pros than cons. Students should play competitive sports because they make them adapt better to this competitive society. However, schools should take effective measures to avoid destructive competition.

Essay Plan
Intro: Discuss intro
Para: Advantages of competitive sports
Para 2:Disadvantages
Para 3: In my opinion, competitive sports are good but over competitiveness should be discouraged
Conclusion:

178. In some countries, people are purchasing fewer new items and more second-hand goods. What are the reasons for this? Is this a positive or negative trend?

The used goods market is gaining popularity, and this can be seen through the mushrooming growth of offline and online used goods stores. This essay intends to analyse the reasons of this growing trend. I believe this is largely a positive trend, although there is a small dark side to it as well.

There are myriad reasons for shopping for second hand goods. Firstly, it saves money. Buying anything used is less expensive than the new alternative, sometimes up to 90% cheaper, but generally at least 50% cheaper. So, a person can save twice the money or buy twice the amount of stuff. Secondly, people have come to realise that buying a branded product, which speaks quality, is better than buying a new one of inferior quality. There are many things available in the market, which are no longer of use to the first owner, but are still in good shape and can serve the needs of many others. For example, unique designer clothing can become to a vast majority when it comes in thrift stores.

Shopping for second-hand goods is a very positive trend, especially for the environment. Buying used goods diminishes waste, as it gives a longer life to common household items. There is also less pollution as it cuts down on manufacturing demands. It is a common fact that the growing and producing of things pumps a lot of pollution into the environment, such as toxic chemicals, pesticides, and carbon emissions. For example, a new cotton T-shirt is responsible for one third of a pound of pesticides dumped into the cotton fields. Another big positive effect of this trend of using second hand goods is to the seller. If a person feels that he doesn't need a thing anymore, he can sell it rather than just throw it away and buy something else instead.

The major negative effect of using second hand things is that these don't carry any warranty or guarantee. Secondly, a very careful inspection is required, which may not be possible at times. For example, an used mattress or furniture may have bugs. Despite these cons, I still believe that the benefits of this growing trend of resale shopping outweigh the negative connotations.

To summarise, there are many reasons for the growing popularity of resale shopping, but definitely the merits outweigh the demerit.

Plan followed

Intro:

Para 1: Reasons

Para 2: Positive effects

Para 3: Negative effects with refutation

Conclusion:

179. In many countries around the world, shopping has turned into a form of entertainment rather than a way of getting what people need. Discuss the reasons for this trend. Is it a positive or negative development? Or In many places shopping is becoming a free-time activity, replacing the traditional hobbies of the past. Discuss the reasons for this development. Is this development positive or negative?

Shopping is generally thought of in terms of fulfilling needs. Shopping is seen first as a function and secondarily as something that serves emotional and social needs. As incomes have grown, choices have exploded and free time has increased, shopping has become entertainment as much as anything else. This can be seen as both – a positive as well as a negative development. In the following paragraphs I intend to explore the pros and cons of shopping as an entertainment.

On the positive side, shopping satisfies our needs. Everyone needs the basics of life such as items of food, clothing and shelter. Apart from that, needs vary from person to person. The things which were considered the luxuries of yesteryears have become the necessities of today. For example, the mobile phone has become a must-have for even the lower income group of people. Many businesses and jobs thrive on the connectivity provided by the mobile phone and the internet.

Furthermore, shopping has given rise to the consumerist society of today. This has given employment to many. For instance, people are working in the manufacturing industries and in the retail sector also. Mega stores and malls are also having a mushrooming growth. What is more, psychologists claim that the best way to cope with stress or any kind of strong and negative emotion is to hit the shops and do plenty of shopping. It is called retail therapy and, according to many, it is guaranteed to boost spirits.

On the negative side, excessive shopping makes us pile up things in the home which we don't even need. It also leads to a throw-away society which is detrimental to the environment. To do shopping, people need a lot of money and if this money does not come by fair means people resort to unethical means of getting it which leads to violence and crime in the society.

To conclude, shopping is good as long as it is done for need, but when it is done for greed then it becomes a bane. So we should shop only according to our requirements and then it will be a pleasurable experience also.

Plan followed

Intro: This can be seen as both – a positive as well as a negative development.

Para 1: On the positive side, shopping satisfies our needs.

Para 2: Furthermore, shopping has given rise to the consumerist society of today.

Para 3: On the negative side,   Conclusion:

180.   Some shops are open 24 hours a day and 7 days a week. Do you think it is a good thing for the customers, shop staff and company as a whole?

Today, we belong to a 24/7 society. All 24 hours are ours, and we should take advantage of the given time and do our best. This could be very beneficial because it adds to productivity. Round-the-clock shops are part of this society. Definitely, it is advantageous for the customers, staff and the company as a whole.

Customers are benefited in numerous ways. To begin with, today's work routine has changed. Many jobs require late-night or early-morning shifts. They may range from truck and taxi drivers to police and firefighters, to hospital and manufacturing employees. People are staying up later and getting up earlier and they need a convenient place to shop. Moreover, 24-hour stores also benefit those with more urgent needs, such as patients released from hospitals during the night in need of pain medication, and parents whose sick child needs a prescription. The growing needs of an aging population can also not be overlooked. What is more, this allows parents to shop for family needs almost any time of the day or night without interrupting crucial time with children. They can do the shopping after children go to bed. Finally, such stores are a boon for those who do not like to shop during the day because it is too busy and overcrowded.

The 24 hour supermarkets have benefited job seekers too. Plenty of jobs have been created and there are more choices for people to apply for evening work as there are vacancies for late evenings and early mornings. The option of night shifts arepossible for those who have commitments during the day, such as students. Moreover, the rate of pay for evening work can sometimes be more than that during the day. Additionally, there are staff discounts on the goods sold within such shops as well as other company benefits which is why working in such supermarkets is very popular among many job seekers.

The companies themselves will also gain from opening the stores for 24 hours because it will enable them to get more business as shoppers are welcome to shop and purchase whenever they want and whatever they want. They will also be able to take on staff specifically for stacking and filling shelves because during the day there will be too many customers around to be able to fill the shelves properly. 24 hour supermarkets also enable deliveries for any time of day and night without the need of worrying about late deliveries due to the store having to close.

In conclusion, it can be said that 24-hour-shops are a boon for the customers, staff and the companies as a whole.

Plan followed

Intro: It is a positive development for all

Para 1: Advantages for customers   Para 2: Advantages for staff - More jobs

Para 3: Advantages to companies   Conclusion: Repeat views of intro.

181.   Many people are doing their shopping on the Internet nowadays. Discuss the advantages and disadvantages of shopping online.

Today with the internet so readily accessible to us, more and more people are turning to online shopping for all their needs. Clothes, shoes, a variety of products and even groceries can now be purchased via the internet. This essay shall look into the pros and cons of online shopping.

There are several advantages to shopping online. The first is the ability to shop at a time that is convenient to you, not just when the shops are open. The second advantage of shopping online is that goods are often cheaper as the seller does not have the costs of running a shop and having to pay wages to salespeople, insurance and all of the other running costs of a brick and mortar store.Online shopping can also be a lot more comfortable than real world shopping as you do not have to deal with the weather.

A huge advantage of shopping online is that you have the opportunity to compare as many products and prices as you want without having to spend the time and money to travel between several different shops. You will also be able to read reviews that have been written by other people who have purchased the item you are considering; you will be able to find out about the item from a genuine user not just the salesperson. Finally you will be able to find and buy products all over the world and not just in your immediate vicinity– this makes purchasing of hard-to-find items a lot easier.

The main disadvantage of shopping online is that you have to pay shipping costs and have to wait for the items you purchased to be shipped and delivered. This could take several weeks if you have purchased a product from overseas, and the costs of shipping may outweigh any savings you made on the purchase price. You will not be able to purchase an item you need to use immediately online.

Another disadvantage is that you have to buy the item relying purely on a photograph and description, you cannot feel or see the item you want to buy. It can sometimes be quite hard to judge the size or quality of some items purely from a photograph. The final disadvantage of shopping online is that it is much harder and takes longer to return faulty goods; you will have to repack it and pay to ship it back to the seller. It can literally take weeks to exchange a faulty product purchased online.

In summary, the main advantages of shopping online are convenience and cost savings, while the main disadvantage is that the item is not immediately available, and you cannot inspect it personally before you make your purchase.

Plan followed

Intro: Discuss essay intro

Para 1: advantages   Para 2: more advantages

Para 3: disadvantages   Para 4: more disadvantages

Conclusion:

182.   Ordinary people copy famous people whom they see on TV and magazines. Do you think it is a positive development?

TV and magazines play an important role in our daily life. These are meant to provide information and entertainment to their viewers. With their vast reach nowadays they have evolved into our daily life style and ordinary people generally tend to follow famous people and celebrities being shown through these media. I believe this is largely a negative development.

The major negative aspect of this development is that people are attracted by and follow the glamorous side of these people, which is portrayed more. As a result ordinary people follow famous personalities based on their looks only and not based on the work they do, success they have achieved or their contribution to society. For example, if their favourite celeb has 6 pack abs, they also try to achieve such a body, and to do so quickly, they have to consume a lot of unhealthy supplements, which may not be good for them. Some girls even stop eating altogether to get the size zero figure of their role model. What they fail to realise is that these celebs spend hours in the gym every day to get that sort of figure.

Another negative effect of this development is that if these celebs drink or smoke in public, the common people think it is a sort of status symbol and do the same. They also want to achieve the comfortable lifestyle and costly cars and other such possessions without doing the hard work required to achieve such status. As a result, petty crime incidences are often seen.

On the positive side, these celebs sometimes motivate people to do good things and not let any setbacks in their life lead them to go into depression. The encouragement given by celebrated people can help them overcome such situationsand achieve success as well as help others For example, a famous Indian celeb Deepika Padukone told people how she fought with her depression in a YouTube interview. Many people were really motivated by it and learnt ways to come out of their depression.

To sum up, it is true that people tend to copy famous people who are glamourized by the media. I firmly believe that it is a more negative than a positive development. People should not follow these celebs blindly. They should be realistic and follow only the good aspects of these celebs.

Plan followed

Intro:

Para 1: negative effect

Para 2: more negative effect

Para 3: positive effect

Conclusion